The NEW
GOLF AIMING SKILL:

MIND'S EYE IMAGERY
WITH BIOGRAPHIES

GEOFFREY LUCAS

Revised Second Edition
Copyright © 2006, Published by
Golf Technology Calgary (1984)
An Imprint of A2Z Publishing
All rights reserved

The Publisher: A2Z Publishing
Littlefield, AZ.
Victoria, BC

Typeset in Arial Graphic
Cover Illustration: Photo Credit (at rear)
Cover Design: Prism and Final Details, Inc.
Inside Illustrations: Theresa Chiozza & Kim Johansen
Book Design: JoAnn Hopper, Final Details, Inc.
Mesquite, Nevada

Cataloguing In Publication Data
Lucas, Geoffrey, 1940--
BISAC: Sport/Golf/Exercises/Mechanics.

ISBN O-9692902-5-X
Other ISBN Publisher Imprints in this Series:
0969 2902-4-1
0-9692902-3-3
Published simultaneously in the
United States and Canada.

TABLE OF
CONTENTS

PREFACE

The success of the ideas contained in the book, **The NEW Golf Aiming Skill**, will be ascertained in the coming years of Tour play in golf, at such a time that The Tours futuristic new scoring trend will have run its course. By then a new future will be on the horizon and new thoughts will be sought.

Perhaps what has been referred to in this book about an uncharted, undeveloped area in mental golf, that is, the endurance of staying with the mind's eye emphasis throughout a full 18 holes of golf and the full four rounds of a typical Tour event will always remain a challenge. It certainly is not commonly achieved by the players, at present, which is not to say that much advancement and much accomplishment is not to be found among elite golfers.

It is believed that emphasis has not been placed on endurance in mental golf. Many factors intervene and such factors come at both opportune and non opportune times during the game. Some of us who try to play the game have had little if any success in the area of mental endurance in golf and of course that includes aiming a key skill.

On the other hand, many successes of a smaller or lesser amount on Tour have been reported. Aiming is one of the vital sub sections of such mental endurance and is itself one of the more successful aspects of play. The tuning in of the sub conscious for a full round of play is still not achieved. This tuning in is however not always achievable, simply because it is often subject to non-regular use. So that we often focus on classical swing factors and de-emphasis what is achievable in full mind play golf.

However, it still remains true that golfers will find a way to reduce their average game score especially among those players who take on this special challenge. Certainly they mar run into other barriers to lowering score along the way. It is immensely impressive that this challenge has such an International and widespread core of players and professional & amateur teachers and achievers. **Although it is difficult to gain satisfaction from golf, there are many players that do achieve such satisfaction and become the long time enjoyers of golf. We hope that this new book in some way adds to such joy of the challenge of golf.**

It seems that the future of teaching the player may be improving and this could also signal that such ideas as herein contained are working. Golf enhancement comes from many sources and often it is inspirational and is any exciting and continuing field in sport. What seemed rare a few years ago, is commonplace in present Tour play. Some sophistication is present it seems. Golfers recognize that mind emphasis golf and the mind's eye role in golf leads to improved play, yet a comfort zone for such golf needs to be achieved.

Whereas when the present author wrote a similar set of Preface statements some years ago and included a long list of Tour golfers with special mind control golf skills it seems unnecessary to attempt such a list today. Simply put there are many mental skills out on Tour. Every player has reached some stage of development and every interview produces some evidence of that accomplishment.

Perhaps what has not been achieved, at least to full potential, is the area of researching the impact on score of self success viewing, pre viewing, packaging of self success in one form or another, ways to do so and technical means and economical ways of achieving such doing.

It has been stated several times in this text that what has been accomplished one time in golf and one time in the golf swing can be retained, reviewed and redone. The problem is that each player takes their own circuitous route to this end.

Healthy and avid use of the imagination and steadfast confidence in what one is trying to do in golf is one key to the above stated goals. This book banks on the reader being capable and willing to take on such swing building and game building.

However imagination, it is said, is by far the most neglected and underdeveloped area of the mind. Some athletes have photographic memories, but the majority of people need assistance for developing such skill. It is also said* ... that a psychotherapist expects you to use the mind's eye to further explore better ways of creating a stable mind along with extra skills. Rarely do we consider the full creative potential of the mind. This book intends to aid you in altering this basic and key in your aiming and all around game skill.

*Barbara Brown, Supermind: The Ultimate Energy. N.Y. Harper and Row.

CHAPTER 1 THE NEW GOLF AIMING SKILL IN SPORT AND NON SPORT

Objectives: A look at the occasions when a person uses imagery which this book refers to as mind's eye images; introductory comments about golf and other sport players as mind's eye users; the learning opportunity in imagery; school imagery and sport; some famous early advocates of imagery; imagery and symbolism; modern use of the mind's eye; visual thinking; typical and contemporary usages by celebrities; the self fulfilling prophecy and imagery; health and imagery are analyzed; the relationship between fitness and imagery is detailed; and the MAIN OBJECTIVE is highlighted, that is, **THE CHAPTER CREATES AN AWARENESS OF IMAGERY AND THE MIND'S EYE BOTH HISTORICALLY AND IN DAILY LIFE.**

****

The NEW Gof Aiming Skill is a reference book written about as many aspects of imagery and performance psychology as the reader may find necessary to self-teach or take on an educative experience until successful function in the mind's eye and golf is reached. It is a book about enhancing golf performance. It is a book that can be applied to golf, to sport, and to life in general. The SPECIAL FOCUS of this book is the treatment of golf as a TARGET GAME.

WHO USES IMAGES?

True imagers have developed a rather amazing degree of detail in their images. Their images or mind's eye pictures (that is, brain generated pictures which flash through the mind) can have vividness, detail and timing. An image can be held momentarily in the brain and images occur frequently to a user.

An image can and often does involve many basic senses such as feel, sight, smell, touch and taste. **And images and mind's eye pictures can be improved and applied at the correct time.**

While almost every human being has some ability to create and use images, there are great fluctuations in ability from person to person. Scientists, philosophers, musicians, artists and doodlers, educators and story tellers, entertainers, athletes, bright minded people and healthy; physically fit people and sensitive people all tend to be imagers.

So do injured and imprisoned people who have provided us with some outstanding examples of image ability and applications. Some careers and some life skills, in particular, require image creation ability. Examples of such imagers will be detailed briefly in this first chapter.

IMAGERY is a slightly more complex field of learning than you might at first suppose. Good imagery may provide you with some amazing learning and lifestyle and golf benefits.

INTRODUCTION AND A SELF ANALYSIS OF YOUR IMAGERY

How often have you used an image to direct your action in your present lifestyle? Are you driving a car or are you in a sport situation when images occur to you? Do you see images or mind's eye pictures when you are thinking through a problem?

Perhaps mind's eye images happen to you in connection with hunches or intuitive thinking. But more than likely your images have to do with reactions or emergency situations when a quick mind's eye picture precedes some rapid and often brilliant reaction by yourself!

Have you had the experience of seeing your whole life history flash before your eyes when you found yourself in a real jam or death-arousing scare or situation? If you have had to dive underwater to rescue someone or were pulled underwater by a dangerous current or tow, you probably had a detailed series of mind's eye pictures or movie style images bombard your brain.

Perhaps you have had less traumatic experiences such as a leisurely relaxed afternoon lying in some favorite spot where you preview and review your future plans in life or in sport life. Have you found your images to be ACCURATE? Are your images in TECHNICOLOR? Are you images FREQUENT? Are your images RARE? **If you have had any of the above images, you most certainly may e able to generate and apply positive images to golf and sport that dramatically improve your performance!!**

GOLFERS AND THE MIND'S EYE

Some golfers use imagery while others never use imagery and the mind's eye in any successful way. More than likely the Tour player has had occasional golfers (once a weekers) and regular golfers seeking success in friendly club or amateur golf can improve.

There can be a problem in adequately learning imagery among golfers. This problem can apply to almost all athletes or sports players. The image problem is centered around the lack of quality, vividness or even the absence or repeatability in creating mind's eye pictures at the right time. Perhaps this is due to infrequent practice or a shaky commitment. Besides this, a golfer may not have considered applying their imagery to specific parts of golf, such as aiming or systematic play for every minute of a Tour or amateur event. **Confidence builds slowly but surely in this aspect of golf.**

Unorganized programs aimed at developing this skill are frequent at present. The golfer has little if a readily available help in golf and the mind's eye.

However, as has recently been demonstrated, the development of effective imagery and the accompanying golf skills can occur among golfers. Successful golf imagery is becoming somewhat frequent according to Tour players, and **putting aiming confidence in particular is flourishing.**

Golfers who compete on the Tours are among players seeking to use imagery and its benefits in golf competition and new Tour players are coming from nearly everywhere it seems including several fine development Tours.

In addition, new golfers, occasional golfers (once a weekers) and regular golfers seeking success in friendly club or amateur golf can improve.

One of the simplest ways to improve your golf is to improve your ability to visualize or see clear mind's eye images for golf. Images allow repeatability of little successes in golf. For example, a golfer can rehearse for every golf fairway and green and "see" all their shots land in the soundest tactical positions on those fairways and greens. **By doing so, uncertainty and doubt are eliminated and some pretty impressive golf scores result!**

Some skills are needed to do this procedure successfully. Besides clearly formulated images one needs to be able to relax and stay relaxed on the golf course. It is generally necessary to improve relaxation skills as well as mind's eye skills. **Just close your eyes for a second or two and shrug your shoulders and say relax your mind's eye pictures improve immediately.**

Presently, I have estimated that 20% of the players on the various Tours effectively use imagery in golf. Good golf and especially bad weather golf and other tough situational golf are accompanied by better mental golf and effective mind's eye golf. Good golf is accompanied by mental skills other than imagery of course, but imagery and visualization are particularly important. **Probably 100% of Tour players have used imagery but effective use is a lot less common. At the very least most Tour players see themselves in their mind's eye as successful some of the time out on Tour.**

RECENT IMAGERY SUCCESS

An amazing high proportion of the 20% of Tour players have credited improved image making accuracy and timely use of the mind's eye with their starting and perhaps unexpected string of successes on Tour (and some vast amounts of money earned). Of the names that have received publicity and have appeared in newspapers, golf magazines and television you will recognize such Tour players as Ray Floyd, Peter Jacobsen, David Stockton, Mike Read, Dennis Watson and Annika Sorenstam, Sylvia Bertoluccini and Carolyn Hill.

Many more Tour players have hinted at or given details about their mental golf successes. Their techniques and what is known of their image or mind's eye enhancement practice will be examined in the **NEW Golf Aiming Skill.**

A few of the other 80% have indicated that their images are not accurate or versatile enough to be fully trusted to reproduce during crucial golf game situations. Some of the Tour players do use imagery and understand the role it can play in their sport but likely have not reemphasized, upgraded or worked on their mental or mind's eye golf games. Sometimes players do not have accompanying relaxation skills. Sometime they attribute success to other factors such as superior putting. Often though, the **mind's eye and superior putting go together and one provides for the other.**

Previously, some athletes and Tour players felt a certain stigma or personal resistance to exploring fully the mental edge in golf. Golfers and especially Tour players tend to explore every edge that works and are quite aware of any new strategy or reemphasis which may help them. One editor of Golf Magazine (Desmond Tolhurst) had told me that his magazine has a continuing commitment to the mental side of golf. The magazines in golf which I read, such as, Golf Digest, Women's Golf, Australian Golf Digest and Golf World and the Official Tour Guides, all feature golf performance articles when they are able to.

In addition, true mental edge or image edge ability is not a short term or "band aid" approach in sport or golf and requires extra time and effort. A firm and binding dedication to mind's eye practice time is sometimes a difficult decision to make if one is an advocate of striking hundreds and hundreds of pure practice shots as many golfers of merit assume to be necessary.

Often aiming is automatically within a warm up or pregame practice session such as when aiming shots to targets and momentarily aiming at the corner of the target green or even the edge of the flag.

WORKING TOWARDS GAINING THE MIND'S EYE EDGE

Tour players are currently working with sport psychologists and are among those athletes who frequently take a change of pace week for focusing on other aspects of great GOLF play. Yes they will go to an Academy of Golf facility so they can still hit balls but they want a change in emphasis perhaps. They may work on new goals or simply on sharpening their mental game and general confidence building. Details of such recent efforts will be the main stress throughout this golf performance book. MENTAL GOLF MAY BE THE WAVE OF THE FUTURE, BUT IT IS THE PRESENT STRESS OF UP TO THE MINUTE PLAYERS EVEN ON THE DEVELOPMENTAL TOURS, THE CANADIAN TOUR AND THE FLORIDA TOUR. IT IS OBVIOUS THAT MANY PLAYERS MAKE RAPID GAINS IN TOUR SUCCESS FROM ONE TOUR SEASON TO THE NEXT, GIVEN ALL THE NEW NAMES WHICH APPEAR ON TOUR.

GOLF'S SCIENTIFIC CONGRESSES NOT IN TUNE

Despite the optimism and the current stress on visualization and the use of mental edge sport, we see in Golf and in the Olympic sport disciplines we do not find much support in **think tanks of Scientific golf** such as the Scotland, the USA and the Japan meetings of golf's bright minds. A recent Congress (Scientific Congress of Golf II) focused largely on the biomechanics of the swing, the golfer's equipment, the golf course and the game. Exactly three of forty reports looked into performance routines of any sort including visualizing the path and the outcomes of the shot being attempted.

BIOGRAPHIES AGAIN & SWING FLAWS

The calm eyes closed rehearsal of what the golfer intends to do has always combined rather nicely with correction of swing flaws. So that, generally speaking, image ability in golf is found with other success factors. The Tour player feels a supporting euphoria of experience when these two parts of golf combine with game procedure, game management, aiming and aligning and general Tactics and tenacity.

Recently, I caddied for a top notch and confident Amateur and his ball crushing Amateur buddy in a foursome which included the eventual winner of the Becks Challenge Florida Tour event. Lonnie Nielsen, a former PGA Tour veteran from Buffalo, New York shot two fine under par games at the Ft. Myers Country Club and **showed a calm confidence on the exterior throughout both days.**

What impressed me was that the ProAm format allowed my Amateur player to test his mental golf rather severely. He played steady and unspectacular golf but seemed to know the exact swing flaw that kept his "A GAME" or his best game just under wraps for the two days.

THE SUPPORTING EUPHORIA OF EXPERIENCE: ON THE FINAL DAY

In the Becks Brewery Open final day, we see the mental edge more in evidence by its steady application. **The mental edge and the use of the mind's eye for the runner up leader Lonnie Nielsen, is focused not on his 66 but on not getting caught up in winning or in losing but in feeling real good about himself by playing well on the final day.** Nolan Henke was in the foursome and also had 66 on day one. Nolan is a current PGA Tour exempt player and is a local favorite. His game consisted of superb driving all day and solid scoring and he pulled into a tie after 17 holes with Nielsen, who finally took a bogey on tough 17. The bogey resulted from a poor chip shot and perhaps a misread putt.

When the rather awesome driving Nielsen bogeyed the 17th and Henke made a par saving 15' putt, the two were tied at nine under. On the 18th, Nolan ended up double bogey. Up to that point both players were just cruising along getting better and better it seemed. Henke stated he "shot himself in the foot" so to speak and finished 2nd at 7 under tied with Greg Lesher a Nike Tour player. It was a great day for Nielsen who waited 10 years to win at the Becks. In 1987, he had shot a course record 62 at Ft. Myers CC in his debut but had not won the event. Later Nielsen would reemerge as a awesome Senior Tour player.

THE NON SUPPORTING EUPHORIA OF LITTLE EXPERIENCE

In golf, it is often said, that it is the nature of the game that often determines scoring and winning and losing. Nielsen wins 10 years later. In the same foursome Dana Quigley, a Senior Tour player does not putt well until near the end of the final day and shot par 71 and finished 4th overall. In the same foursome, a young Marc Blais from Ottawa Canada, shoots 65 on day one for the outright lead and on the next day carves out a disastrous 77 playing with the leaders. Blais starts out bogey, bogey, missed drive and then birdie, but nothing can relax his play on this day it seems, even the relaxed and calming comments by Quigley and the laid back demeanor of Nolan Henke cannot penetrate or help Blais' inner game. The mind's eye and the power of visualization cannot come to the forefront.

YET, ON THE VERY SAME SUNDAY OUT ON THE CALIFORNIA VALENCIA COURSE, ON THE OTHER SIDE OF THE USA, ONE BILLY MAYFAIR GETS HIMSELF IN A WINNING ZONE OF GOLF WHICH SEEMS DECIDEDLY MENTAL AND WINS THE NISSAN OPEN. THE NEXT WEEKEND MICHAEL BRADLEY WINS AT DORAL'S BLUE MONSTER IN THE DORAL-RYDER OPEN EVEN AFTER HITTING A 10 INCH PUTT THAT CIRCLES THE CUP AND SOMEHOW STAYS OUT.

FROM HOLE 12, BRADLEY USES A MIND'S EYE OF JUST TRYING TO SCORE BIRDIE WHERE HE CAN AND DRIVE THE BALL WITH THE LENGTH AND ACCURACY, WHICH THE DORAL COURSE SEEMS TO DEMAND. HIS ADJUSTED MIND'S EYE PLAN WORKS JUST RIGHT IT SEEMS.

A MENTAL GOLF MIND'S EYE SCENARIO TO BE SURE
I see this two week period of PGA Tour / Nike Tour / Becks Florida Tour event and LPGA Tour event in Australia as becoming a great mental golf controversy. A two week period that seems to touch on every aspect of performance in golf and question certain mental strategies usually taken for granted. It is not possible to down play this part of golf, if it ever was possible to do so.

THE SCENARIO: NIELSEN/ MAYFAIR; BRADLEY & WEBB
From looking back in my notes made while watching the Doral-Ryder, I see that my new name for Michael Bradley is **"MR. CALM"**. He is exactly like Lonnie Nielsen, another **"MR. CALM"**, no expression of any emotion on the exterior. After every birdie or after a great par save, Bradley doesn't react at all. That is exactly what a mind's eye coach would like to see out of these two players, who are of a similar emotional characteristic it seems.

If your mind's eye sees you as even keeled and icy calm, then see it and evidence it. See your plan, play your plan out. Smiling has nothing to do with icy calm golf or even a long streak of very hot golf. Both these players evidenced their wins, one win worth $7,500 and one win worth $360,000.

But Wait? Should you be calm on the inside or calm on the outside? Should you play better in front of friends and parents/supporters? Karrie Webb won one year later in the LPGA Tours Masters in Australia when Gail Graham had won the same event a year ago, with her parents visiting Australia and supporting her play. Can Tiger Woods win in front of his friends in California if he plays the same event one year later?

But Wait, Wait? Even some more difficult mental golf skills are being challenged during these two weeks. Can you miss a 10" or 12" putt on the final day somewhere around the 11th or 12th hole and still win a prestigious Tour event without some very good mind's eye skills and some mental abilities? It is not to the point that Bradley went on to win but it is to the point that he said to his mind's eye that he could regroup, that he had mental strength and apparently now he was going to use it. The comment, at the time according to the CBS television broadcast crew was "can he control his self talk?" which is a fair and appropriate comment. Maybe he will not be able to control it. Who knows, it is only in Bradley's mind. I know what I said at the time. **Yes, he can control his self talk and if he is as smart as I think his is, he will be seeing his own very reliable putting stroke many times between now and the next putt he makes. His mental rehearsal will reassure him and yes, some reassurance is needed even at this level of play after missing a short-short putt, we all can agree.**

According to my notes made at the time, I saw that Michael Bradley controlled his self talk admirable just back on hole 11 when CBS commented that he did not control his trajectory and let a shot balloon and stop short and in the bunker. He controlled any negative stuff in his mind on 11 and I know that shot bothered him as much as the putt he missed. So I was sure that most Tour players, like Bradley, would still be in control.

I can see a real controversy here for a Tour players skills and his mind's eye abilities. It isn't easy at all as a mental skill. As Jim Nantz stated more than once, at the time at holes 12-18, the missed putt has to be on his mind. We saw so much of athletes' visualization during the '98 Winter Olympics and Jim Nantz seemed to sense Bradley's dilemma. Yet I know I disagreed and sensed Bradley being in control of his putting strategy.

There was some "silly" things happening out there in the wind at Doral during that time it was said. The reference was to some "silly" putts, besides Bradleys, P.J. Horgan misses an 8 footer, Tiger misses three from around 12-16', and John Huston misses one and went back to -9. John Huston shoots an incredible 67 and comes from a long ways back to finish 2nd (tied with Mayfair at -9) and becomes the Tours #1 man.

At the time it seemed that **Billy Mayfair** was the one knocking putts into the hole, but the "some silly putts" comment caught up to him on a longish birdie putt which became a three putt. Tiger Woods mind's eye seemed to see him going for the win, and he was truly after the win. Ray Floyd played some incredible mind's eye golf, especially into the face of the wind and seemed to gain a great deal of respect for a fine performance on his non Senior Tour schedule.

BUT WAIT, WAIT, WAIT: MORE BASIC QUESTIONS

You can be sure that in this book and in all its contents one consistent idea of the mind's eye procedure will emerge in a very basic way and will be listed among the basics of imagery golf.

THAT BASIC IS IN PUTTING, OR AT LEAST SO I CONTENDED AND WILL CONTINUE TO SO CONTEND. It goes as follows and will be developed

more in later Chapters. See an image of the putting stroke in your mind's eye.
Imitate or muscle memory that image in your practice stroke two or three times
before each putt (being sure about your aim line which is another accompanying

 image or mind's eye). Spend 99% of your time on each green
seeing and visualizing that aim line. Thirdly, and most
importantly, strike the putt with the exact same stroke which
you have just prepared. Never vary from this basic notion
and practice an immense amount for feel while on the putting
green with a stroke that is mechanically sound. AND YOU
WILL BECOME A WONDERFUL PUTTER AND HAVE VERY
FINE PUTTING STATISTICS IN COMPETITIVE GOLF. THE
PRESENT AUTHOR FEELS SO STRONGLY ABOUT PUTT IDEAS, THAT HE
HAS A NEW BOOK OUT ON 55 EXERCISES TO MAKE ONE PUTT HAPPEN.
(Title: Six 1 Putts...to cure a sick golf score) (Publication Date: Dec. 2006)
Information at A2ZPublisher@shaw.ca

ANOTHER CONTROVERSY: MAYFAIR AND STOCKTON

**Could such a basic mind's eye procedure be challenged as being
wrong. Yes it could be challenged.** In golf, if you develop a procedure that
works for you then use it by all means. In the next paragraphs, you will see
about two money winners on Tour who have developed better procedures for
their putting and at least one of them may leave you somewhat **incredulous** if
not totally **incredulous**.

1.   For two weeks now we hear the **Billy Mayfair's practice putting stroke**
before each crucial putt is nothing at all like the putting stroke which he uses to
strike the ball with. According to the theory of mind's eye golf, this would not
work very effectively since the mind's eye provides feel and even direction to
perform a correct putting stroke. However, Mayfair won $350,000 and $176,000
over two weeks after going without big successes for some time on Tour.

Not having talked to Billy Mayfair or his caddy, I cannot see a reason for
such a stroke rehearsal unless it is because his practice stroke is on purpose to
practice some other aspect of performance. His putting stroke is described as
a outside in cut motion but that is fine enough with mind's eye theory.
Biomechanically, such a stroke will cause much discussion to be sure.

2.   **In Dave Stockton's new book titled *PUTT TO WIN:* Secrets for
Mastering the Other Game of Golf** I have learned that David emphasizes no
putting stroke rehearsal whatsoever, that is, not a physical or an overt rehearsal
(I do believe that he rehearses 'internally' that is to say that his kinesthetic or
internal feel is superb, probably). It is still a rehearsal or warm up stroke to the
golfer as you might have done yourself, it just lacks outward movement. This
may explain the Billy Mayfair system of putting as well, puzzled over above.
Basically, David Stockton's stroke has won big money on both Tours (11 wins of
the Senior Tour as well as that many on the regular Tour) and **feel and rhythm**
is supreme in his stroke. His golf has always been based on an overwhelming

stress on mental golf and a great confidence through skill in putting and short game play. His book is a sensational boost to mastering the other game, that is the putting game and the short game. You will see later that my belief is that there are two great books including Stockton's needed for your library in the section of your golf book collection titled performance golf (as well, I hope, as the present **Golf Trilogy** of including the *NEW Golf Aiming Skill*, making five books in total).

DAVID STOCKTON SAYS **"no Practice Stroke Needed, Thank You"** and goes on to cite the belief that the practice strokes takes your mind off the line of the putt, the image of the ball going into the hole, and the feel for the speed of the green". He states that even one practice stroke puts your mind onto mechanics and that detracts from your goal. As well he cites slowness and tension build up which detract from the goal of making putts. **As stated above, I do not agree for the reason that a stroke rehearsal is a feel refreshed or what is called a kinesthetic rehearsal and does not detract or take your mind off the line, the image and the feel.** In this book, we agree mostly with David Stockton and have many statements about spending every possible moment on the green with your eyes in contact with the putt line and the ball entry to the hole, which is totally mind's eye putting. **I agree that sometimes a putting practice stroke can be motionless or virtually lacking any real movement since your mind easily enough 'includes' that physical motion.** That idea is really what the mind's eye is all about. If that is the interpretation, then we agree even there, but I would never say *no practice stroke thank you* since I want rehearsal of some sort.

He is also a great teacher as mentioned elsewhere in this book and a long list of his students are found in the Tour ranks. For example: Paul Azinger calls him a great putter and a great teacher and recommends his book; Lee Trevino states that Stocktons' putting rhythm never changes, short or long putts get the same and that is the key; Tom Weiskopf is impressed most by the speed at which the ball leaves the putter head and David himself states that when you putt a Surlyn ball, strike the ball softer to create a slower ball motion since that type ball comes off the face faster that does the Balata golf ball (He prefers Balata of course).

Finally, **Michelle McGann** says he taught her that putting is mental and physical and **feel of the line of the putt lets you believe that every putt is makeable.** Not only that, but she credits David Stockton with teaching her the essential tools necessary to be a Champion putter, which is discussed further in Chapter 6 of this text.

As my writing in Chapter 6 states, I have found David Stockton to be a **personable and helpful coach type** and his communication skills are in the upper echelons. In his text, he touches on his father's communication and his father's theory on teaching golf. His father also showed a finely tuned way of titillating David as a non golfing and as a golfing son and golf project. **Davids' own son is earning**

his way on to the PGA Tour and that comes right back to David Stockton' approaches to teaching it seems.

****

Even in the first Chapter of this book, you had best understand that if you are not a relaxed golfer then it is **unlikely that you will become a mind's eye applier low scoring golfer.** Relaxation immediately improves the quality and view ability of the image pictures in your mind. It is not said you could not become a golf champion. Sometimes a golfer like Michael Bradley is said to bottle up his emotions yet he is now a big time winner to be sure. Yet it seems his images will be absent.

This book is being written in Lee County, SW Florida and they are proud that Bradley was born here and that John Huston is a Floridian as well from the Doral-Ryder Tour event. Not to speak of Raymond Floyd, TerryJo Meyers, Nolan Henke, Tommy Tolles and others from a long list of Tour Players which I am hearing about each day.

NO MATTER AT WHAT LEVEL OF GOLF OR SPORT OR SPORT FITNESS YOU ARE AT PRESENTLY, YOU TOO CAN BENEFIT FROM PROCEDURES AND PROGRAMS FOR IMPROVING YOUR PURE IMAGERY SKILLS AND GOLF SCORE ENHANCEMENT.

THE CHAPTERS FROM HERE TO CHAPTER 6 WILL GIVE YOU THE GOLFER OF ANY ABILITY LEVEL, THE MENTAL PRACTICE YOU SEEK. CHAPTER 6 WILL ATTEMPT TO PULL ALL THE MATERIAL INTO JUST HOW THE TOUR PLAYER CARRIES OUT SKILLS FROM THE MENTAL AND PHYSICAL POINTS OF VIEW.

A WORD ABOUT THE GOLFERS COMMITMENT

The program of imagery improvement and mind's eye applications in this book is for exercising in a new way, the mental way with skills coming next, not first. Your tactics and mental tenacity will pull it all together. This involves a modest investment of time and effort. A few hours per week during the preseason and about the same in the playing season with a few minutes during the critical post game rework will be enough. The idea is to be ongoing or in with the actual golf games you play and not just a one time reading, logging and journalizing.

If a golfer wishes to use self success videotapes as a sort of cybervision-like resource, then more time will be needed. Our experiments with repeated viewing of successes such as putts falling into the hole and greenside and sand shots going in the hole have been positive and have reduced scores in golf. These videotapes are not at all like *Sybervision* Sport tapes which are commercially available products which focus on the golf swing needed with various golf clubs, if that is what I understand Sybervision to consist of.

An intensive aiming set of practice sessions such as putting may also be repeatedly necessary.

A WORD ABOUT THE SPORT PSYCHOLOGIST OR PERFORMANCE ENHANCER PROFESSIONAL

The mind's eye program outlined in this book does not encourage the golfer to hire a sports professional like a sport psychologist or performance enhancer. However, such resource person may be available at a golf center or sports clinic or through a University evening program of continuing education. Reading this book will provide short term benefits in sport and in golf and more benefit would arise as more time is spent in improving and applying such concepts to your sport. Most Tour players have what they call a "shrink" or psychologist to talk to. Often they telephone this person during a golf event. Often they mention great and immediate success after some of these consultations. David Stockton's book presents two such memorable occasions during Major tour events.

These days it is not unusual to have a personal coach or fitness instructor so that a personal performance person can be sought out as well.

BRAIN POWER IMAGERY STARTS EARLY IN NON SPORT LIFE

The development of our imagery systems takes place very early in life. An infants initial impression of the world around them takes the form of images. These images are constantly changing as new experiences and information is encountered in life.

Although a young child's image system may get a good start, there is some evidence suggesting that images become inflexible and less productive in learning. An image system can lose its unique ability to adjust. If this image system involves rhythm and feel for things, then that might disrupt those emerging skills and abilities. This field of learning is also known as visual learning. Visual learning likely would enhance sport movement learning or at least might prosper such skill development.

IMAGE SELECTOR

Be that as it may, as time moves forward more and more evidence is surfacing and being reported on the positive and varied use of visual learning both inside and outside of sport. Viewers interface so strongly with their worlds that perhaps it is little wonder that a 3 month old person shows preference for novel spatial patterns, as Paul Quinn reported in *Child Development* and as Jerome Kagan, a visual learning writer has found.

Kagan recently compared 4 month old infants in Bejing, China in Boston and in Dublin on the same battery of visual, olfactory and auditory cues and found Chinese infants significantly less active, less irritable and less vocal than the Boston and Dublin children. The Boston infants showed the highest level of reactivity.

Another article reported in the *Journal of Film and Video* only recently published, called for an enlightened understanding of how viewers actually interface with motion pictures. Surely, they suggest, the still picture in motion as they put it, is only of Historic interest and the myth of a passive viewer is long overdue for being discarded. Another writer, John Fraser who wrote a #1 Best Seller on *The Chinese: Portrait of a People* showed that Chinese Opera viewers get animated and chatty as they come to enjoy the Opera more and more. Silence means that the Opera or stageplay is a poor one, not that they are being courteous viewers, as in Western society.

In the field of language arts and in creative writing, students simply cannot cope with verbiocentric educational experiences for knowledge acquisition. *Lessons from Douglas* illustrates this concept where Douglas, a young art student challenges his teacher to let him use Art to stabilize and give shape to his thoughts. Douglas' cognitive process and knowledge development simply could not operate without visual learning. Jean Ann Clyde reported about Douglas and noted how learners and teachers expand their vision of what it means to learn something.

The development of language and word meaning as part of brain power imagery can become locked onto words which tend to deter overall visual perception or visual understanding of that which we observe and imagine. As a result, our view of the world can become closed. We have to leap past concept words.

Soon, and it cannot be too soon, we have to practice things such as golf right where the game takes place just like a good old fashioned playing lesson that takes place right out on a golf course. It seems we have to learn about golf ball trajectory when we view how that ball interfaces with the real landing areas or a good facsimile of a golf course. **Like Douglas, perhaps we need 'our Artform' which is ball striking and ball flight to learn from. Always have I contended that we need a 21 hole golf course, with the first 3 holes to refresh our visual golf minds and warm up our kinesthetic or inner feel for the game. Then 18 holes to follow. The first golf course I design will be built over 21 holes, in my visualized design at least. A VISUAL LEARNER NEEDS NOTHING LESS!**

DEVELOPING OUR GOLF VISION

Our golf vision and our mind's eye imagery can also become locked in and inflexible. In golf, we can become closed rather than open to new experiences and shot situations.

For example, we accept certain flight patterns of the golf ball. In the western hemisphere, we get used to high flight patterns with our mid irons as long as we don't balloon ball too high and short. For new golfers, there is great frustration at not getting the ball up high until the mechanics of loft and contact are explained and used.

But play golf in Scotland or in any windy setting and that will require us to develop a new type of mind's eye with low flight with our mid irons. Before striking that same shot, we must mind's eye a low flat shot shape for success. The wind blows and the fairways demand a rolling shot. Otherwise, we end up going too far over the green and into some gorse or heather or other tough growth, usually on a little incline to make the next shot even harder. No longer do we have

IMAGE MONITOR

the soft, wind protected golf green to hit into. There the greenskeepers dry the greens out and don't like lush green grass like North Americans have come to expect.

In Scotland, a low wind boring shot with lots of controlled spin and roll is required. So that the image must be adjusted for the brain to work with the body to maximize the particular golf requirement.

WHAT ARE THE NAMES OF THE BASIC IMAGES PEOPLE USE?

Just to clarify the various images or mind's eye the definitions and a summary chart will follow.

To mentally practice a motor skill requires a "movie picture" set of images without any accompanying physical movement. For years that imagery has been named *Mental practice imagery* although *Kantian imagery* is the common practice of thinking in pictures to precede thinking in words.

To use cognitive imagery is to accompany thinking and analytical skill with image or mind's eye pictures. We use this form if imagery in analyzing a computer output, a horse race form chart, a computer menu, and a complicated recipe book which has accompanying pictures due to the recipe complexity, and problems in science and other school subjects.

In trying to learn to accept new social acquaintances, new cultures, new attitudes, new mental health patterns and fear and stress reduction skills, we are using images that are called *guided affective images.*

If we are trying to make smart decisions on the golf courses, we are using *Tactics imagery.*

When we are trying to see a clear pre-hit picture of a certain golf swing before swinging, we are using *Technique imagery.*

When difficult and demanding situations face us in life or in golf or sport, we are using *Tenacity imagery.*

Television has, of course, been credited with forming a vast amount of the images we take for granted. While golden arches mean one thing in many countries, another set or arches means cathedral or expect Gothic architecture to somebody else in some countries. One can name hundreds of images which instantly stand for a meaning. Some images have become Universal and many images have political meanings.

Television advertising attempts to play with our interpretation or with our fixed image systems. Art, drama, music and some sport and skate-dance and dance forms do just the opposite, that is, they want our image systems interpretation to grow and flourish.

TYPES OF SYSTEMATIC* IMAGERY

NAME	MEANING
MENTAL PRACTICE	NO OUTWARD MOVEMENT
KANTIAN IMAGERY	THINKING IN IMAGES/PICTURES
GUIDED COGNITIVE I.	IMAGES THAT MASTER THINKING
GUIDED PSYCHOMOTOR (GALYEAN)	SPORT, MUSIC, KEYBD. SKILLS
GUIDED AFFECTIVE I.	ATTITUDES, EMOTIONS, ET AL
TACTICS IMAGES	RISK DECISIONS IN GOLF
TECHNIQUE IMAGES	SEEING GOLF SKILLS
TENACITY IMAGES	DELIBERATE MIND TOUGHNESS
AIMING IMAGES	SIGHTING TARGETS

****

*SYSTEMATIC means that in all types of imagery, one plans and tries to continuously use mind's eye mental images. From a paper developed for the Los Angeles Scientific Congress of Olympic Sport .

****

FIXED MODES OF IMAGERY IN ADULTHOOD

Barbara Forisha while at the University of Michigan, once reminded us that fixed patterns of imagery do predominate in adults. For example, your career may foster certain images. Groups of individuals have patterns of similar imagery. These patterns of modes are related to creativity or lack of creativity. Such a relationship between imagery and creativity varies by gender, academic standing and level of education attained.

A study of British Youth by Hudson led to the idea that boys' image systems can become fixated, fixed to some standard, or peer fixated. What this means is that instead of adjusting your image system to progress or reorganize the way you view the world, you would terminate this reorganization and take on a fixed personality. **You may become quite inflexible and rigid.**

This finding has led to some enormous changes in how young women and young men view themselves. Role models that hope to reverse these image fixations have become even more important in society. Television advertising in sport and in computer sales have been most aware of such images. One should learn to filter out which ads are which and what they mean when we don't think them over. **Value systems in golf and sport and even in non sport should not be taught by television. Otherwise our future is belly up, so to speak.**

Personally, I find it very encouraging when the NCAA has the guts and courage and responsiveness to use television and athletes messages to impact and interface with us with images on topics like betting, leadership, responsibility and other values which are missing in some of society.

The same is to be said for the Press and Media when they continue to demand that those athletes who trash talk, trash Olympic rooms and trash Coaches, should have to bring forward some new images to explain their actions. These are all images of society.

Isn't it fascinating that images are the central focus of much of society and will probably be even more evident in society in our children's future.

SYSTEMS FOR RATING YOUR IMAGERY

There is a system for rating yourself on rigidity of imagery. One example is the general quality labelled image fluidity-consciousness versus image rigidity-inclusion.

A few years ago, golfer X may have rated themselves as 0 or 10 on fluidity-consciousness of golf shot shape or trajectory (that is, they never had any image ability or awareness or watched for height of shot and lateral or other ball movement). Now because every 25th word on television golf is 'trajectory' that golfer rates a 5.5 of 10. Perhaps Tiger Woods rating of golf shot shape in 8.75 of 10. That is, even though, his shots travel some enormous distances he has acute mind's eye images of his golf shot shape, for the various situations he faces on the golf course.

LAURA DAVIES, JOHN DALY, TIGER WOODS, KARRIE WEBB, LORENA OCHOA, AND OTHER PLAYERS WHO ALL HIT THE GOLF BALL INTO ORBIT, MAY HAVE NEWER SHOT SHAPE CONSCIENCES THAT REGULAR GOLFERS DO.

As we grow and develop in adulthood, we go through stages of image development such as receptive to images stage; autonomous image stage; assertive image stage (i.e. strong, stubborn images); and finally, to an integrative image stage (that is, images are flexible and mesh with your view of the world).

Golf aiming is similarly an integrative stage and often very advanced. That is, interface as best you can in aiming to be an advanced mind's eye player.

MEN NEED TO WORK ON IMAGERY

A golf putting research project done among women, junior and men golfers showed an interesting insight into **stage.** Using Sliver Springs (Calgary, Canada) private golf club members, their putting green, videotape compared to straight  image exercises for the 'memory' mind's eye cards we compared, separately, junior golfers, women players and men players all of low and medium handicap. We measured putting to a 15' target. The Research Assistant for our study, Lloyd Boody, soon enough found out that imagery improves putting and that videotapes of players own repeated successful putts, when committed to their mind's eye brain was functional in improving putting to that 15' target.

Women improved significantly, juniors improved somewhat and men and lean improvement. Men feel that their games are fixated it seems (Boody, Lucas). In another study, championship senior women players also improved.

FAMOUS EARLY ADVOCATES OF IMAGERY

Some famous advocates of the mind's eye in early history included Aristole and Pythagoras. Aristotle suggested that thought was housed in image form, brought on emotions and indicated inner knowledge. **Aristotle discovered that the world was a vast treasure house of entrancing mystery into which man's reason could enter and find knowledge.**

Pythagoras, on the other hand, taught mathematics by evoking dream imagery. Dreams and fantasies for sport will be reviewed later.

Famous scientists-imagers included Einstein who is said to have used his senses of perception and feel to interpret inner images that led to solving complex physics and mathematical problems. The image poster of Einstein is extremely popular.

Kekule is said to have discovered the benzene molecule and its structure by imagining a snake following its tail. Complex mathematical problems were solved by the Frenchman scientist Poincare in moments of visual reverie it is said.

VISUAL THINKING ADVOCATED

Rudolf Arnheim, an American visual thought and art professor who was Berlin trained and educated prior to 1940 has been recognized as an expert on visual thinking.

Arnheim has said that we suffer from "perceptual pellagra" which is a disease that is caused by lack of sensory experience. He says that too often we come to associate our senses with sex and sensuality and not with higher pursuits of mind and body. Arnheim also adds that our curious perversion started in the 18th century when learners and children were taught to doubt the immediate evidence of the senses.

ARNHEIM STRESSED SENSORY EXPERIENCE

Aristotle had also mentioned the problem of doubting the senses in early Greek thought and in science. Doubting the senses led to deterioration in both ability and frequency of accurate visual experience. Petersen liked the statement Arnheim best had made in stating that: "each culture seems to have developed a linguistic Nationalism that obscures the universality of most experience". **Some golfers have mentioned that doubting the senses and obscuring vital information is a problem in their golf play.**

Two examples of great visual or mind's eye image clarity that have been experienced by most people may illustrate our over dependence on the word rather than the experience. When you vividly remember someone's face despite not having seen that person for years, you are using visual mind pictures. Remembering a small town from years ago, or a smell that a word often has not been associated with, and the like, is a frequent visual mind memory.

If you attempt to describe that town in words to a son or daughter or other visitor that has never seen that town, when it was vibrant and alive in your impressionable childhood and youth, will lead to some startling conclusions for the new viewer. Often they will say that there is nothing there any more since their images for that place are not available.

TYPICAL CONTEMPORARY USE OF THE MIND'S EYE

Shelley Long once explained her use of psychology and visualization in her life. Perhaps you remember her from *Cheers* or from some movies such as *Irreconcilable Differences*.

Much of her work life has been undertaken to deepen experiences she has had. Earlier she visualized her desire 'to make Los Angeles career wise" and she got there. She visualizes fears away with equal dedication it is said. She feels her use of the mind's eye is highly successful. She mentions that fears are to keep us on our toes, but we must not dwell on them. If we do, it tends to make them happen. She believes that if you think things are going to go wrong and you visualize that, they will, because we affect our world. An extension of Murphy's law from Cheers bars eh? Whereas on the other hand, if you see things going right, and expect them to go right, they do so. At least according to Sutton of the Calgary Herald who wrote up some of Shelley's philosophy of life.

One other statement Long has is very important to golf and other creativity and energy requiring life-styles. She feels we should spend time alone and rebuild our creative energy. We agree and know several people who need this time. **It is the belief of the present book that intense experience with imagery programs and their workings can and does deepen one's own knowledge.** It enriches because it involves experience and accurate visualizing. Self-disclosure is enhanced and is generally healthy.

THE SELF FULFILLING PROPHECY

Any mention of the self fulfilling prophecy in lifestyle has a large tie-in to sport and performance where a number of prophecies exist. Self-sufficiency or the strength on one's conviction about oneself and one's performance, both physical and mental, are the basis for reaching new performance levels in sport. *Efficacy* is the belief you have in yourself and self knowledge are basic to overcoming any negative prophecies or thoughts. Many athletes appear to be vulnerable to weakened convictions about performance, especially rabbit eared golfers who sometimes listen too much. **The popularity of staying channeled or focused is very evident however and is growing as a counter technique in sport performance.**

IMPRINTING WITH SUCCESS IMAGES

The self-fulfilling prophecy has been demonstrated to be on accurate idea. It is a true phenomenon according to researchers such as Maclean, Gray and LaViolette. The phenomenon is studied via the limbic neocortical connection in the brain. The power of the self-fulfilling prophecy uses the limbic function for success images ("can do images") as an imprint to permit a person's actions to follow positive direction. The right hemisphere of the brain is connected richly to this specialized brain known as the Wemotional or Brain W. Right brain function has a lot to do with patterns or wholes and many people today are intuitive in this regard. Intuition is often mentioned when Tour golf performance is analyzed.

IMAGERY IN THE SCHOOLS AND UNIVERSITIES

Galyean, whose Academic field is integrative learning cites the wide usage of systematic guided imagery in all aspects of the school and higher up curriculum. Often a school day can start with basic centering exercises as in relaxing, deep breathing and sensory awareness general activities. Next, perhaps, the teacher sets the mood for the day with longer guided imagery excursions to favorite places and natural settings.

Students take naturally to shorter focusing exercises with the general idea of quieting mind chatter, dispelling distraction and sharpening mental attentiveness. According to Galyean, focusing techniques are being adapted in some school districts along with parallel training to focus parents and the child care generation.

GALYEAN IN THE SPORT FIELD AND TEACHER TRAINING

Applying systematic imagery to the sports field results in an effective learning tool. As well I and other educators have used it to sharpen the abilities of teachers, coaches, and performers by applying imagery to sport and physical education (Coaching Workshop, New Mexico S. Univ., Lucas).

Many National team coaching programs have spent considerable time on imagery as part of training team prospects. An ice luge training program was such an example for guided imagery. Our indoor program in driving sleds had athletes sit in sleds, eyes closed and steering all the way to the memorized track that they had been on many times before the warm weather melted us down. Every turn and every nuance of each curve was steered and timed through. An exact race time was sought. A 59.5 seconds may have been our repeated target. Confidence starts to surge in such athletes and then their natural talents can arise.

Our sport was natural luge or 'naturbahne' (not quite like Olympic luge called 'kunsbahne') and we added famous and competitive natural mountain valley tracks in North Italy and Austria. The best prospects went

there and thus were better prepared. **The guided imagery was like a library of golf course settings that are imaged as well** (Natural Luge H'dbook, Lucas).

LEARNING BENEFITS FROM IMAGERY
There are several learning and confidence building benefits currently associated with imagery. School Districts like it since it expands and deepens mental performance while not weakening basic subjects like math and science.

Summarized benefits are said to be:
1. **Retention of fact**
2. **Retention of accuracy**
3. **Effective learning of definitions and new ideas**
4. **Language proficiency**
5. **Interpersonal relationship via sharing ideas**
6. **Motor skill areas**
   6.1 Technical skill
   6.2 Refined sport skills
   6.3 Tactical skills
   6.4 Aiming skill
   6.5 Tenacity and attitude skills

In addition, the use of imagery education is said to prepare learners for learning, to reduce mind chatter, and thus focus and economize our schools, our golf centers and our sport development efforts. For many it is a more interesting way to learn. Advocates also predict trends of diminished academic achievement. Integrated learning while having to be selected carefully likely may be vital to schooling and learning of the future done now.

Golf classes for University age students and community golfers in both introductory and advanced categories are marked by greater interest in learners who thrive on self knowledge. Contracts for learning, keeping journals and inner golf experiences can allow students to play and learn golf on the **GOLF COURSE RIGHT AWAY AND FREQUENTLY!**

IT CAN BE A POWERFUL LEARNING EXPERIENCE WHEN A HEALTHY SELF-CONCEPT LEADS A PERSON OR GOLFER TO FEEL THAT THEY OWN THEIR OWN LEARNING POWER AND RECOGNIZE THEIR OWN PREVIOUSLY LATENT CAPABILITIES.

UNIMAGINATIVE PEOPLE VS. HEALTHY IMAGINATION
It is noticeable that unimaginative people are easily **bored.** In fact, Jerome Singer, a clinical psychologist from Yale University USA, has said that the problems can be worse. **Unimaginative people** are less relaxed and independent than highly imaginative people. In addition, the risks of an undeveloped fantasy life may include delinquency, violence, in overeating, and the use of dangerous drugs.

The scientific study of our mental lives has reaffirmed that **human beings are "thoughtful, curious and purposeful creatures"** something that early civilizations such as the Tibetan, Central American and the Chinese applied long ago. If you have ever had a Rorschach or inkblot test and you associate ambiguous ink blots with human figures in action (the human movement response) then you tend to extreme imagination and physically controlled or inhibited behavior. However, we also now understand that an imaginative person can drive themselves to problems such as despair or self concept complications in nutrition and eating disorders.

FITNESS AND THE IMAGINATION

For years jogging, cycling and other exercise programs have been proposed to improve fitness measures and to change the state of one's mind. Fitness programs mesh well with the imagery enhancement programs proposed in this book. Fitness studies have confirmed that one's mind (and especially FACTOR M: Imagination) can be altered and the imagination factor can be increased by exercise such as those for middle aged men and women. Brisk walking is likewise beneficial.

Little advantage is gained by riding a cart over any *fit* Tour player in my view. Very few handicapping conditions will allow the benefits of a training effect and if anything, a normally healthy Tour player always has the potential to benefit from training whereas someone like Casey Martin cannot have the same 'training-effect' advantage, at least in this writers opinion.

Despite this opinion, several PGA players state that use of a cart equals not having fair and level playing field. I can see some point to this, such as the cart allows the player to speed away from the spectators, which may allow brief benefits. Also, the player might be fatigued on occasion and the cart equates with a rest, it is admitted.

In fact and I heartily agree, Lee Trevino has stated on the USA based Golf Channel interview that he favors bulldozing all golf carts and getting back to a walk and golf mentality. Performance enhancement golf and golf carts don't mix well. Riding carts cause one to miss key environmental clues and cues along the fairways... **Aiming needs these clues and cues. Such clues can be stored in the imagination and can lead to lowered golf scoring.**

GUIDED AFFECTIVE IMAGERY

It is said that imagery programs are important in developing healthy self-feelings or the constituents of mental health. Psychologists such as Jourard and 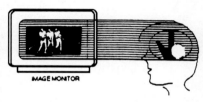 Rogers have cited the benefits of healthy self-determined concepts such as the ability to look within oneself (introspection) and to tell or share innermost stories (self-disclosure) with one's confidants or friends. Images stressing "successful me" are quite powerful and tend to imprint mental pictures of the self as capable, productive and well received by others. **To be comfortable with ones self and to accept others as they are is said to improve mental health. Story telling is vital in many ways and that is one area that golfers and tour caddies are good at.**

It is said that common biofeedback forms, such as tingling sensations and warmth in the hands and upper body, are also indicators of group unity and warm feeling among fellow participants in sports or other activity settings.

TANTRIC (T YOGA) AND HOLDING IMAGES IN THE MIND'S EYE

One of the ancient forms of the yoga-type or Tibetan Buddhism is the Tantric form. In Tantrism, there is a **highly developed procedure for holding an image** in the base of the brain. According to **Samuels and Samuels**, Tantrism clearly applies to modern persons who are not in direct contact with the truth and are separated from the truth by their obitual use of labels.

Paul Theroux, my favorite travel and cultural writer, in his book, **Riding the Iron Rooster,** commented on just how powerful Tantric rites and mind's eye images are in Tibetan Buddhism.

Some of the basics of this application of imagery are used for golf mind's eye enhancement. For example, the use on inner **screens or viewing rooms** and creative imagination while attempting to maintain high self control and perfect lucidity are used. So called viewing rooms are helpful for mind's eye practice and solidarity. The popular use of terms such as screens or windows of opportunity comes out of this idea.

An aspirant of Yoga must visualize images that have been seen and codified by the Masters rather than what his personal imagination might project. That idea is a **perfect application to golf** where the swing must follow the basics of most of the master golfers or especially the proper biomechanical sound and natural to you. Also we should follow the Masters from other fields such as religion, philosophy and lifestyle/health.

Two of my favorite Biomechanical professors and advisors, who confirm the above for golf are Richard Schmidt and Benno Nigg. **Nigg is from Switzerland and Calgary and has pioneered many concepts in engineering and physics that apply to sport and golf.** As I stated elsewhere modern swing technology for the PGA instructional model accepts the biomechanics of motion. Nigg, near #1, in biomechanical circles, confirmed this idea. Schmidt has explained them well.

Visualization or imagery in **Tantrism** is aimed at spiritualism but another principle applies fully to golf imagery. Images are to be based on past experience and not thought of as an intellectual exercise. Tantrism is similar to yoga and is a psychology of the mind, body and the spirit, according to Ramachandra Rao. **In golf, we use the images of the Masters and the experienced first and**

then and only then switch to your own self generated image models.

SEEING WITH THE MIND'S EYE

A complete description of seeing through
he use of visualization and imagery has been
written by Nancy and Mike Samuels. Their
book is devoted to introducing the reader to an
understanding of the nature of the visual process
and its importance in life. Their book is a very important one for our current
topics.

They view visualization and the mind's eye as the "other side of human nature".
That is, as **a sort of energizing, non-rational flow and as a path to enhanced
use of the right hemisphere of the brain.** One can experience this idea by
attempting to become familiar with the Ten Insights of the Celistine Prophecy
(see James Redfield-author), where we are encouraged to hold a vision with the
mind's eye as a further adventure. Here in Redfield's application, we see a set of
applications and adventure within imagery as a basic communicator and can call
it mind's eye imagery.

The most important procedure that one can undertake for improving imagery/
visualization according to the Samuels, is that of looking with awareness and
alertness at whatever is in one's visual field. **Go beyond everyday labels and
concentrate purely on visual images for mind's eye enhancement.** For
example, on your next visit to an art gallery, look for visual images and bring your
own interpretation to what you are viewing. Disregard labels. Do not read labels
too early.

Of course, one can grave a lifestyle without choice. Walter Kaufmann once
wrote a book about that very subject. A **very inactive imagery system** would
be one that could lead to a situations labelled **Decidophobia.** Golfers are in a
category where certain situations in golf call for a standard response and often,
no variation.

Golfers are also in a game requiring the utmost in creative imaginative
responses. **Many golfers are absolutely lost in this situation and it is sad
that golfers, mostly men, don't use creativity. Tom Watson, Marty Scoles
and other Tour players like Ben Crane, Mi Hyun Kim, and Michelle McGann**
certainly are creative however. Kim has six career LPGA victories in four years.
Her 9 wood is considered to be a closer aim than her 9 iron! She carries six
metal woods while most of us carry one or two hybrid metal woods. Aiming skill
has and is changing.

A recently published *Official Tour Guide* mentions some very creative golfers
who can handle bad weather play because of their extreme creativity and use of
the mind's eye and so golfers or at least **Tour players
are showing creativity it seems.**

SUMMARY
KEY WORDS AND NOTIONS OF CHAPTER ONE.

*THE ABILITY TO PRODUCE VIVID IMAGERS IN THE MIND'S EYE VARIES FROM PERSON TO PERSON BUT MOST CERTAINLY THE ABILITY TO GENERATE AND APPLY IMAGES IN SPORT CAN BE DRAMATICALLY IMPROVED AND AIMING IS ONE SUCH VITAL APPLICATION IN GOLF.
(See the Resources Section for Mind's Eye-Visualization Exercises)

*THERE IS LITTLE IN THE WAY OF ORGANIZED PROGRAMS AIMED AT DEVELOPING IMAGERY SKILL FOR GOLF. YOU ARE BEST TO CULTIVATE THIS SKILL YOURSELF AND REAP SOME SURPRISING BENEFITS IN GOLF AND IN LIFE.

*RECENTLY SOME TOUR PLAYERS HAVE UTILIZED ENHANCED IMAGERY AND CONCENTRATION SKILLS TO INCREASE THEIR MONEY WINNINGS AND THEIR SATISFACTION ON THE TOUR.

SOMETIMES THEY HAVE NOT HIT ANY SHOTS AT ALL FOR A FEW DAYS OR UP TO A WEEK. APPARENTLY THEIR BODIES RESTED AND HEALED AND THEIR INTUITION GOT INVOLVED AND THEIR MENTAL GOLF STABILIZED AS THEY RESUMED TOUR PLAY.

*GOLFERS AS A GROUP ARE KEEN ACCEPTORS OF THE MENTAL EDGE BUT MEN ARE OFTEN LESS RECEPTIVE WHICH IS TO THEIR DETRIMENT.

*THE MOST COMMON WAY TO IMPROVE YOUR GOLF SCORE IS TO IMPROVE YOUR MIND'S EYE ABILITY; TO DISCOVER AND CORRECT SWING FLAWS; TO IMPROVE SIMPLE GAME SYSTEMS AND TO ALIGN AND AIM BETTER AND USE SHOT PROCEDURES ON A REGULAR BASIS. **INTEGRATE AS MUCH AS YOU CAN REGARDING AIMING.**

NO MATTER WHAT LEVEL OF GOLF OR SPORT OR SPORT-FITNESS YOU ARE PRESENTLY INVOLVED IN, YOU TOO CAN BENEFIT FROM PROCEDURES THAT IMPROVE YOUR PURE MIND'S EYE SKILL AND ENHANCE YOUR GOLF SCORES.

*ALTHOUGH A YOUNG CHILD'S IMAGE SYSTEM NORMALLY DEVELOPS WELL, THERE IS EVIDENCE TO SUGGEST THAT IMAGES CAN BECOME INFLEXIBLE AND NON PRODUCTIVE. IF YOU ARE ONE WHOSE IMAGES ARE INFLEXIBLE, THEN IT IS OBVIOUS THAT YOUR BENEFITS COULD BE MINIMIZED.

*THE MANY GROUPS OF IMAGES WHICH VARIOUS PEOPLE USE ARE FULLY OUTLINED.

SUMMARY
<u>**KEY WORDS AND NOTIONS OF CHAPTER ONE**</u>
<u>**CONT'D**</u>

   *****ARISTOTLE AND PYTHAGORAS** ARE AMONG THE EARLY FAMOUS ADVOCATES OF IMAGERY. WHO KNOWS IF THEY PLAYED ANY BALL-TYPE GAMES BUT IT IS SAID THAT THEY DID BY SPORT HISTORIANS.

   *****DOUBTING OR NOT DEVELOPING THE SENSES CAN LEAD TO DETERIORATION IN BOTH ABILITY AND FREQUENCY OF VISUAL EXPERIENCE.** ADDING TO YOUR VISUAL EXPERIENCE WITH GREEN SIDE SHOT PRACTICE SUCH AS DEB RICHARD, LPGA, STRESSES ON THE GOLF CHANNEL CAN AUGMENT THE TYPE OF SHOTS THAT YOU SELECT AND THAT YOU COMMIT TO YOUR MIND'S EYE.

   *THERE ARE SEVERAL LEARNING BENEFITS CURRENTLY ASSOCIATED WITH IMAGERY. LOTS OF TIME IS NEEDED TO FULLY BENEFIT IN THIS DOMAIN THE NATURAL ABILITIES WE POSSESS ARE QUITE SENSATIONAL!

   ****

CHAPTER ONE
BIBLIOGRAPHY AND RESOURCES

Academy of Golf (Calgary)., Development & Tour Aspirant Workshop Series. Self Success Videotape Curriculum. Gdoclucas. 1991-1993

Adams M. and T. J. Tomasi. To Play Better Golf. Journey Editions, Charles E. Tuttle. Vermont, Rutland, Tokyo, 1993

Arnheim, R. Visual Thinking and A Conversation with Rudolph Arnheim, Psychology Today, 1972.

Anderson J. and B. Anderson, The Myth of Persistence of Vision Revisited. Journal of Film and Video, 45 1993.

Clyde, Jean Ann. Lessons from Douglas: Expanding Our Visions of What it Means to Know. Language Arts, 71 1994.

Cameron, Julia (with Mark Bragan), The Artists Way: A Spiritual Path to Higher Creativity. Putnams. New York, 1992

Cole, J., Florida. LPGA Player: Series of Reports and Consultant Reports, Hills of Lakeway. Academy of Tennis & Golf (Texas). 1990

Canadian National Luge Team. Naturbahne Sledding. Practice Sessions and Psychological and Performance Coaching. Canada, Northern Italy. Winter 1990 1993

Forisha, Barbara. Patterns of Creativity and M. Imagery in Men and Women. J. of Mental Imagery, 5 1981

Hudson G. and Galyean, B.C., Guided Imagery in the Curriculum. Educ. Leadership, 3 1983

Hogan, C., Five Days to Golfing Success. Meri Miller Assoc., Multnomah, Oregon 1986

Jourard and Rogers cited in Galyean (above).

Jacobsen, P., with Jack Sheehan, Buried Lies. Penquin: Middlesex, England. 1993 (1st pub. Putnams).

Kaufmann, W., Decidophobia, N.Y.: Random House, 1975

Kagan, J. and others. Reactivity in Infants and a Cross National Comparison, Child Development. 65 1994

Lucas, G. and L. Boody, Effects of Pos. Imagery and Success Videotape Viewing on Golf Performance, Cdn. Psych. Assoc., Canada: Banff, 1989

Lucas, G. and L. Boody, Golf Improvement Intermediated by Imagery Training or Success Videotape Viewing, Finland: Jvaskyla. 1990

Lucas G. Images for Golf: Visualizing Your Way to a Better Game. AZ Academic Sport Resources Press, Canada: Edmonton. 1987

Lucas G. Imagery Strategies and their Impact on Shotmaking Accuracy and Game Score in Golf. California: Los Angeles, 1984 (Olympic Congress).

Lucas G. The NEW Images for Golf: The Fundamentals of Visualizing and Scoring, Victoria B.C. and Littlefield, AZ; AZ Edge Publisher, 2006

Lucas G., Sanchez Jr., F.F., and J. Borro; Six 1 Putts...Minimum to Cure a Sick Golf Score. (55 Golf Exercises to make one putts happen). AZ Edge Publisher, Victoria B.C. and Littlefield, AZ 2005, 2006

Lucas G., Natural Luge Imagery & Performance Handbook, (Contract: Cdn. Luge Association) Calgary: AZ Edge Publishers. 1990

Laurence, J., Woburn, England. European PGA Tour report to G. Lucas 1993, (series of consultant reports).

Nisker, W. Bhudda's Nature (A Practical Guide) Bantam Books, N.Y., Toronto, London, Sydney, Auckland, 1998

Ramachandra, R., The Tantra Psychology., India, New Delhi, Heinemann Pub., 1979

Maclean A., Gray B. and Laviolette C., New Theory: Feelings Code, Organize Thinking. Brain and Mind Bulletin. 7 1982

Redfield, J., (with others): 1. The Celestine Prophecy (An Adventure) N.Y., Warner, 1993   2. The Tenth Insight., N.Y., Warner, 1996   3. An Experiential Guide., (The Celestine Prophecy), N.Y., Warner, 1995.

Singer, J., Fantasy: The Foundation of Serenity. Psychology Today. July, 1976

Stockton, D., E David Stockton's Putt to Win: Secrets for Mastering the Other Game of Golf. With A. Barkow., Simon Schuster., N.Y., London, Toronto, Sydney, Tokyo, Singapore. 1996

Schmidt, R., Motor Control and Learning. Champaign, Ill: Human Kinetic Publishers., 1982

Thurman, R., Infinite Life., Riverhead Books, Penguin Group, N.Y., 2004

University of Calgary. Continuing Education Golf Series. Self Success Videotape Curriculum with Elite Senior Women Players. 1990

Workshop Series. Canadian Junior Girls Golf Program. Canadian Ladies Golf Union. (Pinebrook: Calgary) 1989. 1991

Golf Week, Read It. Live It. www.golfweek.com Orlando, Fl., 2000-2006

CHAPTER 2: FAMOUS AIMERS AND HOW THEY AIM

Objectives: How non golf athletes and golfers use imagery and sport psychology concepts.; examples of the mind's eye imagery studies; tapering off- a new concept at least in golf; fantasy and sport effort; the mental build up; mind over matter; anti attitudes; joggers and the mind's eye; overall approach and imagery; scientific scrutiny; and psyching out and playing matchplay in golf with modern humanistic approaches.

****

Athletes in all sports are taking charge of their images and turning them into sport performance successes. Every athlete desires to be self-dependent. Very few athletes and Tour players do not wish to be creative in their methods of training. The majority need support to perform well. Such support is in addition to the athletes self controlled skills.

Perhaps one of the strongest reasons Tour players turn to mind's eye imagery and other mental strategies is that they want to take charge of themselves. Sport psychologists note that such development assists the athlete who decides to reduce or end their sport participation. Since they have developed lots of mental skill, they can usually adapt and adjust to new sport participation patterns and, indeed, new challenges in life. Furthermore, the work ethic becomes somewhat more of a factor in sport as they thrive on the work ethic which can be rewarding to them.

IMAGERY SUCCESS STORIES

Some of the imagery success stories which follow show precisely this independent quality. In addition, as experts in psychology contend, athletes have developed techniques for practice and play while using the mind's eye in positive and effective performance. The can produce, use and control their images in a myriad of effective ways as in aiming.

Viewers of baseballs World Series, have a distinctive insight into the mind's eye and visual superiority. Cameras installed being the catcher's area are utilized electronically to show the pitched ball to the viewer. The pitches are rerun in super slow speed. Most impressive are the pitches that tumble towards you the imaginary batter. The "tumbling' motion and the incredible dropping flight path make this view seem as if we could see the same pitch at regular full speed. It in no wonder the most common form of imagery in baseball is that of a "larger" ball moving to the batter. **Here is aiming skill personified. The electronic baseball pitch information gives flight path and speed and is just**

like the mind's eye that can and should track a golf ball.

It is said that legendary Stan Musial could see and imagine a baseball pitch with heightened awareness. He saw in "super slow motion" without the benefit of any camera, slow motion or freeze frame electronics. Musial did not guess where the ball was, he could actually see it. **He said that he could see the seams of the pitched ball. So that, Musial would likely be able to visually catalogue the pitches of each pitcher he faced -- a decided advantage indeed.** Actually, Musial is known to have mentally classified **320 types** of distinct pitching deliveries.

Wayne Gretzky, the fabulous Canadian and USA based ice hockey center has **extraordinary visual skills** which enables him to play game upon game without missing any passes at all. He is equally precise at making passes. His mind's eye imagery skills appear to be linked to an ability to pre locate teammates, opponents, and body checkers. His passes seem uncanny in their aiming and consistency. The best defence men still don't often take his body out on the boards simple because he is pre locating them it seems and will embarrass them perhaps. Dealing with Gretzky's wizardry on ice appears to be virtually impossible. His assist totals are always superior it seems.

Gretzky has stated that he "sees" hockey puck, position and player movement patterns as a series of constantly changing angles and patterned re-angles. His aiming skill seems to mesh with his "seeing" skill.

Other athletes are well known for tending to be highly aware of the mind's eye player location on the courts, fields or the other surfaces of sport. Pele in soccer and Cousy and Jordan in basketball are three such famous athletes. Imagery and visualization skills give these athletes a natural superiority in court and ball location awareness.

Progressive coaches are redoubling their effort to include visual development drills in their practices. Recently, sport vision experts and optometrists have linked visual superiority to these outstanding athletes and to natural or aware athletes in general.

However, just the opposite has been investigated recently when ice hockey goalies who were assumed to possess superior vision have been found to be guessing at blurs or in-error puck location. Of course the movement of the highly speeding puck in ice hockey seems not to be seen by many viewers and as a result an electronic blip which follows rapid puck changes in direction in being experimented with in televised hockey.

Imagery rehearsal or pregame imagery warm-up may be assumed to be easily carried out by a visually superior athlete. In golf, what is that warm up to be like? Vision labs are working with athletes to improve ball watching or flight "tracking" skills which may not be available to all peoples visual skill.

"Tracking" ability is subject to improvement. As vision skills improve, so does the basic imagery ability of a golfer-athlete and aiming may get better. The emergence of the optic or the half colored ball (and the colored ball of various

makes) is related to this development (although golfers tend not to utilize such a basic advantage in ball technology at the present time, or for game play at least).

In our University golf camp and classes, we believed that having students observe optic golf ball flight patterns was a basic underlying skill of golf fundamental. If your brain has dealt with visual ball tracking information, it will be able to visualize effectively and use club take away skill to accommodate such flight. A golfer will be more likely to develop such skills with their golf swing.

Jim Thorpe, the famous American First Nation athlete was an all around natural athlete. It has been noted that he had such acute imagery and mind's eye ability that he could duplicated another athlete's sport movements or skills the very first time he tried to do so. Apparently, he would often be superior to the other athlete even on the first tries of that sport.

Repeated tests show a clear relationship between best performers and visual aiming and imagery data in visual or tracking sports (golf, football, hockey, tennis). Self accounts written by great athletes tend to confirm this notion.

DO FAMOUS AIMERS HAVE SUPERIOR VISUAL SKILL?

Superior athletes and Tour players may have superior visual skills which in turn may allow them to be superior mind's eye players with high self confidence.

In fact, speaking of Tour players, who are superior visualizers and aimers? **Germany's Bernhard Langer** has been found to be a visually aware athlete and one of the best putters on the PGA and the European Tour. It probably is not a coincidence that a recent study has shown him using visual lines on the greens for the highest percentage of time of any male golfer on Tour.

That is to say, if we count the **elapsed time** for each golfer reading the putt line on each green by coding for each five second block of time spent on the green, we find that Langer is the top one at this part of effective putting. **So that, we consider Langer a famous aimer in golf. A majority of putt reading can be done before it is your turn to putt, you will find that Langer is not a slow player.**

NBA PLAYERS AND GOLF LESSONS

A case study of a NBA player, who had a shooting accuracy problem, has shown a startling relationship. After a golf lesson consisting of training in visual lines and aiming skills the player improved in shooting in basketball and his season shooting statistics. **AIMING SKILLS ARE SAID TO BE CLOSELY LINKED TO SUPERIOR VISUALIZATION. APPARENTLY IMAGERY REKINDLES FURTHER USE OF MUSCLE-MEMORY AND DEVELOPS EVEN BETTER MIND'S EYE IMAGES. HOW COULD THIS BE SO? PERHAPS WE PROMOTE OR DEVELOP OUR AIMING SKILLS IN SPORT.** Professor **Joan Vickers,** a Visual Kinesiologist, and other scientists have shown that vision in sport is subject to eye movement including the involuntary blinking or closing off of the visual "signals" of aiming or shooting or striking in sport. Perhaps training is indicated here in the phase of visual sport as well.

TRANSFERABLE SKILLS IN IMAGERY
Athletes find that imagery rehearsed off the field of competitions in immediately transferable to on the field situations. A gold medal winning archer uses a simple "posture" image of herself as a steel stake in the ground. A top biathlete goes from the stretching of the cross country skier to the stability of a target shooter by imitating the Rock of Gibralter.

Mark Blencarne, an archery Gold Medalist, has been using imagery as a performance review, a method taught by John Syer and Christopher Connolly. Blencarne and soccer players from professional Tottenham Hotspur show an "extra ordinary degree of detail" in postgame memory. Athletes recounting or re-imaging a game or competition discover new information and insights. Less tangible items such as when the athlete got up, how they dressed, and their routine turned out to be extremely important to the athletes performance. **Performance review done in this way assists reworking an image program aimed at future competition.**

REWORKING AN IMAGE PROGRAM
A tennis player on the International circuit used a clear image of a famous tennis player like Ivan Lendl moving to and hitting a superior passing shot to improve her own speed of moving because she felt she was lacking a movement and had a hard time duplicating it in practice. Such mental practice routines allow movement to start earlier in a shot situation, the athlete knew she could hit without specific physical practice.

IMAGERY PRACTICE 3 SINCE THE 800's!!
Kurt Krueger founder of the Practical Sport Institutes located in New Delhi, Los Angeles and Melbourne, has adapted imagery practices that appeared in textbooks in India as early as 800 AD.

Workshops run by Krueger's Institutes include visualization, meditation, warm up, cool down and nutrition. As a result, an Australian rules football team has accomplished outstanding improvement by using mind's eye or visualization in the their team development. Swimmers have also accomplished prodigious feats.

FANTASY IMAGES VS REAL IMAGES
Psychiatrists have noted that everyone has a vision of what he or she looks like when they play a game of tennis or golf. However, they also contend that the image is usually a misleading illusion of mastery and control.

Usually players discover the gulf between fantasy and reality and their self-esteem can be endangered. A book written by Cobb, Kahn and Cath entitled *Love and Hate on the Tennis Court,* details this 'misleading' mind's eye notion.

JIM MILLER: NATIONAL POWERBOAT CHAMPION

Athletes such as Jim Miller have not only set world speed records but have used mind's eye images in unique ways. Bennett and Pravits, have described  how Miller designed a new mystery engine speedboat in his mind's eye until those plans were elaborate enough to cast, machine and build his engine part by part. When he completed the project he set a new five mile world speed record with his 'imagined and completed speedboat'.

REPRESENTATION OF LOCATION (OR THE MIND SELECTING INFORMATION)

Researchers, such as Kyle Cave, are involved in helping us understand how visual cues are used by humans and golfers in their image or mind's eye selection. Most people use location information for mind's eye representation in a lot of ways including, just prior to making a golf shot or other sport target decision. A golfer may see a row of mounds and several mound-appearing sand bunkers as they walk up to the green. **Golfers can face quite a lot of location information.**

LOCATION INFORMATION FOR GOLF

When a golfer sees a lot of location, such as those 'mounds and sand bunkers', the golfer then should eliminate the unnecessary overkill in information. Sometimes a golfer can be overwhelmed by a 'new look' golf course and not eliminate enough location information. **Researchers are just now finding out how we humans select information and that is why they are studying mental rotation tasks and other visual selection procedures that we carry out even when we are as young as infant age.**

Getting back to our example, only those mounds that could directly affect the approach of our shot are selected for the pre shot mind's eye setup for aiming.

Since the golfer just wants the ball to land on the green so it will release in the direction of the pin placement, **it follows that feel for distance and shot shape is every bit as important as image selection.**

In fact, the golfer should keep their image or mind's eye as simple and clear as possible and of course, should see the ball in flight and especially see the ball landing and spinning and rolling tot he hole. **Often this complete procedure produces unexpected and pleasant golf results and lower scores.**

FAMILIARITY WITH ALL BALL FLIGHTS

That is why the golfer should watch and become familiar with shot shape and golf course landscape. By this, I mean, such watching as going to a Tour event and standing near the target areas or greens and repeatedly seeing balls hit towards them; the watcher. By watching balls flying towards you as you stand beside a green or landing area, you may become fascinated that you know little about this phase of ball flight.

Familiarize your visual field with high flight, medium flight, wind flight and the various shots one is capable of hitting with some additional practice.

FEARLESS FRED COUPLES

When Fred Couples, one of the Pacific Northwest's best contributions to Tour golf, was interviewed after winning a recent Kapaluaa Hawaii golf event, he said he did one thing effectively in the final round...that being keeping his shots "below the wind all day". Here Couples is combining his knowledge and ability for shot shape with selective viewing in his golf mind's eye system. **Of course, his reputation and ability to keep the game simple is very evident in this example of golf kept simple.**

SO THE GOLFER IS A VERY SELECTIVE VIEWER OF THE LANDSCAPE THAT MIGHT PREVENT AN EFFECTIVE SHOT FROM HAPPENING. THE GOLFER KEEPS THEIR VIEWING SIMPLE AND CHANNELLED, AS IT WERE.

GOOD GOLF IS AIMING WITHOUT COMPLICATION

Early evidence by researcher Cave indicates that we code our new images via the retina rather than some complicated spatial transformation or other brain skill.

The coding appears to be easily accomplished by the retina in a natural way.

So golfers soon learn not to be overwhelmed by golf course architecture. Try like they might a golf course designer and course builder should understand that the mind's eye aiming' golfer sees very little of any wondrous mounding, bunkering, railroad tie water trimming and shaping of holes. Strictly aside from this designers' apparition, we can still concede that the signature hole or holes are a great advertising medium for attracting the golfer.

KEEP VISUAL INFORMATION SIMPLE

I suppose one could say that a golfer keeps their visual information as simple as possible. For the golfer even the signature hole or holes requires strokes which count for one stroke, just as the other holes count in score.

IMAGE SELECTOR

PRACTICAL SUGGESTION

To prepare for a Tournament walk, fast-walk or jog the course's holes that are visually 'wicked' or rich in mounds, sand bunkers and water trim several times before playing that course. Then practice hitting the shots for the course and the expected (and unexpected) weather and the wind. Play the course as many times as possible even though you often will have to depend on the other means outlined in this section.

Hit balls high, medium high and low by controlling the club face angle of the club as it passes towards the ball. Control the angle of the take-away of the club and soon you will establish some control of ball shot shape.

Another practical suggestion is to remember to do ball rotation exercises to memorize ball flight or roll patterns for your favorite ball label. Move the ball away from your eyes as you rotate it. Rotate the ball with open eyes and rotate the ball with almost closed eyes for improving your memory in the mind's eye. (See also the Section at the rear of the book labelled: **EXERCISES FOR VISUALIZATION SKILLS**).

Soon all of this type of visual location information will be easier for the golfer to accept. It is just like the rest of today's information overkill, look at how much of it we filter out, reclassify, or deal with later or in some other form.

By all means, watch shots from the landing places for shots, as mentioned above. Perhaps you will see something new from behind or below the shot, or about shot height and shot descent.

One day after caddying on a practice day at a Canadian tour event, I got to play a few holes just ahead of two Tour players, Dennis Harrington of USA and Paul Devenport of New Zealand, both super nice guys. All of a sudden, two balls, one 20 seconds after the other, went flying over the top of my head and descended about 20 or 30 yards down the fairway. I knew they were teeing off, but thought I was out far enough and a rise in the fairway prevented them from seeing me. Ho, ho, ho!! When a drive lands it sounds like a rocket taking off, but instead it is a decelerating sound---like nothing I had ever heard before and really scary.

Maybe all you have been doing is playing and maybe you need to review some the wonders of modern ball shot shape dynamics. I sure did!

TUCSON'S RANDOLPH: A GREAT DRIVING RANGE

After doing a lot of watching of shot shape, a golfer will find that a great driving range or practice facility is an especially good help. Even public or city recreation facilities, such as Randolph in Tucson, Arizona USA, are immensely useful. There, the golfer, will have rows of palm trees among many, many mound shaped targets. This provides multiple aim lines for the golfer. Such palm trees and mounds greatly enhance your chances for aim practice and good information selection golf.

Not only that, but Tour players, such as Annika Sorenstam, have laser binoculars to help such practice in aiming and I have seen her go back to the practice range at Randolph after her round and measure the exact distances to various palm tree targets and then hit shot after shot at each

distance.

MORE REPRESENTATION OF LOCATION (ATSV)

Another line of research, involving grade 7-10 students in science class, has found support for our ability to handle complex information in the mind's eye. Science students can quite naturally develop visualization strategies for involved information quite on their own and later construct strategies with novel new information added in. Students (and golfers) can do a lot of transferring. **This newly acknowledged skill has been named analogically transferring specific visualizations (more simply ATSV).**

Of course, this ATSV can apply to several new golf courses we seem to all have played on lately.

TRACKING: OVERHEAD OR UNDERWATER

An effective form of the mind's eye, adapted from an underwater slalom canoe 'tracking or mechanical track' has been the image of a helicopter's low level survey for each golf hole and golf green that a golfer is about to play on. This enhances the memory of the hills, ridges and hummocks immediately surrounding the green. A canoe-slalomist at the World Championship level is said to have done a similar image exercise. The canoeist's conscious mind would not accept increased high speed canoe travel until the competitor imaged

or did a mind's eye of a mechanical underwater track for the whole course. He became accustomed to this new high speed track and 'brain-power' canoeing turned into better competitive performance.

A golfer can have exactly the same experience. Their mind will accept better ball placement attempts and more pinpoint accuracy only when they show the right brain that each hill, ridge and course characteristic is well known and acceptable to their golf performance brain.

Just imagine how simple the mind's eye images are that any well known Tour player uses. They use pinpoint accuracy when playing well and that image of accuracy cannot be cluttered with complex visual information.

COURSE FAMILIARITY BREEDS ACCURACY

Along with pinpoint accuracy, remember that distance control via the swing feel or kinesthesis and swing speed is far more important as a factor here. Like Annika Sorenstam perhaps we must practice for this part of golf.

CADDIES ON TOUR USE LASER BINOCULARS

On Tour, when caddies arrive at the next Tour event, they can be seen on Sunday night or early Monday using various distance checkoffs for visual cues. In small groups or even husband and wife teams, they use laser binoculars and pacing to verify accurate distances. They also write down or sketch slopes and front to back variation in greens. One caddy on Tour appears in an ad for binoculars and gives a testimonial for his brand of equipment.

AIMING: SHOT SHAPE AND TRACKING: THE FACTORS

Another factor which affects aiming and shot shape and tracking is how your golf equipment matches your own swing requirements. So that, while discussing various shot shapes and trajectories of swing, it also should be kept in mind that, "how a shaft performs is a main indicator of its quality" (see Bibliography). Therefore, if you are trying to improve accuracy and consistent accuracy, you may have to pay much more attention to factors such as shafts, flexpoint and torque or your basics of club selection.

Poorer quality shafts usually have inconsistent balance and flexpoints (so called kickpoint), which can result in inconsistent shot shape and distance control even with the same swing. A high quality graphite shaft (high % graphite fibre and low % fiberglass) and a good steel shaft (which has more work gone into its development as a shaft, than the shaft materials) with a consistent flex will be able to assist a fundamentally sound golf swing produce consistent shot shape and distance. Golf shots are much more than how HOT or fast a ball jumps or leaps off one's club face. **Consistency with shot shape and with distance control is a big time winner on Tour, you can be sure.**

AIMING: FACTORS AFFECTING YOUR ACCURACY

Some other points to assure you know why shots traject high and not so high involve flexpoint or kickpoint. Flexpoint is the point where the majority of the shaft bending occurs since the lower the kickpoint the higher the resulting shot (since the shaft kicks in later in a swing).

AIMING: FACTORS AFFECTING SHOT SHAPE: TORQUE

Of course, the ability of the shaft to resist twisting (that is, torquing) is related to your ability to not contact off center hits. Off center hits have little accuracy going to a target which is quite fare away. Perhaps you will have to get shafts which include some boron near the tip of the club which will resist twisting or even use titanium, an expensive alloy that has little torque and even dampens shock at impact. Such shock is not pleasant to feel.

AIMING: SHOT SHAPE AND AGE OF THE PLAYER

If you are over age 50-60+ or are losing your golf fitness or for other reasons are having trouble with hand-eye coordination, you may ready not getting enough on-center hits, then you may have to work more on this part of the game. You may have to pick up on doing more repetitions on the practice fairway to warm up for a game. Take a nonpermanent **flow pen marker** with you to practice and every now and then put a coin sized patch of marker ink on the sweetspot of the iron you are hitting with. Hit a shot a see exactly where the dimples of the ball marked the ink.

If you find you are only rarely near the sweetspot then you will be having trouble with shot shape for technical or athletic reasons. Don't worry, stay relaxed and practice a little more. Even a well coordinated golfer will benefit from such extra practice.

Of course, try to let swing feel include the feel of good ball contact. Hit lots of practice shots that have a purpose. **A pleasant by-product** will be a new state of golf fitness and that, combined with good technical equipment will help you become an accurate striker of the ball.

Shot shape and perhaps better aiming may become a consistent part of your game.

AIMING: SHOT SHAPE - A CASE HISTORY

One golf season, I had not hit many accurate shots and I simply was hardly ever striking the needed center of gravity hits and as a consequence, landing on few greens in regulation.

The next winter, I joined a good indoor golf school called Allreds, which had swing instructor golf professionals and also had video swing checks three times a day. The golfer could work on  **swing corrections and almost immediately get feedback on how they were doing and see the swing on videotape with professional commentary.**

Also, that winter I made a lifetime purchase of good shafts and custom clubheads and grips. Notice that shafts came first in the order of purchase. The golf school club fitter worked with me for one week off and on and finally it was settled the ALDILAHM series with HM40 shafts might be best for my swing and speed of swing and fitness for golf. The recommendation of HM40 was specifically for average or above average players to maximize distance and accuracy. They are premium grade fibres and some of the lowest torque ratings available. All that series has mid point flex ratings except the HM55 for lower trajectory and they felt great with the mid graduated cavity back clubheads the fitter recommended.

Top amateurs and Tour players do not use the HM series preferring the ASD series for frequency matching for even greater consistency when they have chosen ALDILA, or other great shaft makes. Most shaft makers have superlite series for seniors, women with medium speed swings and any player needing a light shaft (that is one that is one half the weight of steel) AND extra whip and therefore distance, given that kind of swing speed. With lightweights you can swing slower without losing distance whereas accuracy might be a little less, but still plenty acceptable.

If you can handle longer shafts (grip one inch down the grip ntil you are swinging the same time after time) and swing slower by all means do so, as the 'bullwhip' or 'fly rod' effect will give more clubhead speed and thereby enhance distance. **Commit all of this to the mind's eye, for sure and rehearse with the mind's eye and pleasant results will come your way.**

The author once owned a Golf Technology Golf learning center (Idaho/Mr.

Bud Blankenship-inventor and developer) and found out via the electronic swing analyzer sensors that one mile per hour clubhead speed=almost exactly two yards distance. New golf club technology may have enhanced this ratio of speed=distance for a normally fit golfer. It was very unusual to find a golfer who could swing with clubhead speed over 115 mph, they were the exception since 90 mph was respectable for a developing swing.

SHOT SHAPE AND GRIPS
Of course, I wedded my new shafts and clubheads with proper grips, another vital equipment factor. Avon golf grips of the correct thickness for medium-small men's hands and so called 'cadet fingers'. AVON GRIPS have an incredible cushion core for firm positive gripping power ("holding a child's hand-power"). CHAMOIS type grips are claimed to be the world's #1 air cushion grips and chamois feels good in hot and cooler conditions. For rainy places consider cordlines with alternating soft grip materials. See Golf Week Magazine for advertizing on grips for sale.

IN SUMMARY THIS SECTION: THE FRIENDLY FLOW PEN
SO GUESS WHAT? DO YOU THINK THAT FLOW PEN COMES WITH ME TO PRACTICE SWEET SPOT HITS EVEN WITH THIS SOPHISTICATED GOLF EQUIPMENT? OF COURSE IT DOES.

OFTEN THE FEEL OF THE SWEETSPOT CONTACT IS AN INNER FEELING OF THE MIND'S EYE CALLED A KINESTHETIC IMPRESSION (correctly spelled kinesiology or kinaesthetic). Such an inner feeling is a big part of aiming on the golf course. So if you can feel where the clubhead and the shaft is at all times in your swing combined with mind's eye skill, you probably are a great golfer and we all wish we could be like you in golf!

SHOT SHAPE: TWO KEY POINTS
Two other summary points are included here:
(1) When you work hard to be able to vary shot shape, you may find your energy level and golf fitness of your body will also be something you have to deal with. At least you can do something about this state of affairs in fitness. Often, you will find you can hit balls productively (and creatively, that is, with mind's eye aiming) for hours on end instead of minutes. Now you will find that you do not have to grind your body and mind to be successful. Instead, overall, you actually could do less ball striking.

(2) Understand that all aspects of aiming are governed by simple aiming mind's eye imagery. Simple procedures of aiming (like aiming using knee line, shoulder line, hip line and keeping them is agreement or the myriad of other aiming devices reviewed in the book) and some proper skill of golf mechanics (one author calls that Classic golf vs Quantum golf - see Bibliography) as well as good equipment suiting your own body requirements. **ALL AIMING MIND'S EYE**

IS REVIEWED IN THE NEXT CHAPTER.

*Although this Section consists of pretty basic golf knowledge, and article in **AUSTRALIAN GOLF DIGEST** (May, 1994) assisted in developing the parts on golf equipment along with my own material on Shot Shape. Acknowledged are Ross Derham (True Temper), Craig Waldon (Quality Golf) in an article: Looking for Mr. Goodbar and also New Shafts: Adding Order to Chaos by Guy Yocum and Brett Parker.

MENTAL PREP--NOT SO SILLY AFTER ALL! AND TAPER OFF PHYSICALLY AND BUILD UP MENTALLY

Athletes who develop strong mental prep programs are learning more and more about tapering off physical prep in the two or three days prior to competition, especially in highly exhausting sports or events. For the Tour player this can mean ProAm play and/or special preparation practice.

Not only does this give them a physical advantage but it gives time to prepare mentally. Mental preparation through the mind's eye involves low level muscle excitation and it appears that such low level muscle excitations are suitable preparation for whole-body efforts like **golf.**

But not all athletes believe strongly enough in a mental program and thus they can easily do too much physical preparation. The injury lists continue to grow on Tour. Of course, it is not uncommon for confidence (and therefore; consistency) to suffer under these circumstances.

MIND'S EYE WARM UP

These types of problems may be solved in the future. Apparently, Soviet sport scientists believe so strongly in tapering off physically and maximizing mentally that concentration testing is being used immediately prior to competition, in the belief that designating starting lineups or competition entrants should be based on which athlete is concentrating well immediately before playing (or can you imagine, even before teeing off in the Walker Cup or in National amateur or high school and college golf play, which essentially is the same format as counting only three of the four best scores from a four person golf team).

This would be ideal for two goalie systems common in lots of sports events. Two goalie systems have existed for a long time in ice hockey, and goalie rotation could be subject to scientific guidance. However, just yesterday, one of the most experienced general managers in the NHL stated that he probably would get better goalie play over a full season by a one goalie system rather than being forced to use two goalies for roughly one half of the games each per season. **There are also many variables and unknowns in sport performance that it may be that golf will be left out of such science and intuition based decisions in sport.**

However, since the mind's eye is basic to concentration it still may

not be preposterous to assume that mind's eye warm-ups (at least) prior to competing could be monitored or at least checked off by a golfer-athlete.

BUILD UP MENTALLY THE DAY PRIOR ON TOUR

BUILDING UP MENTALLY THE DAYS BEFORE COMPETITION HAS BEEN MENTIONED AS AN EFFECTIVE PREPARATION STRATEGY. REST AND THE TOUR GRIND ARE ALL, OF COURSE, MULTIPLE FACTORS. **See a discussion and proposal for winning by a system in Tour Golf in chapter six of the present book.**

THINK TANKS ON GOLF

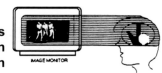

In the last few years, World Wide Congresses or think tank meetings on golf science, have been held at St. Andrews at the Olde course in Scotland, and in Tokyo, Japan. The topics have included mental golf among other topics, as well as all facets of the expansion and development of the wonderful sport of golf and have included: fear reduction; anxiety loss and most performance concerns which a golfer encounters. Other than these topics, there has been very little indeed regarding the mental aspect of golf performance.

AIM LIKE THESE MODELS: GUNNER GUNN AND LAURA DAVIES

Sometimes your image system can be highly tuned into precise accuracy. Often time spent watching a fine precision and rhythmic golf swing can pump up your mind's eye applications. Target aiming can become very inspired, even for prolonged periods of time. So can golf performance.

Recently, Graham Gunn from Toronto, playing in the National Club Professionals Championship of Canada and known to his friends in the Gallery as 'Gunner', shot either 67, 68, or 69 in all four rounds at tough Priddis Greens in southern Alberta. His swing was so compact, precise, and repeatable that after observing a few hours of his target aiming golf one could not help but get pumped up in their own golf. Sure enough, in the next 3 or so rounds of golf I played, I had much more accuracy going for my golf.

I didn't even have to think of Gunner Gunn (gun...bang...target...bullseye, etc., etc.). I just had aim mind's eye imagery and better modeling I would guess. Unfortunately, it didn't last forever. **According to my present text on mind's eye golf, this should not extinquish unless your mental effort is not there. You guessed it... no, it is not easy or automatic.**

The effect of watching such a golfer, seems to automatically influence one's subconscious brain, the source of our ultimate energy in visualization.

Maybe another book on the mind's eye in golf should not be ***Mind's Eye Golf: Greenside and Putting***, but instead should by ***The Ultimate Energy: Golf's Last Challenge.*** Even Tiger Woods fails at this part of golf as does most every Tour player.

LAURA DAVIES AT TUCSON

Laura Davies seeks pinpoint accuracy to go along with her long hits which at a recent Ping Welchs LPGA Tour event, were only matched by three or four of her opponents. Now Korean and perhaps Scottish and more Asian-born athletes are doing precision aiming. The US is also developing some precise aimers it seems. Nothing stays the same everything changes--even golf.

I started suspecting that maybe Davies was super accurate when the editors of **Woman Golfer** in the Australian Golf Digest stated she should get credit of pinpoint accuracy with her iron play. She recorded a hole in one recently in the Tournament of Champions final round. She aced the 8th hole with a 130 yd pitching wedge. **Long and accurate was the suspicion!**

By now, I have watched Laura Davies practice just prior to teeing off many, many times and know her caddies somewhat. I am positive in this practice she is seeing none of the intimidating mounds and palm tree targets in the wedge distance target zone of the practice area at Randolph, Tucson LPGA event. Instead, she is openly disgusted with her shot mechanics as she hits a few (just a few) especially with wedge. She flicks a cigarette butt into the grass or stomps on the butt to work out her evident frustration or imagined frustration, and says a word or two. **She was quite disgusted one particular morning at Randolph.**

She spends more time trying to do better, but soon enough, has had enough and went over to the putting area. But, I also take note that nothing bothers her very long at all and she is friendly and businesslike at the same time. She smiles and says cheery things to her friends and supports the golfers just like many of the Tour players do. The caddies take their cue from this behavior mode and are cool and friendly too. **Later, I realize that for Laura Davies, this little tour of the practice area and the putting green is like a social ritual which readies her to play.**

Overall, she may be a somewhat concerned with swing mechanics (who isn't on Tour?) and she works only on wedge and driver while most of the a.m. draw players work thoroughly with each club and pay lots of attention to alignment and solid, repetitive contact with the ball.

Still and all her concern, is only superficial it seems and her pinpoint accuracy may be a thing she knows she can reproduce later. Her images for golf seem to be at a good and simple level for her aiming procedures. She portrays the image of a winner, one can be sure of that, even if wins are fewer and further between with the LPGA International Stars like Annika, Karrie, Si Ri Pak, Kelly Robbins, Helen, Liselottle, Lorie and Allison and on and on.

LAURA DAVIES GOES ON TO PHOENIX

She is happy with her putting these weeks because Karsten Solheim (the Senior golf patriarch around Moon Valley, Phoenix and the developer of Ping technology) although rumored to be under the weather health wise

this week, comes over from his house and has been seen on the greens coaching Laura. Later, I see Karsten on the green, sure enough coaching some of the Stars. It is said Laura is using a new Ping putter with an inset in the face surface. Sure enough, that is true also. She putts well just now.

Some of her wedge play is pinpoint to be sure and her putting is good but overall **her great season** is just getting underway it seems. Later in the season, as in most of her career, she wins again and has top finishes and continues a great battle with Annika Sorenstam (of Sweden and University of Arizona) and the impressive Australian non-youngster Karrie Webb for the honor of being the first woman on the LPGA Tour to win a million dollars in one season.

Notable is the special attention paid to reading the greens by both players. What the caddies or the Tour player reads on each green is usually putted right into the middle of the cup. No problem it seems. Both Webb and Sorenstam seem to use their caddies to verify read or add information to the read of the green (more than other players use their caddies for this part of competitive edge striving).

All three of these top competitors are dynamically good at putting. Maybe Laura Davies is less dependent on the caddies read but then her caddies may not have much in the way of golf background from what I have observed, or Laura and some other Tour players cannot handle outside help. Some studies into women's competitive personalities show that self-dependency (Factor 'X') is common in addition to the factor of being a highly organized person (Factor 'Y').

MORE PERFORMERS USING THE MIND'S EYE

The images form the mind's eye are useful in other sports, as well as golf. Completing a gymnastics routine, skiing a course or race and completing a skating

or synchro swimming program, are ideal occasions for the mind's eye. Jean-Claude Killy, a television sport personality and sport figure in France and former three time Gold Medalist, once prepared for a race with the mind's eye only. He was recovering from an injury so he decided to not risk further injury beforehand. **After that race, Killy remarked that it turned out to be one of his best performances.**

Richard Suinn, the psychologist who started working with USA skiers and Olympic athletes, has noted how athletes can learn to relax, even under considerable pressure as they wait for the next event.

Athletes awaiting the next round of a competition can concentrate on a mind's eye such as accurate alignment or can shift attention away from the prior hole. Alignment is said to be an illusive concept in golf and a vital one. As stressed previously, a lot has to do with directing the athlete's energy of preparation to the correct cue.

One of Jack Nicklaus' more famous dictates, is a belief that it is mind much more than method that makes the golf champion. This belief is given credence both by the number of years taken to start winning on Tour and the number of Champions over the age of 25. However, as stated elsewhere, there is confounding evidence that shows that this is less so on the Men's Tour and more so correct on the Women's Tour, where, currently at least, older players win proportionately more. YOUNGER LPGA WINNERS WOULD COME FORWARD SOON ENOUGH FROM EVERYWHERE IT SEEMS. REPRESENTED BY MEXICO'S LORENA OCHOA, USA'S MORGAN PRESSEL, MICHELLE WIE, PAULA CREAMER (more on her later), BRITTANY LANG, AND JAPAN'S MIYAZOTO.

MIYAZOTO WINS Q SCHOOL BY AN UNHEARD OF 12 STROKES OVER SIX ROUNDS AND IS SUCH A POPULAR TV STAR (with a winning and ready smile!) THAT SHE UPSTAGES ICHIRO SUZUKI AND HIDEKI MATSUI OF THE YANKEES AND THE "SMILING ASSASSIN" SHIGEKI, THE PUTTING MACHINE.

By now, ANNIKA SORENSTAM has recorded a 10 victory LPGA year and seems to be closing in on the 88 win record or KATHY WHITWORTH.

PAULA CREAMER BECOMES A ROLEX ROOKIE OF THE YEAR AND DOES WELL VS. THE EMERGING GLOBAL WOMEN AND YOUNG WOMEN AT THAT. CREAMER RANKS AS HIGH AS SECOND FOR THE YEAR AND EARNS $1.53M BY THE '05 FINAL STATS.

By now the Tour would have six millionaires win the formerly rare $1M including Annika S., Paula Creamer, Cristie Kerr, Lorena Ochoa, Jeong Jang, and Natalie Gulbis, the former 14 year old trying to qualify out in California at the Long's Drugstore Challenge. Every one of these players on the LPGA Tour has impressive stats in AIMING AND DISTANCE AND RESPECTABLE PUTTING.

In addition, it is noted the developmental Tours have soon enough shortened this need among players. Of course, some players have had to return to the developmental Tours and players like Scott Verplank reemerge with successes on the big Tours. There are more exceptions and it is difficult to generalize.

As well, some College trained golfers are receiving early exposure and develop skills in mental golf early. Many can relax out on Tour for a brief period at least . There are several examples of this occurrence at events as large as at the Masters, The British Open and major LPGA events. However, the grind of the full time Tour soon enough asserts itself on the players easy going ways in golf performance.

DANIEL GOULD: ILLINOIS GEM

A modern day sport psychologist, Daniel Gould was at Illinois as a baseball player, wrestler and football participant and completed a historical study of Griffith. This sport historian study talked of Griffith' film making equipment; leadership among baseball players and teams; training; personality profiles; motor learning tests; and various social-psychology factors.

Griffith filed a final report which Wrigley shelved since he decided to call off the study. This was due to the players reactions to psychological interventions.

They felt that they would be viewed as flaky and subject to ridicule if it was known that they had such help. **Nowadays, Tour golfers sometimes contract part-time psychological or performance assistance.**

The players in the Cub's teams were reported to have cursed and made fun of everything Griffith attempted. The general attitude to player assessment is to this day not all that imbued with support for testing and the like. Some Professional teams have staff psychologists.

KARRIE WEBB PREPS AND TIGER WOODS PREPS

Hockey teams at the NHL level have suffered through some resistance to the use of sport psychologists. Some teams have part-time staff. Some have more need. As Harris pointed out, there is a great deal of sport performance enhancement possible in team sport, as well as in sports such as golf.

Some golfers, such as, Tiger Woods and Karrie Webb, are well prepared mentally it seems. Where aiming problems come up for these two performers, and that problem does arise, especially with Tiger Woods, one really does contemplate the benefits of mind's eye strategies. This whole area is reviewed in the present text, as stated previously.

Despite the somewhat resistant attitude in these sports, hockey and baseball should no longer be considered sports without psychological assistance. A majority of players seek maximum performance and potential.

Recently, Pat Lafontaine and Ed Olczyk, former US Olympians, worked with Craig Farnsworth, a sport vision program expert in Colorado. After participating in visual activity training, the players expressed publicity they feel improvement in movement skill, passing-receiving, and in overall recognition. **Some amazing improvements have also been cited in football and volleyball players.**

The National Football League has shown recently that several coaches are attuned to the mental sport game. They are on the lookout for the new edge. They shape their team system on the basis of their talent acknowledging their mental skills.

SELECTIVE VIDEOTAPES

Coach Pat Riley of the NBA and former NHL coach Bob Johnson noticed the mind's eye connection and they developed selective videotapes for their players to view in those sports. Imagery videos can build on visualization powers and are used to expand the players' power play options or to enhance team understanding and acceptance of teammates outstanding individual moves in basketball.

Team unity or team affiliation is said to be enhanced through sharing of ideas gained in visualization.

Early research at the San Diego Golf Academy, where young PGA teaching and business candidates train, showed that selective videotapes of self improvement in golf skills when coupled with music resulted in enhanced putting performance. This improvement even occurred under competitive pressure simulations.

SELF SUCCESS VIDEOTAPES

AT OUR OWN GOLF **ACADEMY** FOR NON SCHOLARSHIP UNIVERSITY GOLFERS, WE MADE UP SELF-SUCCESS MIND'S EYE RESOURCES DESCRIBED IN THE FOLLOWING PARAGRAPHS.

These self-success videotapes, as we named them, found that golfers improve after viewing their own shots falling into the hole, repeatedly and time after time, when recorded on a videotape.

Later on, we provided greenside and sand shots by selecting out and editing shots that holed out or nearly holed out for each of 14 Academy golfers, all of University age players and PGA candidates.

These tapes would then by viewed at home while in a totally relaxed viewing posture. Such selective or self success videotapes did take a long time to make up since we did four types of greenside shots for all of our Academy golfers. Currently, the present author is checking out long term benefits of self-success mind's eye training.

We wanted our players to have a set of mind's eye visualizations for their sub conscious or image acceptor brains acceptance of positive videotaped images shown to it successively. Each player had about 40 of their own shots going right into the hole, the players loved to look at the tapes, and out on the course the visualizations could pour out for that preview, so vital to a positive pre shot image.

JOGGING AND THE MIND'S EYE

Whether you are riding a stationary bike in a drab exercise facility or jogging in a pavement jungle, you will likely use imagery to enhance the surroundings. You will probably find use for training tactics from the mind's eye as well as imagery related to 'ease' of persisting or improving.

. Triathlon competitors report such techniques for the mind's eye as well. Good programs of jogging training such as those by the late Jim Fixx (the Complete Runner), Joan Ullyot (Women Running), and Jeff Galloway whose text was a recent purchase for this non jogging author, are enhanced in various ways by such visualization.

It has been suggested that joggers and walkers let the mind's eye inform them of everything they do and that imagery be utilized in trying new or different training as well as for seeing that personal limits in training can be adjusted.

It is also said that here is a momentum to be developed in a good jogging, walking or other program just as there is in a golf improvement-enhancement program.

STREAM, RIVER AND WIND IMAGES

Michael Murphy, author of **Psychic Side of Sport,** has commented that joggers utilize flow images in the mind's eye as 'stream flowing with you and the like. By maintaining the mind's eye as you jog or walk, one finds the workout easier to complete. Encourage those images and relate them to the Hawaiian Marathon or other training that you might have contracted yourself to complete. Look at using some cool down images.

This is generally sound advice according to jogging authors. Michael Murphy also cites some classic occasions of utilization of the mind's eye in **Golf and the Kingdom,** a must read for golfers.

A somewhat similar mythical character golf book, **Quantum Golf,** features 'Linc St. Clair' (vs. Chivas Irons), and focuses nicely on the mind's eye, by author Kjell Enhager. This little text may also help your inner rhythm and overall confidence as you move away from classical golf. A very enjoyable journey of a read as well.

EVERY GREENSIDE SHOT CAN HOLE OUT JUST AS EVERY PUTT CAN HOLE OUT: SOME DIRECTIVE CASE STUDIES

Sport psychologists are spending hours in case studies with athletes problems and performance improvement. The case study illustrates the mind's eye procedure and some specific cues associated with such imagery.

NEGATIVE AIMING IN ICE HOCKEY

For example, Silva reported that an ice hockey player who used the stick excessively to slash (penalty), had gained too much penalty time and used imagery and 'new' cues to reduce a former behavior which was hurting the player's own team. The program involved selecting cues and pairing images to change a 'retaliation set' or way of thinking and reacting to a new behavior acceptable to the player and the team.

In this case, the cue was stick to the ice which, if you are a hockey player, will realize has several effective hockey meanings. *TO THE PLAYER, IT MEANS THINGS LIKE STAY COOL, STAY ON THE ICE, DO NOT TAKE SILLY PENALTIES.*

PREPARING TO IMPROVE PERFORMANCE

The mind's eye imagery used in the hockey players program was to visualize the self in various game situations where the player did not come up with the puck. Visualization was to include the feeling from within-self (internal image) as well as just how an observer would see the player (external image). Later, the player moved to a phase of visualizing where the arch rivals were visualized in the scene. This was the start of preparing the mind's eye for interventions or actions in future games.

A golfers aiming improvement can thus be visualized, especially with

**selective golf success videotapes. The idea of including situations in golf
is very evident.**

Golfers can enjoy such success just as a hockey player can. In the case of
the hockey player, the program occurred over several weeks and then was given
a transition period of fourteen days. The player cut his penalty time to just over
two minutes per game from five minutes per game during the last 10 games of the
season. As well, the player got to play two more minutes per game on the ice.
An amazing gain to be sure. **ANY ATHLETE SOON ENJOYS SUCH BENEFITS
OF THE MIND'S EYE.**

The potential of such sport behavior modification programs are rather immense
when one considers the frequency of certain habitual behaviors in sport. In golf,
the player can isolate out these behaviors easily enough. Golfers focusing on
repeated successes and good skill can soon enough believe that every greenside
shot can go into the hole and that every putt is makeable.

**The athlete or the golfer establishes a belief in the potential benefit of
any change and this is fundamental to gaining improved performance. If
it is self initiated, it usually is even more believed in by the golfer.**

RESIDUAL BENEFITS

The impressive benefits of organized mind's eye programs have also been
demonstrated with such athletes as basketball players who have particular fouling
behaviors (patterned fouls) or foul shooting accuracy problems; football players
rated as having high levels of stress preventing all out performance such as jaw
tightening just prior to running a pass route and being thrown passes to.

Relaxation problems with figure skaters and the general effect of stress or
the rate of wear and tear within the athletes' body are also areas for effectively
utilizing the mind's eye. But there is some suggestion of residual benefits over
and above these. It is thought that:

1. **Athletes may be more relaxed;**
2. **More control over specific tensions;**
3. **May exhibit less minor injury; and more
   attention given to practice.**

OVERALL APPROACH NOT LIMITED TO MIND'S EYE

Imagery programs as outlined in sports books almost always include a
relaxation component. In addition, there are verbal cues that will be used
frequently. The use of the mind's eye can be a small or a large undertaking but at
the very least involves self-knowledge and a certain amount of athlete analysis.

Fitness and overall physical or mental health may aid the athlete to become
a strong mind game performer.

USING SPORT IMAGES IN THE PSYCH OUT

**Psyching out an opponent is a rather common way of upsetting the
concentration of the athlete. You will have noticed the 'external' psych-
out or the experienced athlete utilizing a technique against an unsure or**

less experienced opponent.

One summer, a British Columbia golf course held a golf team challenge match between **Fuzzy Zoller - Andy Bean** and two fine College golfers. **The apparent clinking of coins and keys was seen to upset the concentration of the younger golfers.** Golf Team play and Match play or hole by hole play are both more likely to foster "psyching out" practices. Both forms of golf competition are reappearing in several parts of the golfing world.

One of the newest and most effective ways of psyching out in golf is to prepare a mental-physical game plan for a golf course and adhere to the game plan no matter what.

A well thought out plan involves playing the course not the opponent or playing partners and using the mind's eye to stick with the plan.

Even a highly skilled player who is not prepared mentally will usually be upset by his own game plan shortcomings. This is the same as a supposedly poorer team defeating a better opponent.

TENACITY through the mind's eye is a method that is resistant to this aspect of team play, or **skill tampering.**

Generally, the psych is less common in todays' sport world but an 'internal' feeling of being psyched out or being out of control is all too common and quite understandable.

USING THE MIND'S EYE TO ENHANCE AIMING, IS OF COURSE, A MORE PERSONAL, PRIVATE AND CONTROLLABLE USAGE OF TENACITY.
PERHAPS A TENACITY OF PERSISTENCE!

SUMMARY
KEY WORDS AND NOTIONS OF CHAPTER TWO.

*Athletes are self-dependent, imagery wise and future life skill adjusters.

*Superior athletic performance goes with effective mind's eye skills.

*Improved ability to align, aim and checkoff-aim appears to be extremely significant to improved golf scoring.

*Representation of location involves a natural and perhaps a learned skill for using new information from visual cues and location information in our representation or reality.

*Athletes have extraordinary ability to recall in detail and because of this, they can gain new information and new insights for future competition.

*Golfer-athletes can learn to memorize images for ball trajectory of oncoming or exiting ball flight, which can be called shot shape. Golfers have their own skill and concepts for shot shape.

*The conscious mind will accept new and better performance by the athlete via the imagery medium.

*Golfer-athletes can learn to link imagery to performance of ball flight.

*The new tournament approach in golf as is other sports, is to taper off physically and build up mentally, while to taper off varies with each individual golfer due to psychological and psychomotor reasons.

*The mind's eye can be used to augment concentration and future performance and aiming. Concentration is an elusive skill for golf, however many ideas are available in this book.

*The new athlete accepts psychological help even if limited to a mind's eye program.

*Golfer-athletes get extra messages via the mind's eye.

*Organized mental sport development programs are currently under development and research.

*Relaxation, self-knowledge and fitness & strength are key components fostering mental performance in golf.

*ATSV stands for analogically transferring specific visualizations. This means natural simple strategies to handle complex information and to construct or transfer strategies of visualization. **It is one of the newer skills for golf.**

****

CHAPTER TWO
<u>BIBLIOGRAPHY AND RESOURCES.</u>

Price Nick. Australian Golf Digest. "The Basics: Put It All Together" (Final Section). August, 1994

Kostis, Peter. Australian Golf Digest. "The Basics: How to Hold the Club". May, 1994

Farnsworth, C., Personal Communication. "Sports Vision". 1984

Krueger, Kurt. Personal Communication. "Practical Sport Psychology". PSP Institute, 1984

Cave, Kyle. Cognitive Psychological Journal. "Representation of Location in Visual Images". 1994

Cave, Kyle. Journal of Research in Teaching. "The Construction of Analogical Transfer of Symbolic Visualizations". 30.10.1993

Lucas, Geoffrey. "Images for Golf: Visualizing Your Way to A Better Game". Edmonton: AZ Edge Publisher, 1987. (ISBN 0 9692902-0-9)

Enhager, Kjell and Samantha Wallace. Quantum Golf: The Path to Golf Mastery. New York: Warner Books, 1991

Harris, Dorothy and Harris, B., Sport Psychology: Mental Skills for Physical People. New York: Leisure Press, 1984

Syer, John and Christopher Connolly. Sporting Mind: Sporting Body. England: Cambridge University Press, 1984

Cobb, N., Kahn, A. and Cath, S., Love and Hate on the Tennis Court. Philadelphia: C. Scribner Sons, 1976

Bennett, J., and Pravitz, J. The Miracle of Sports Psychology. New Jersey: Prentice Hall, 1982

Suinn, Richard. Psychology Today. "Body Thinking: Psychology for Olympic Champions". 1976

Derham, Ross and Craig Waldon (Editorial Staff). Australian Golf Digest. "Shafts: Looking for Mr. Goodbar". May, 1994

Murphy, Michael. The Psychic Side of Sports. Reading, Maine: Addison-Wesley. 1978

Silva, John. Behavior Modification. "Competitive Sports Environments". 1982

Yocum, Guy and Brett Parker. Australian Golf Digest. "New Shafts: Adding Order to Chaos". May, 1994

CHAPTER 3: TACTICS FOR AIMING AND TARGETING

Objectives: The "I am smart" golfer concept; further illustrations; four types to Tactics and management in Golf; playing the course; pre-practice; energy-equipment harmony; match play and special competition; special Tactics; Tactics interventions; target guides; target shooting; and driving the golf ball as a Basic.

****

TACTICS imagery is the most important of the three basic imagery exercises outlined in this psychology of golf book. The majority of famous Tour players agree and, as has been pointed out, the stress on this type of golf is increasing.

TACTICS imagery provides pictures or models of the golf course you are playing on or the golf hole you are teeing off on. Combined with AIMING TACTICS, this is one sure way to improve golf score.

It is just as if you are seeing a mini-movie of each golf hole in your mind's eye, from tee box through to green. The mini-movie includes too, side and aerial views. As in any movie or videotape, it can be replayed any number of times.

The minimum standard for your mini movie ought to include an image of the landing area for your tee shot, the main hazards and features of the fairway as well as the slopes, green size and shape and general situation around the green.

IT IS WHEN YOU, THE GOLFER, SEE AND USE THE DETAILS OR NATURAL FEATURES OF A GOLF COURSE THAT THE SCORE IS REDUCED AND THE SATISFACTION IS INCREASED!---a sort of see it and aim it.

The following chart indicates the composition of TACTICS IMAGERY and suggests that a golfer remember the GAME TACTICS I through GAME TACTICS IV are needed to score to the best of your ability.

COMPOSITION OF GAME TACTICS TO BE USED IN GOLF

****

Game Tactics I - **Imagery used to review key landing areas, contours, ball rolls and situations on the course.**

Game Tactics II - **Imagery used as exercise to review contour of all apron areas around each green.**

Game Tactics III - **Imagery to be used on the greens such as slope, overall shape and grass types as if they affect ball roll.**

Game Tactics IV - **A management Tactic consisting of journal entries**

written post game to record actual game shots. To check up on the on-imagery and off-imagery golf performance just completed. To learn from past errors. TO MAXIMIZE SCORING.

****

Most of the imagers that you will recall for Game Tactics I, II, and III, are **external** images. They are the same as would be provided by a movie or video camera, but you use your mind's eye 'camera'. That is, you do not feel them inside your body as in a kinesthetic feel which are internal images.

Log books can be a key to improvement

Illustration 1

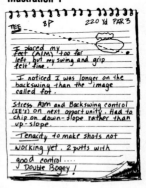

The first activity you should do is to make a complete visual review of your regular or home golf course. This is best done by walking your course or the course you are preparing to compete or caddy on either forwards towards the greens or in reverse without playing. Visualize your way through a game where you hit your regular type of shots.

When we do this in caddying in groups of two or three of us, one of us has the laser binoculars and we check various landing areas and useful distance approximations and then verify the main distances. Use the course booklet if one is available. ALSO, CHECK OUT THE *Caddy's* BOOKLET WHICH USUALLY COSTS $10. Make sure it is the caddy-made booklet instead of the commercial one if possible (only at Tour courses/ask one the regular caddies). Keep your own notes with your own system. I learned not to clutter such notes up with anything extra that my player would not ask for later.

Illustration 2

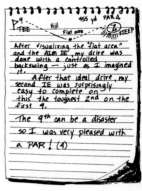

Why walk in reverse from the green to the tee? This idea came from walking natural luge courses in Northern Italy upwards so it was safer. A luge sled and driver can crash into you just like a golf ball can fly into you when walking and visualizing with mind's eye in a forward direction. So, I quickly pace off 50 yards and turn and face the green, then I go to 100 and 150 yards from the green and turn and do the same thing. **When I do so, I am focusing on the green which is like the focus of scoring in golf, which it surely is.**

Also, I got to see typical golf shots this way from the early Monday morning practicers on the LPGA Tour like **Dale Eggeling, Patty Sheehan, Marissa Baena** (NCAA Champion from Tucson), **Helen Alfredson** and other early birds. **As well it is the most serene and beautiful time to be on the golf course for completing your visualization review,** also, we got some rest later in the afternoon that way since we got our work for

Monday and Tuesday on Tour done early.

As a player, it is important to be honest with yourself so that you plan your own regular shots. In that way, you will capitalize during games with your best score. So you do a mind's eye of playing within your own game on all par 4's and par 5's. If your game **TACTIC** is to play par 5's so that your 2nd, 3rd, or even 4th shot is a lay up (perhaps to just behind a water hazard which protects the green) **then so be it!**

REDWOOD MEADOWS

Your **TACTIC** is very smart because you are setting up an easy or well thought out shot that will end up very close to the flagstick. **You are very smart since you will one putt several times during the year in this golf situation. You will be mind's eye CONFIDENT perhaps.**

The par 5, 14th hole at Redwood Meadows (Calgary, Canada), demands such respect. Very few of the best players score five on it despite its easy logic. Even **Lee Trevino, Barbara Bunkowsky and Burt Drysdale (Course PGA & fine competitive player)** played the 14th that way in a two day exhibition there. But to lay up short on the 2nd shot and then hit a little wedge stiff after a mind's eye preview, is the smartest golf it seems. **You also get on a roll and your confidence builds and that is the only way to play scoring golf, they say.**

A PAR 5 DEMANDING TACTICS IMAGERY

Not only is the hole below difficult up around the green, but it is guarded on either side of the whole bending fairway by creeks, hazards of small fresh mountain water mini lakes and trees all the way along its 600 yard length, some of the length which is cut off by the correctly place drive.

Your **TACTIC I** mind's eye is very important here, as an image shows a nice large landing area to the right if you don't cut off some of the distance by driving left and bold. Very little can be cut off.

An unplanned or poorly imagined attack on the 14th hole is deadly! Review this type of hole with an external mind's eye a few times prior to going to the golf course.

A complete **TACTIC 1, TACTIC II, AND TACTIC III** attack on such a golf hole will leave your brain at ease and your creative subconscious relaxed.

A Game **Tactic II** for all the apron and contour of the 14th green includes, in the case of the hole some large boulders that surround the front of the green right at the waters edge. These boulders are just eight to ten steps from the green and there are large conifer trees over the back of the green.

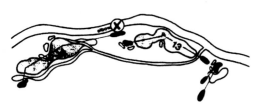

Seeing **Tactic II** is helpful because this green tends to hold only high soft shots.

Tactic III is reviewed in the mind's eye just before hitting the shot onto the green. After seeing **Tactic II and Tactic III, the analyzer brain** tunes out and the **shot selector brain** takes over. This is where Technique mind's eye imagery takes over as YOU feel and imagine the actual golf swing you have selected.

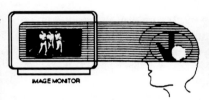

IMAGE MONITOR

Tactic IV comes later. Write down in your journal the KEY imagery that worked well (all three types). More important, record the mind's eye performance that was off base or did not materialize well and did not assist your performance. You may find that you did not have all the swings that your imagery wanted you to perform or that your mind's eye was a weak one.

After the game, check over or evaluate your cognitive mind's eye and your affective mind's eye imagery. In cognitive imagery, you are supposed to see yourself as an analytical golfer through as many as possible of the 18 holes.

Cognitive imagery wants to prevent you from 'mentally daisy-picking' especially near the last three, four or five holes of a typical golf game. If you saw strong cognitive thinking golf images for the last one-third of the game, you will almost always post a score that you are pleased with.

In affective imagery you want to see a mind's eye image of yourself as having an effective attitude and awareness of you and the other golfers in your group. You are aware of the others as being there, you may be courteous and respectful, but you are not competing with them, since in the mind's eye, you are much more 'into' competing with self and completing your imagery plans.

In affective imagery, you see a clear picture for you to play the golf course via shot shape and your golf skills. You also see you as playing each shot, even the easy ones and each one requiring and getting your best effort. YOU SEE A HIGH LEVEL OF GOLF EFFICIENCY AND YOU ARE THE ONE DOING IT. YOU ARE IN CONTROL OF GOLF FACTORS.

BASIC EXPECTATIONS OF TACTICS MIND'S EYE

For the most part, ask yourself if your images were clear and accurate. Did your images include the details that you required to make an effective golf shot? Were you capable of timing your images so that you could stand at the back of each tee box and call up the same mind's eye images you reviewed before the game?

Out on the golf course that is easy, since you can see all of the environmental cues before you. You don't have to close your eyes to see your mini movie, instead, just click off or check off the whole scene.

Can you include all the blind features of each hole that is out of sight or too far away to see? Great course designers often hid golf course features in an effort to test severely your tactics mastery out on the course.

In this regard, I once watched two great amateurs, Blaine McCallister and Richard Zokol, duel each other in the final of the Canadian Amateur and display the best putting I have ever seen. Hole after hole, Zokol, then of BYU in Provo, Utah and a Texan by the name of McCallister knocked in putt after putt and remained tied even after the regulation 36 hole final. Sudden death overtime started immediately at Calgary Country Club, a fine test, with some tricky greens.

HIDDEN GOLF COURSE FEATURES

Both golfers used what I can only describe as department store putters with doctored up grips. That did not matter. If anything, they putted better and both were several strokes under par. On the first playoff hole, Blaine lay two just eight or ten feet below the cup on a grinding up hill Par 5, in a slight trench-like part of the green.

Watching from well back and in line with the putt, the putt looked very much like one that would be made. I was standing beside PGA Professional, Burt Drysdale, who had once worked at the golf course being used, who nudged me and said, "I'll bet he didn't see break for that putt" (it was well known to some).

Apparently the break was totally hidden. Sure enough, McCallister hit the putt right where he intended to and the speed was just right, but the expected putt line just didn't materialize. **Zokol, also lying two, had a shorter putt that he made and the Championship was his.**

PUTTING: TRACKING AND ACCURACY

This type of illustration is familiar to every golfer. Even when the correct mind's eye is used as a ball roll preview, the information has to be correct. The read of the green must be accurate. It is when the image is based on accurate information that a putt will roll directly to the middle of the cup. In games, you putt well in your invariably are into mind's eye imagery that is good and ball roll which is tracking well.

MORE BASIC EXPECTATIONS OF TACTICS STRATEGY

Three other expectations for the mind's eye, require the golfers attention. One is **COMPLETENESS.** Did you see your image complete itself (swing finish or ball in hole)? Or in tracking or seeing shot shape, did you see the start, the middle and the end of the flight or roll (or swing)?

Did you see the landing, direction of bounce and the roll? If you 'saw' a sixty yard wedge bounce and roll into the cup, you will be surprised when you make the shot more often than previously! Try to hole out. Every time.

Another expectation is **POSITIVE-NEGATIVE** for your image. Did any image or mind's eye suggest a golf disaster? Could you re-image to a positive image in such a case? Did you get over to your shot situation so you had enough time to prepare in a positive way?

Third, did you have any **MIND'S EYE ENDURANCE?** Could you image holes 16, 17, and 18? Did you visualize the clubhouse, your family, going home, or that well earned after game break too soon? Actually, it takes real effort to do mind's eye and use muscle-memory all the way around 18 holes. **It may help you to think of your overall game performance as occurring in three hole or six hole segments of the game. As far as the mind's eye and imagery are concerned, you are playing 18 holes. The subconscious is agreeable. TRY TO USE TACTICS FOR MORE HOLES EACH SUCCEEDING GAME.** If you can honestly say, that you only used good TACTICS for six holes during one game, then attempt eight holes the next game. Eventually, you may get to 18 holes but it is not easy. Tour players may come close. Some Tour players may not come close.

JUDGING YOUR SUCCESS

Sometimes, you can use other parameters to score success by. You will always have an 18 hole score of course. However, you can use those other success parameters or means according to recent sport psychologist thinking. For example, "...today I played with good Tactics for driving for 14 of 14 holes and I am pleased with that" or "...my effortless ratio was pretty high today and I did feel my energy spreading".

THE AFFIRMATION FOR THE 'I AM SMART' GOLFER

Another way of using TACTICS, TENACITY AND TECHNIQUE MIND'S EYE, is to use a simple version of affirming your 'great golf skill' by constantly seeing yourself as an 'I am smart', 'I am tough', and 'I am good' golfer. A number of years ago, Gary Wiren (former Director of Education of the PGA of America) suggested a Competitive Edge card, which is a small card containing your current and your best affirmations.

Affirmations are used to plant the seed of an idea in your subconscious. Affirmations are powerful psychologically, and Kurt Kreuger, of the World Wide Institutes of Sport Psychology, centered in Los Angeles, once told me to use strong positive statements that something is already so and to use those statements ten minutes each day. You can totally change what we create for ourselves--we can transform attitudes and expectations for life (personal communication). IN THIS SENSE, WHAT YOU SEE HAPPENING IS WHAT YOU GET AND AFFIRMATIONS ASSIST YOUR MENTAL GOLF POWER TO GAIN IMPETUS.

AN AFFIRMATION LIST FOR YOU, THE 'I AM SMART' PLAYER

@**See a self-image and say to yourself,** "I get birdies on as many Par 5's as there are on the golf course because I place my drive and second shot nicely".

@**See a self-image and say to yourself,** "I land all my shots in the best

landing areas to set up the next shot".

@**See a self-image and say to yourself,** "I always place my shots so that I can putt up hill".

IF YOU AFFIRM, YOU IMPROVE
Say some more affirmations....

@**See a self-image and say to yourself,** "I am a smart golfer because I try damn hard to do all of the above and especially...not to make the same error in golf twice".

@**See a self-image and say to yourself,** "I always see the mind's eye needed for the situation".

@**See a self-image and say to yourself,** "I see absolutely every putt going into the center of the cup...I try for less than 18 putts each round".

****

TEE SHOT TACTICS AND STRATEGY
When Craig Stadler, everyone's favorite out on Tour, was a light weight Masters champion and discovered he was driving between 40 to 50 drives out of bounds each Tour season, he decided to drive for less distance and keep the ball in play as much as possible. Amazingly, he later stated he drives..."only three or four out of bounds all season long it seems".

KEY ON ACCURATE LANDING AND CONTROLLED FLIGHT
It has been calculated by Golf Technology engineers (Bud Blankenship-Idaho) that a driver striking a ball on the club's center of gravity produces five percent more distance than one struck just one third on an inch off center. A controlled swing produces good contact and loses little in the way of yardage.

BECOME KNOWN AS YOUR CLUB'S ACCURATE GOLFER
Taken together, if your TACTICS mind's eye produces great aim and fine ball landing area skills and you swing easy, then you stand to lose just twenty five yards distance YET, YOU GAIN BACK ten to twelve yards by consistent ball club contact and you will become known as an accurate golfer around your club. This is quite a smart golf TACTIC.
Your imagery will likely take away the desire for long driving at least when some other benefit buoys your confidence on the tee box from smart tactics previously executed by you. LIKE CRAIG STADLER, YOU CAN ALWAYS GO AFTER EXTRA DISTANCE WHEN YOU HAVE TO.

HOW MUCH TIME OVER EACH SHOT: A TACTIC
A good general tactic is to not spend too much time over each shot. After you start using the mind's eye on a regular basis for pregame and game, you will see that you can move through a shot routine rapidly, while still not hurrying. **Too much time over a shot is said to result in muscle tension build up.**

As has been mentioned by sport imagery experts, a mind's eye regimen or routine which works well for you will eventually materialize.

Keep recombining the elements of the three basic mind's eye types to find which works best for you. Don't be reluctant to change your regimen. Like a good coach who makes practice interesting by changes or by inserting new wrinkles, you also tailor your program.

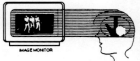

TARGET SHOOTING AND TARGET GUIDELINES

In golf it is necessary for you to have a carpenter's square mind's eye as well as an aim-line image. With this notion you can use the mind's eye to aim your body and clubs towards targets.

TARGET GUIDELINES

(Chart by McGregor-Tourney)

McGregor-Tourney Company advises that when lining up with the body to align targets when the golfer is 1 degree off perpendicular to target the player will end up increasing putt distance by six feet in a typical 100 yard golf shot; and when 3 degrees off at 150 yards one will be left with a putt some 25' longer than it might have been without line up error. This is truly an area for the mind's eye to assist posture which aims at targets in golf. And truly an area for having good golf clubs.

Golf Technology (Idaho) is a golf manufacturer who produces Electronic putting Analyzers as well as swing analyzers and game simulation electronic wizardry.

In their putting machine a pad of sensors reveals tracking while trying 10 ft. and then switching to 20 ft. putt simulations. An engineer has calculated that at 10 ft., you can vary your putter face alignment up to 3 degrees and still make a putt aimed at the center of the hole.

WHEREAS, for a 20 ft. putt, you start to lose the 'tolerance for error'. In all you lose 1.5 degrees and so must aim the putter far better.

IMAGE BIOFEEDBACK PUTTING

For this reason, we practice as follows: imagine a 0 degree putter in your mind's eye with eyes closed, open them and take a little waggle or two and immediately putt on the Electronic machine and find out from the machine just how closely you can duplicate or imitate the 0 degree putt angle you had started out visualizing. IN THIS CASE, IF WE CANNOT MIND'S EYE ACCURATELY, WE CAN NOT PUTT ACCURATELY! This is well demonstrated in this simple "image-biofeedback-linkup" for putting.

LESSONS ON ALIGNMENT

If you are inexperienced with a carpenter's square alignment (that is, visualizing a large carpenter's 'set over your body' and then do a mind's eye for it) do the following:

1. Work with a PGA teaching Professional for overall body and clubface alignment and agreement (i.e. everything that you line up agrees). It is common that your shoulders align one away and perhaps, your clubface or your hands another way. Use natural body positions, that is, positions your body easily accepts. BECOME AWARE OF THIS IN GOLF SINCE EVEN EXPERIENCED GOLFERS CAN MISALIGN.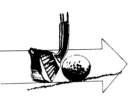

2. Once you reach the level where you are, 'feeling from within', THIS SO CALLED BODY ALIGNMENT, YOU ARE NOW ABLE TO HOLD ALIGNMENT THROUGH THE SWING + START TO REALLY DEVELOP 0 degree ON THE PRACTICE FAIRWAY.

Start from behind the ball and pick out an AIM-LINE which 0 aligns with the target....the exact middle of the target... **and do not stand for any fuzzyness in aiming!!**

NEXT: 3. Learn to step up to and into the ball with a consistent routine, including what you did in 0 degree (above). ONE EXPERIENCED TOUR PLAYER I WORKED WITH, FEELS SHE ALIGNS ONE WAY YET HER BODY DOESN'T GIVE HER A CONFIRMING FEELING WHEN SHE HITS SHOTS. THIS DIFFICULTY TAKES A HUGE AMOUNT OF TIME TO WORK OUT OF BECAUSE IT INVOLVES RE-TRUSTING YOUR FEEL WHEN THAT FEEL IS NOT RELIABLE TO THE PLAYER.

As mentioned earlier, Dennis Watson, an earlier Tour surprise, who won a truckload of money in a six month stretch of time with an alignment routine in which he set his right foot first, THEN his clubface AND THEN his body followed by his foot. He also was said to have developed some effective mind's eye skills.

CHECK 0 DEGREES

NEXT: 4. You can check 0 degree alignment in one of two ways. Verify your internal feeling for the accuracy of your own Carpenter's SQUARE image. Soon you will be able to feel an exacting alignment position. Do this for every shot you hit on the practice range and soon enough you will be capable of aligning well out on the course.

Michelle McGann, the Hat Lady, so called, can align out over a dangerous and long Lake and pound out a drive right along that line, or at least that is what she did in the Wednesday ProAm in California when I caddied in her foursome. She had a finely tuned alignment routine which seemed to be very reliable. Donna, her caddy, verified that routine.

Carolyn Hill and Lisa Kiggens are two other Tour players who couple alignment and the swing in motion with the mind's eye and intuition.

CHECKING OUT ALIGNMENT: OTHER KEY METHODS

There are methods to augment and test your skill and mind's eye feeling for alignment. Commonly recommended procedures are:

1. Start from behind and pick out a grass line target to the target, checking it all the way to the aim point and back again several times, NEXT, pick out a short version off of that line and use it to position your body lines and clubface lines (i.e. golf club scoring lines) as you step up to the ball.

Use your aim-line mind's eye and carpenter's square to visualize and complete your physical set up. You should also have a teacher work with you on setting woods and irons behind a ball with the purpose of having you understand the skill of club face positioning, grip, and arm and body alignment. **This procedure applies equally to beginning golfers right through to Tour players.**

Look back to the McGregor-Tourney Chart and notice what a drastic error 3 degrees is in golf aiming.

2. The second way to test your skills and mind's eye and its feeling for alignment is to use your putter and putter alignment skills. The alignment of a suitable marked putter (e.g. T line type, Zebra or Rossie) can act as a miniature version of the alignment used with any of the golf clubs.

In putting, your clubface, hands, lower body and shoulder-line are all involved. A simple device such as putting in a trough formed by two small boards will help. In the first place, this simple aid will help with square to square club path in the region of the ball contact.

Secondly, it will help square up the clubface to 0 degrees as you strike the putt. Use the aim-line mind's eye and the carpenter's square as you practice. Test your perception of feel for your image and the actual stroke. Close your eyes every second or third stroke as your practice. Practice these golf skills for repetition to groove the skill's motion.

Go to the putting green for actual practice or use a super smooth indoor carpet. In this way, the skill can transfer to all iron and wood alignments.

You will become a greatly improved putter. **To complete a putting improvement program, you will need to cultivate a feel for putt distance as well as the ability to read greens and grass types.**

FINAL GOAL IN ALIGNMENT

If you have a fairly normal inside-out swing path (say 1-1.5 degrees) with your 150 yard club and if you are constantly twenty-five feet or further away from the cup than you think you should be, you are misaligning by up to 3 degrees, as we said previously.

You must get your image and alignment down to 1/2 degree to 1 degree.

DEMAND A LOT MORE OF YOUR GOLF TENACITY BY SELECTING A DIFFERENT TARGET FOR EACH PRACTICE FAIRWAY SHOT.

THE GAME NEVER GIVES THE SAME TARGET TWICE IN A ROW IT SEEMS.

SUMMARY OF MIND'S EYE REQUIRED FOR TACTICS

*Tee view, side view, aerial view

*Landing area mind's eye (Tactic I)

*Green situation (Tactic II & III)

*Ball path mind's eye

*Carpenter Square mind's eye

*0 degree

*Grass line mind's eye

*T line PUTTER mind's eye

*Alignment agreement

*Shoulder line mind's eye

*Body Line mind's eye

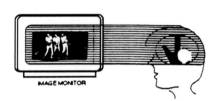

IMAGE MONITOR

Theory only, in REALITY A SINGLE LESSON OR INFREQUENT PRACTICE IS YOUR ENEMY. EXPECT LITTLE IMPROVEMENT

TACTICS TO ADOPT FOR LEARNING FROM GOOD GOLFERS

It is recommended that you the golfer adopt a general TACTIC for learning and developing further mind's eyes by watching other golfers, mostly golfers with natural swings and natural scoring senses. Because visual experience is turning out to be a powerful way to golf improvement, you might wish to implement this TACTIC.

As it turns out, it is not possible to use a certain shot in golf without some prior experience with that shot. For example, Tom Watson's great golf from fifty yards in is famous because he is confident due to experiences..

To hit the shots he does, you need a lot of visual experience with the swing-shape and knowledge regarding the lies and situations he has had. Earlier, we wrote about the deep grass shot and varied shots around the green. **As indicated, a mind's eye cannot be stored until the golfer is very clear about that shot.**

So that, we recommend that you observe good technique as much as possible. It would be a disservice to you, the reader, if it was not indicated that the Champions Tour is by far, the best for this.

In particular, Don January and Hale Irwin absolutely exude the type of swing quality that you want to expose your image maker brain to. Try other Champion Tour players.

Additionally, you can pick up a lot of short game demonstration by watching the Tour players. Often they spend hours working at some unnoticed spot around the main practice areas.

Peter Thomson practiced his short game incessantly two years before rebounding to virtually dominate the Senior Tour for a period of time.

Another source for seeing fluid golf swings in the LPGA Tour. The regular Men's PGA Tour is excellent but power swings are too much in vogue and not particularly well suited to learn model mind's eye from. No doubt, any opportunity is excellent. Go out to your State, National or Zone or Provinces Championships and certain players will exude those great swing qualities too.

A videotape or two is an excellent mind's eye builder as well. You can find such videotape sales recommended by major golf magazines, in particular **Golf Magazine, Golf Digest and Golf World. Two other favorites of the author's are Women's Golf, and Australian Golf Digest. Also, it is recommended you buy Official Tour Guides books as much as possible.**

TACTICS TO ADOPT

Before doing a lot of PP practice (PP=pure physical) a learner in golf should visually expose themselves to that large amount of golf modelling just discussed.

Experiments comparing modeling alone (i.e. demonstrations) or in combination with brief instruction are emphatically conclusive, modeling techniques are important as effective aids in learning motor skill such as those required for golf.

A VISUAL VERSUS A VERBAL EXPERIMENT

Complete this experiment by yourself or with some golfing friends. Take six golf magazines at random. Look at all the swing pictures in them, even just ever so briefly, and focus in on some key swing postures and movements.

Try and compare and develop a mind's eye-recall for several parts of the swings you saw. Don't do any reading at all.

Look only at the cue words under the pictures which captions the swings. These cues will direct your mind's eye to certain swing keys.

Don't spend any more than 1 hour doing this, better yet, just take 25 minutes.

Hit balls while the imagery brain keys in on your refreshed visual-image bank of fully understood mind's eyes.

Practice imitating the mind-pictures you have developed via the magazine study.

DRAW YOUR OWN CONCLUSIONS.

YOU WILL BE STRIKING THE BALL VERY EFFECTIVELY AFTER THIS TYPE OF VISUAL PRACTICE.

The second part of the study can be done one week or a few weeks later. Read the same magazines that you did the visual study-practice of. Read and only briefly glance at the pictures. **In other words, key in on the verbal and key out on the visual. Now go out and practice the same amount that you did after the first experiment.**

Usually, your practice will be dominated by confusion and lack of purposeful activity.

The problem is that you are using the left brain and analyzing far too much while your performance selector brain is being under used. **The net result is that you are swinging at the ball with a great lack of feel and muscle memory preparation.**

IMITATING AOKI, DAVIES, DUVAL AND THE GREAT WEDGE PLAYERS

The best golfers that I know among golfing friends and Tour friends and two who have tried the Tour, have an image catalogue of swings stored in the sub conscious part of their brain. For example, they can show off it asked, a swing like Asao Aoki, Fred Couples, Laura Davies, David Duval, Jim Furyk and they can hit with the distinctiveness of each of those players. They can switch to the Tom Watson wedge swing.

This type of imitation is an excellent way of expanding your swing knowledge.

It shows the cause-effect chain in a golf swing. Until you really have a good internalized mind's eye feel for your swing, you might consider imitation of this type as too advanced for you to attempt.

Remember, however that imitation is a powerful way to learn a motor skill.

POWERFUL IMAGERY INCREASES YOUR GOLF SWING VERSATILITY YOUR OWN GOLF SWING: A TACTIC

Of course, you can learn to use modeling to improve your own swing. Pick out a model who is about your own size and has similar flexibility and uses a swing tempo that is possible for you to emulate.

Don't be concerned about age differences. It is not difficult to expose your swing to good modeling by going out to watch as many Tour or top amateur events as possible.

It has also been found that low skilled golfers should watch a peer-model but one who is slightly better at the golf swing. A peer MODEL is better than a teacher-model with a high level demonstration since the peer model is readily acceptable to your mind's eye bank of stored swing images.

For example, a 18 handicapper should watch and play with an 8-12 handicap who is playing well at the time.

In addition play as many golf events as possible with somewhat better golfers than you are. You could play in ProAms or some good amateur events. **The ProAm Tour player gives tips as part of their appearance.**

Send your budding 12-14 year old out to watch top 20 year olds or to be a Tour spectator. Florida high school and junior school players have that advantage many weeks of each calendar year.

GOLF TACTIC: NATURAL GROWTH AND DEVELOPMENT

One key point about modeling bears stating. Many parents worry about getting their pre 12 year olds started in golf. I was just the same. They may insist on several lessons. I have seen parents acting as personal coaches every day at a good City driving range. Those 'coaches' are not even hitting balls themselves. They are not showing any evident enjoyment of the game at all.

Just last week, in the hitting bay beside me, one little girl of no more than age 10, was coaching her chum, who had never swung a club before, and was telling her all the correct things that she had been taught about her swing. Her model swing was very floppy and inaccurate but her coaching was very good.

A parent was videotaping a little boy who had a pretty solid swing. They stayed for at least one hour before going putting.

The above examples lead to a certain amount of controversy regarding what age and what style of learning is appropriate for pre 12 year old players.

It is pretty laudable that parents are taking time to coach their youngsters. It is vastly favorable to a situation where a kid has nothing to do with their time.

We all know, that throwing activities, full body activities like road skating (inline) etc. and hanging and lifting activities make the young body grow healthy and strong. The idea, from a parents' strategy point of view, is to get their girl or boy to be a future lover of golf or tennis, so that their swing is their own focus of improvement. Perhaps swing refinement can come later.

Learning research and observation, shows quite conclusively that pre 12 year olds learn a great deal from observational learning and mimicking, without formal lessons at all.

A good guideline, particularly in golf, is to never hurry children into golf until they start being positive to your giving them some junior size equipment. Once they go out to a pre-age 12 'jamboree' or golf intro Saturday, they will be ready.

Remember to provide modeling. A good place for modeling is out on the golf course. Parental attitude is absorbed through family participation more than direction. Life long attitudes are formulated early.

Good modeling is especially found out on the practice areas and around the putting green. Good players are to be found there and they are practicing.

Growth and development experts remind parents and teachers that golf, tennis, bowling and similar sports have

little in the way of large muscle activity for the 9-12 year age group. Compare mat gymnastics, hanging and rotating type gymnastics and other two person weight or resistive activities.

Youth who have gone through and loved such activities can become excellent future golfers especially if a lot of their early growing years took place around a golf course.

There are lots of versatile all-around athletes in Tour level golf these days. Greg Norman, the highly successful Australian Tour player, was once asked by a parent of a 12 year old, who loved all sports and played football and baseball, if his son would develop detrimentally in golf, due to his 'other' sport participation pattern.

Norman advised the following, saying in effect that love of sport and strength from football type games, would actually help in golf. HE NOTED THAT GOLF MECHANICS CAN BE DEVELOPED OVER A RELATIVELY SHORT PERIOD OF TIME. (Golf Magazine: Champs Clinic). Most importantly, "attributes such as sportsmanship, discipline, and competitive drive develop best playing with other boys and girls in team sports".

A recent sport psychology finding may shock some parents and counselors. It has been noted by youth sport advisors, that at age 15+ level, any force or pressure by a parent to have their daughter or son play a certain sport, almost surely drives such youth away from pursuing SERIOUSLY that very game.

The TACTIC A PARENT HAS TO ADOPT IS ONE OF ENTHUSIASM FOR THE GAME and what is called, very simply, THE 'OSMOSIS EFFECT'.

GOLF TACTIC: NATURAL GROWTH OR CHILD PRODIGY?

Beverly Klass, an LPGA player from Boca Raton, Florida a number of years ago, had modest winnings of $52,0000 and no wins but at least one top three finish. She had not won outright on Tour but had come close.

Beverly was one of the classic child prodigy's in golf, apparently. It was said that she was pushed into golf, especially by her father. After six years on the Tour, she finished an event with a superb third place finish.

When she phoned home with the news, she was apparently asked why she had not finished first. That didn't bother Beverly since she noted that, "that is what being a Tour player is all about" and that is true, it is surely an all out go for broke profession.

Later on, it became known that she was a very well adjusted person and a 'pretty happy cowpoke'. Just recently, when we arrived at Twelve Bridges, California for a LPGA event, we found that Beverly Klass was in

the news again. This time, the *Sacramento Times* newspaper was comparing her to Natalie Gulbis, a 14 year old, from Granite Bay, who was trying to qualify for one of the last available spots in the Longs Drugs Challenge LPGA event, at the beautiful ranch country Palm lined valleys around Lincoln City, California.

BEVERLY KLASS, NATALIE GULBIS & MARISA BAENA

Marisa Baena was at University of Arizona and has won NCAA Women's golf titles twice already and placed highly in the US Amateur as well as having a top finish in a major, at the **Dinah Shore Nabisco** event. Until just recently, she was an undergraduate.

When Gulbis did qualify at Twelve Bridges, a LPGA official confirmed Gulbis was the youngest player to compete in a LPGA event. This proved incorrect. Later, it was reported that Beverly Klass had, amazingly enough, played in a LPGA event as a 9 year old and at age 10, had official Tour earnings of $31.00, in the 1965 LPGA season, Klass had played in the US Open at age 10 and had earned $100 but did not qualify to play rounds 3 and 4. However, she was reinstated as an Amateur and went on to a distinguished amateur career and eventually a 13 year Tour LPGA stay.

Both Klass and Gulbis could hit 250-260 yard drives as youngsters and both played on boys teams at high school. Gulbis is a California State Women's Amateur runner-up. Later, she would be the LPGA Calendar Girl and become a frequent top ten finisher.

Marisa Baena, from Columbia in South America, drives the ball past some of the reputed long hitters currently on Tour. She says her younger sister at home in Columbia drives the golf ball even further. Cristina has made it big in the Future Tour.

Marisa appears to be unflappable in competition and had an incredible run of golf success over two consecutive weekends during the NCAA's and the US Women's Open amateur.

Perhaps the reason Baena is so successful, is because FACTOR P, so called Purpose for Life, is so fundamental to her. While Baena's parents are both doctors at home in Columbia, the income for all citizens is near poverty and even the high profession career path is not a monied one. Thus Marisa and other athletes like her, do not have extra money at all. Maybe in the future, she will be able to send money home and in fact, she recently joined the Tour full time and is doing alright it seems.

Recently, Marisa Baena, whose original goal was to earn a LPGA card, has moved up 120 placces to 24th. Then by the end of a full year, she was 12th, thats right, 120 places. She won the HSBC World MP Championship.

It appears Marisa's purpose of life is very clarified and when I caddied for her at the Dinah Shore, this indeed seemed so.

TACTIC: A BALANCED APPROACH TO THE GAME

A child prodigy in golf and the ordinary player requires a balanced

approach to the game. You need the swing or to accept the limits of your swing plus 'oh so much more'.

The mental approach is needed and so is the balance that it infers. Often the child prodigy is unprepared and ill-prepared in a balanced way, simply since they swing the club so well, so soon in life.

Having not needed a mental game early on, they suffer needlessly on Tour or when they try to compete week after week.

Other factors can creep in. **Self-efficacy** is lowered and therefore conviction that they believe they will succeed may be too low. The emotional components always require attention for the balanced approach as well.

PERHAPS THERE ARE EXCEPTIONS TO CHILD GOLF OR ATHLETE PRODIGIES IN TERMS OF DEVELOPMENT. OCCASIONALLY A TIGER WOODS, MARISA BAENA OR SI RI PAK COMES THROUGH.

AUGMENTING THE YOUNG GOLFERS TACTICS

Get your young golfers onto a golf course. Teach them the codes of behavior so they are welcome. So long as adult golfers and the PGA staff are aware of the youngsters and are given a chance to work with them, they will accept and support them.

Then their mind's eye programs get a natural and an early start. To augment their imagery, make sure that really young juniors have two shortened and weight reduced golf clubs such as an iron and one putter or a junior set. **At least two golf courses nearby our community have 3 to 5 hole short courses that often are reserved exclusively for them.** Check for these special places.

They will see models and they will imitate. Often they are seen together in groups and that will improve them too. Later on, or right away, get a junior club set, of which there are two sizes, pre-age 12 and then the regular junior size set. Sign them up for a junior or pre-junior set of classes. Look out for golf camps if they get interested.

RESTRESSING VISUAL EXPERIENCE AMONG GOLFERS

Adults can re-stress the amount of observational practice they get in golf. A basis for better mind's eyes can be formed. It is said that most of us have lost touch with our visual senses. Golfers have an excellent opportunity to be visually superior.

Out on Tour, the vision skills of many of the players is superior and they often see shot details and the ball ending flight which their caddies do not see in as much detail. You can be sure that such vision assists aiming skill.

If our schools have a tendency to 'de-school' our visual opportunities, we have ample visual enrichment in golf to make amends for such a shortcoming. As noted previously, the best golfers tend to be great visual athletes. There are few exceptions to this fact.

When Rudolf Arnheim, the art and visual perception expert, went to JAPAN, he was enchanted by written 'Asian' characters they use instead of alphabet types. The verb 'to see' is a picture of an eye running on two legs and the dentist's office sign is a mouth with teeth in it. The root word for a daisy is a beautiful word-picture, days-eye. Most words originated as visual perceptual experience. **Thus it is that some societies stress visual experience more than other societies do.**

Visual enrichment in golf can be as follows. When I go to the practice area at a Tour event to watch the great Tour players hit balls, my mind almost explodes visually. My eyes *explore* -- for example, of six or eight Tour swings I concentrate on, I explore a new world of sound, a sound of an iron, titanium, graphite or steel that is like nothing I have ever heard -- I try to store this for my later imitation; and my eyes *select* as I seek out Payne Stewart or Bobby Clampett or Michelle McGann with their wildly extravagant color and clothes and attempt to understand these colors and their personality and their golf swings......even Payne Stewart' memories.

......and my eyes *simplify* -- for example, it is now easy enough to understand the concept that took me forever to try to appreciate, that the clubs of almost all the Tour players move at such a leisurely pace in the swing that it totally defies the blow the club delivers; my eyes *complete* -- for example, my notions of correctness are put at ease and all kinds of false notions I had about the golf swing are laid to rest; my eyes *compare* -- for example, I see uniformity and precision, even as everyone has their own way of getting the club to the top of the swing, not one of them does not literally PAUSE at the top and then start the club back down with the same grace of motion of all great athletes; and my eyes *surprise* -- I see arms and shoulders so flexible in a golfer like Phil Mickelsen and Karrie Webb, that the thrust they deliver should almost break the ball apart; and then I see some other Tour player with their arms set up totally wrong or in reverse and then I realize that *the 'classic golf swing' I so desire to see, isn't even necessary for some of the players--the Tour wonders!*

The rationality of all I see on Tour practice fairways, is based on immediate experience rather then verbal process or theory mongering. My TACTIC here is clear enough.

Visual experience is a basic component of the imagery and mind's eye and imitation I seek and all golfers seek.

That is why I am watching!!

Mr. Arnheim is correct when he suggests that our senses are capable of abstract thought. **When we see the Tour golfers and their swings, we either grasp the essential qualities of those swings with our visual senses or we miss that quality completely. No book or description can replace this experience.**

TACTIC: THE LOOK OF KNOWING WHAT YOU ARE DOING

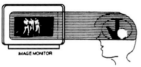

Cultivate a mind's eye for the look of knowing what you are doing in golf.

By previewing your **TACTICS** before a game in your special mind's eye viewing room, you feel yourself getting ready for the game. You build up confidence and relaxed concentration. You know your preparation is complete.

Make it look as if you know that you are going to do what you set out to do! Select your final mental game plan and stick to it. **If a non aggressive Par in one of the first three holes is what you need to get your scoring going for that plan, then don't aggressively putt for a birdie and have to take a bogie.** Stick with the visualized plan. Don't give up on it. Many times when you miss out on a simple game plan, you regret it and your scoring does not go well. That whole scene sucks, as they say. In golf, it makes you sick. Why do we succumb so often to 'brain dead golf', ...good players do not do so.

Your game plan is totally responsible for how you play. See yourself as knowing the physical golf you are capable of delivering.

Your golf movements are precise and leisurely and strong, your energy is perfect for the sustanance of effort required to complete a score you can accept as a true reflection of your ability and effort.

The mind's eye of knowing what you are doing is not difficult to find time to accomplish. If you are a golfer-homemaker with household, family or social duties, you can find time to daydream or for imagery time. A career person or business executive involved with a job and developing career has the same time.

Your recreation and golf is sacred just as your body is and your inner spirituality is. So is your preparation for it. Just think of the time, waiting to pick up your children, wife or husband in your car, time at the fitness center, standing in line at the supermarket or bank. We all do chores and we all take some sort of 'coffee breaks'.

TACTIC: MAXIMIZING SUCCESS AS A GOLFER

See a mind's eye of yourself maximizing success. Do the exercises such as -- overfilling the cup and do success chipping to show you can maximize success. Make you game plan while you

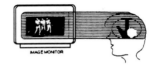

watch your own self-success videotape. Link up game plan + success. Smile!

Carry out the modern way of practicing in which you give yourself some practice situations in which you maximize success to such a great extent that your subconscious see only a successful me image or mind's eye. **How can it be that when I caddy in a ProAm on a Wednesday for the President of a**

New York bank group that the same person who maximizes success every day in their job in New York has absolutely no confidence out on the golf course here in Arizona or California. It doesn't make any sense. The dust on one of the clubs gives me a hint. Did they do any planning at all for this potentially wonderful day out on the golf course at the LPGA Tour? Yes, Michelle McGann, Joan Pitcock or Penny Hammel will inspire some good golf but what is needed is self-success maximizing.

Maximizing success activities is a fine way for your brain 'agreeing' to give you more success in golf. Stand 3' or 4' from the hole and putt as many balls into the hole that the hole is overflowing (with success). This suggests to your  visualization brain that you are confident and prepared and 'accustomed to success'. Do a success chipping drill where every shot is rolled near or over the hole and stops within 24" of the back of the hole. Start short and easy and use your best and simplest putt-chip action. Go right back to putting and overflow the cup again. Take a minimum of 14 nice and loose practice swings with your driver that feels identical to and imitate your very best and very simple swing action.

Practice maximizing success just before some big competition that you are lucky enough to be entered in. Be able to recall your maximum success mind's eye. Show your subconscious that you can putt any number of putts right into the middle of the hole. The cup is 4 1/4" wide, but show your brain that you only use the middle 1" of the cup to roll in your putts.

YOUR MIND'S EYE OF YOU AS A MAXIMIZER OF SUCCESS IS TO SHOW THAT YOU ARE 'MASTER' OF MANY GOLF SITUATIONS.

SELF RECORDING OF SUCCESSFUL ME ON CASSETTE

It is of enormous importance in golf to play the first hole well and to hit effective shots right away on holes 1, 2, and 3. There are, however, many reasons why we are not prepared to play well on the first hole.

The first hole on a former home course is extremely well designed Par 4 with a dogleg left from a 'gunbarrel' tee which, when played from any of the tees, requires a long hit that is rather well placed. A river borders the left side all the way down the fairway. When facing this type of situation, you have to have a strong TACTICs mind's eye to use and you have to be well warmed up and ready to maximize success.

In addition, a ball striking **warm up** of the minimum 15-20 hits is crucial to our reaching a plateau for the golf swing, which would be the same length of warm up required for any motor-skill. Before completing 15-20 strikes, all swings from 1 on seem erratic in nature. In **motor skill learning lab**, we try various motor skills for hand-eye coordination and then chart a graph to see when coordination errors level off. We know this also applies to larger motor skills, called closed loop motor skills such as the golf swing.

This is one area where many golfers for one reason or another fail to capitalize.

Sometimes, there is not driving range or practice area or the practice tee is closed for the season and practice balls are unavailable. In our geographic location, City owned golf courses have installed, starting just this season, commercially made warm up bays just at the first tee. In a pinch, just make sure you swing two clubs 8-10 times and your driver 8-10 times, since this will loosen up your shoulders, to be sure. Just swinging does not warm up your hand-eye coordination, however.

Just two days ago, I played with a 70 year old former caddy who is a clubmaker, and is known as the best greenside player and putter at his club. Both of his shoulders had surgery done during the hockey days, and even though he had a fine swing, it was hole 12-14 before he 'got back' some semblance of his full swing. **He suffered too much even though he stretched out somewhat on the first tee.** It was an early morning game with a minor frost delay of just a few minutes.

*Listen to and recall a mind's eye of Hole #1 Success

In situations where you can not warm up for the #1 hole, you could use an **IMAGE-TACTIC** as you travel to the golf course. It has been found that a cassette recording which you make up yourself is excellent, even for a physical warm up. If you want to, record some tempo-inducing music followed by a number of 'I SEE MYSELF AS.....' statements. In this case, 'I SEE MYSELF AS WITH MY SHOULDERS GOING THRU A FULL RANGE OF MOVEMENT IN MY GOLF SWING' and 'I SEE MY ALIGNMENT AS BEING VERY GOOD AND IN AGREEMENT' and 'I SEE THE MIND'S EYE SERIES OF HOW BEST TO PLAY THE #1-3 HOLES'.

If you stood in front of a mirror as you worked on a full shoulder, turn swing 25-30 times the evening before the game, you will have an easy time of seeing an accurate, vivid mind's eye in your preparation. Your first hole success is much more likely.

A GRADED SERIES OF CHALLENGE TACTICS

Once you become a regular player, as opposed to an occasional golfer, you are eventually going to want to play some of the famous and difficult golf courses in your country or in golfing nations such as the USA, New Zealand, Scotland, Sweden, Australia, England, Canada, Spain, Ireland and other favored area. **In another chapter, we showed mind's eyes for the four courses at St. Andrews, Scotland where summer golf weeks are held by the university in that town.** We recommend that you challenge yourself daily on a different level of golf course and often these can be found in the same location. Sometimes play the shorter course in the a.m. and the main course in the p.m.

*Develop a mind's eye of you playing some of the toughest shots and holes in the golf world.

This will allow you to develop a new set of mind's eye images that will further challenge your golf game. Most golfers have a challenging set of golf courses within a 100 mile radius of their own home. In North America, when I drive through Arkansas, Missouri, Montana, Georgia, Tennessee, Alberta and British Columbia, to name only a few areas, one sees all kinds of new golf developments. **Local area 'amateur golf mini-Tours' seem available almost everywhere.**

Recently, two Trent-Jones courses opened near by the Rocky Mountain range in Alberta. The area is named Banff-Kananaskis, now known because of the Winter Olympics held there. By using several sets of tees on the Mt. Lorette and Mt. Kidd golf courses, there are in effect four separate challenges on these two new courses. When you have to know several sets of TACTICS, you will test your mental game in many ways. The greens, the trap situations, and the shapes of these courses, are wonderfully varied, to say the least.

Every golfer probably would enjoy the challenge of Pinehurst, North Carolina; the Carolinas including Myrtle Beach area; Florida Coastal golf; the various Scotland Links courses and various Sunshine Coast courses. The psychological advantage can be available to the golfer since you have played some of the toughest holes and your mental comfort zone every day courses much better. **Experience is enhanced.**

Mind's eye experience is gained while playing difficult courses. **Playing Pinehurst** can be beneficial because you tend to play especially well due to the strong sense of suggestion of good golf and golf history. At least this accompanied my play at Pinehurst.

Once, when I joined **Carnoustle Club in Scotland** as an overseas playing member and went over there, I played the first five holes of the course under par and then floundered on the sixth hole (so called Hogans Alley) because I had developed a set of mind's eye images that focused on all the difficulties of this famous hole. Exactly where the ditch and dykes were on the right of the #6 had eluded me and I played right into them, in avoiding the out of bounds left. Also, the fearsome hard flat green can take its toll on the number of putts you play. Simply, I did not deliver the strokes. The whole new experience was a little too overwhelming for total preparation. And then, of course, numbers 9, number 12 and number 14 and 18 where yet to come!

PRACTICE FOR FAMOUS HOLES VIA MIND'S EYE
Your imagery for fairway situations can be used on the practice fairway if you have a creative mind. It is fun to try various tee shots to their imagined situations. Constantly try to land shots on the landing area which is correct for you. By being demanding of your shots on the practice area, you will be repaid enormous dividends on the golf course.

Your shot selector brain will be required to get a good workout. If you are a little fatigued, hit just 14 drives for each of the 14 non-Par 3's that you will face.

Practice these simulations. In addition, practice with the wind and vs the wind and adapt your mind's eyes to shots for special conditions. If you are really serious, practice in weather not to your liking and have some interventions for wet weather golf.

GENERAL REVIEW OF GOLF TACTICS

Generally speaking, a review of the mind's eye tactics for playing sound golf will include the following:

1.   Check for clues about the wind at the height that the shot will be traveling. A common way is to look for wind at tree top level and to recall that wind is in zones or layers.

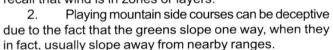

2.   Playing mountain side courses can be deceptive due to the fact that the greens slope one way, when they in fact, usually slope away from nearby ranges.

3.   Watch the bounce of the ball so that you can ascertain the slope of the fairway nearest to the green and the slope of the green itself.

4.   Know the times of the season when the fairways are harder and when they are soft in your locale. Know grass types and their play characters.

5.   Look for clues from other players on nearby fairways for the bounce and roll and other near green shot landings and the like.

6.   Remember to visualize mind's eye for the fact that golf course designers leave off-the-green-spaces at the back of some greens, whereas trouble can be very quick off the back of some greens. Know the length of the green for blue or black flag placements which often require that extra club or two length of club.

7.   Relative to green hardness, know the watering pattern and frequency of watering the greens. See how fast the ball rolls. The clubhouse putting green watering may be different.

8.   Use the 150 yard markers and pace the distance to be sure you know where this distance was cabled to and from. Know your 150 yard pace-off actually may be 152 or 153 yards. Use sprinkler covers for markers, check them for tags indicating distance.

9.   Try to know where soggy spots tend to be. Plan mind's eyes for avoidance where possible.

10.   On new courses, the course design may have exact driving distances for a ball landing zone to avoid fairway sand areas for your TACTICS. The preferred flat spot for the 2nd shot is often part of a pattern as well.

11.   You may find that you can get true roll or straight roll off of certain landing targets. On the contrary, certain landing areas may redirect the ball to a difficult follow up spot.

12.   Try to know the reputation of the green for the type of shot reception it

favors. Know which shot approach angles are best to leave the shot near the hole.

13. Understand that it is not against the rules of golf to ask for information, which is not advice, about all play on a course.

14. Almost all good 18 hole scores come from games that start conservatively and patiently and then gain momentum of scoring.

****

SUMMARY
<u>KEY WORDS AND NOTIONS OF CHAPTER THREE</u>

*Game Tactics I, II, III, and IV are necessary to score to the best of your golf ability.

*Cognitive mind's eye imagery wants to protect you from mental daisy picking in golf.

*Affective mind's eye imagery is related to strong attitudes about yourself and others and how to require the best efforts of yourself.

*The qualities and expectations of TACTICS MIND'S EYES re detailed and feature Completeness, Positive-negative and Endurance or re-image Endurance.

*An 'I am smart' in golf affirmation is much detailed.

*The motor learning skill called modeling is a key to your mind's eye golf success.

*Using the putter for alignment and all alignment is outlined for improving your communication between your skill level and the mind's eye.

*Parents and golf supporters should be aware of a TACTIC for their children's growth and development in golf.

*You can be a maximizer of your golf success. You can be a master of many golf situations.

*A number of famous golf holes are used to demonstrate TACTICS mind's eye imagery.

****

CHAPTER THREE
BIBLIOGRAPHY AND RESOURCES.

Krueger, Kurt. Personal Communication. "Fear: Practical Sport Psychology". PSP Institute, 1984

Yocum, Guy and Brett Parker. Australian Golf Digest. "New Shafts: Adding Order to Chaos". May, 1994

Norman, Greg. Golf Digest. "Champs Clinic". August 1984

Cave, Kyle R. Journal of Research in Science Teaching. "The Construction of Analogical Transfer of Symbolic Visualizations", 30. 10

Dec., 1993

Lucas, Geoffrey. The NEW Images for Golf: The Fundamentals of Visualizing and Scoring. Victoria, B.C. and Littlefield, AZ. A2Z Publishing, 2006

Lucas, Geoffrey, Frank F. Sanchez Jr., and Jerry Borro. Six 1 Putts Minimum...To Cure A Sick Golf Score: 55 Golf Exercises to Make 1 Putts Happen. Victoria B.C.and Littlefield, AZ. A2Z Publishing, 2006

Lucas, Geoffrey and Lloyd Boody. Canadian Psychological Association. "Effects of Positive Imagery and Success Videotape Viewing on Motor Skill". Banff, Canada, 1989

Lawrence, Jennifer. European PGA Tour Performance Report and Documentary of Communication on Improvement. Woburn, England. 1992

Hogan, Chuck and Dale Van Dalsem/Susan Davis, 5 Days to Golfing Success. Lake Oswego, Oregon: Merl Millar Associates, 1986

Quinn, Paul. Child Development. "The Categorization on Above and Below Spatial Relations by Young Infants". 65.1994

Kagan, Jerome. Psychology Today. "Reactivity in Infants and a Cross National Comparison". 1989

Clyde, Jean Ann. Language Arts. "Lessons from Douglas: Expanding Our Vision of What it Means to Know". 71. 1994

Peter Jacobs and Jack Sheehan. Buried Lies. Middlesex, England: Penquin Books, 1993

CHAPTER 4: TECHNIQUE IMAGERY
FOR TARGETTERS

Objectives: Accurate and suggested key technique images are detailed; tie-ins are explained; expectations are relayed; technique exercise and turn ons and turn offs are detailed; accurate aiming through wedge play is related to the mind's eye; swing speed is analyzed; 'my technique' is good is developed; swing style; posture and imagery; and aiming; a last word.

****

Most golfers blame swing mechanics and believe in swing flaw correction to an excessive degree for their bad shots and as a matter of fact, many Tour players will tell you that mental preparation for the shot is often at fault.

BASICALLY, however, if you can think of your mind as an IMAGE SELECTOR or small TELEVISION MONITOR it can give the selector brain correct swing images, and the swing can become consistent and accurate as well as start to develop swing feel and THEN IT LEADS TO LOWERED GOLF SCORES. LATER, YOUR BODY WILL TELL YOU BY FEEL (KINESTHESIS) when your swing is in swing flaw.

IMAGE SELECTOR

However prominent LPGA Tour Player Marisa Baena took 6 years on Tour before being able to self correct with a coach at that.

In this chapter, the application of good mechanics is enhanced by clear, concise mind's eye images. The swing is made in a manner keeping with solid biomechanics and pretty much with the golfers notion of a correct golf swing.

The golf swing is done while the subconscious brain is actually using a clear golf image or mind's eye picture. As the notions of the swing become clear and exact, so can the performance of the swing be exact! An exacting swing produces shot CONSISTENCY and consistency augmented by TACTICS AND TENACITY gives lowered golf scores....golf scores more in keeping with most players development and promise.

The present book is not a Technique book and there will sometimes be assumptions made that the reader understands the **basic swing** presently in vogue among many Tour players. To the author in vogue means biomechanically natural and the swing that is found in the modern golf Textbook titled *PLAY BETTER GOLF*, by PJ Tomasi and Mike Adams (the Swing Doctor) of the PGA Academy in Florida. **In general, this type of swing is all about natural and biomechanically solid swing position, posture and motion.** The basic swing is the one that the mind's eye can call up from memorized swing images which are not fuzzy or inaccurate ones. **There are many basic swing images.**

Inaccurate images lead to muscle memory and a golf swing which varies or is inconsistent. Lower golf scores would not usually be possible.

TECHNIQUE IMAGERY DEFINED

This type of mind's eye or imagery functions to provide accurate pictures and feelings of the golf swing. The images clarify for the brain and body the actual movement.

For example, four images for technique usually required are: 1. stance (with alignment); 2. top of the swing including a nice platform arm/club position; 3. position prior to impact; and 4. extension and follow through. THESE POSITIONS LEAD TO ACCURATE AND REPEATABLE GOLF SWINGS.

WHY SPECIFIC ACCURATE MIND'S EYES HELP

According to image-theory, models and accurate pictures provide clarification for the brain and the musculature for body movements to specific sports techniques. In addition, as Barbara Brown, author of **SUPERMIND**, pointed out not only is imagination the **ultimate energy**, but a detailed and specific image gives specific effects. If you see yourself swinging your driver with a nicely paced 1.8 second golf swing, if you see accompanying full shoulder turn, then you will get specific effects, according to Brown. Namely, the effect will be center to center bail-clubface contact and long, accurate drives. Since the brain is using specific impulses, you can excite and generate these impulses once again. By generating the same impulses repeatedly (via the mind's eye) you recall a former performance of your own.

In addition, imaging makes your body do biomechanical work and it is extremely important in golf (essentially a repeating motor skill game) to make your swing muscles work as often as you possibly can.

Even if a player has time and dedication to repeat every day multiple golf drives, say 150, plus 150 other shots plus putting and short game, they still and especially require accurate imagery for recalling muscle memories and swing feel.

PATTERN, PATTERN

There are additional ways in which the mind's eye works for a technically accurate swing and makes your body work for good golf. Rapid learning of sequences and timing is augmented and your body can work more efficiently. **Small muscle forces are firing off during imagery. Practice is being accomplished and accompanied by 'internal feedback' at a very high level in the central nervous system.**

Of course, your psychological **arousal level is better** (set more appropriately, it is said) and you are generally ready for a good performance attempt. *The pattern set off in the CNS by a specific image of swing technique is important and that pattern is strongly associated with the action.*

SO THAT, AS BARBARA BROWN HAS POINTED OUT, A SPECIFIC IMAGE OR MIND'S EYE HAS VERY SPECIFIC AND BENEFICIAL EFFECTS.

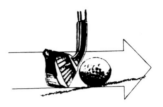

ASK YOURSELF ABOUT YOUR TECHNIQUE IMAGERY

Normally in a golf game, you will step up to the tee box fourteen times to use your driver (or sometimes a lay up club of some other choice, which caddies and players sometimes debate over a little). You will attempt to hit each drive in the best **TACTICS IMAGERY** ball position to enhance your second shot. Four times you will step up to the tee box for a par 3 hole.

Your game objective will be to get 14 of 14 drives in position and to get 4 of 4 par 3 shots on to the best part of the green for the follow up putt attempt.

Now let us look for the minimum expectations for the mind's eye as you use your driver for those 14 key hits, thinking of both ball position and some pretty good distance, even for a senior.

BASIC EXPECTATIONS OF IMAGERY AS YOU USE YOUR DRIVER FOR 14 KEY SHOTS PER GAME

VIVIDNESS:

Is my mind's eye vivid enough to include the details I require to hit a good drive or are some key details missing? Does my image see me relaxing my muscles especially my arms, shoulder and legs, yet maintain the grip with obvious tempo and does the take away get me in a nice hands/wrist/arms/club platform position as my shoulder turn? FOR MY SWING AND FOR MOST SWINGS, DOES THE SWING HAVE A NATURAL FOLLOW THRU THAT IS HELD MOMENTARILY AT LEAST?

As you concentrate on imagery vividness never allow yourself to change back into the 'non image mode or style'. Stay with the mind's eye imitation mode (called muscle memory) and depend on it as Tournament Tour event pressure mounts.

VIVIDNESS:

The reader should use their own golf swing and their own driver to set up the basic demands of expectation for the mind's eye. **Use a mirror at home or on the practice area and memorize the natural lever system that you see in your swing. Get someone to help you really see your swing and use their**

set of answers to find out your exact swing positions and VIVIDNESS WILL DEVELOP IN YOUR CLOSED EYE IMAGES. One of the most frequent things one sees on a Tour practice tee is golfers, coaches and caddies in some cases, helping one another, even if  very briefly, with swing positions and check-offs. One caddy would always have a long cardboard box to check his players swing plane, which would be viewed thru as if it were binoculars.

SELF OR OTHER IMAGE

Is the imager you see of your own swing or another golfers swing? Experiment or blend a little here. For example, mine is of my own swing except at the exact moment of impact I have a substitute one frame mind's eye of **Tom Watson** due to great upper body position that he has been shown to have. His physique is realistic and suitable for me and I relate to his muscular arms and shoulders, and I suppose, his High School football background.

COLOR:

Is your mind's eye picture in color or in black and white? Try to use technicolor and make the colors as real as possible. For example, see your driver as what it is --- perhaps a driver as "Powerbuilt" persimmon head of blonde wood grained head meeting a bright yellow optic golf ball or a titanium whatever meeting a white ball with your own i.d. viewing from the top of the ball to you. See a black arrow through the clubhead and see the arrow continue right through the clubhead and on to target.

Of course in TACTICS mind's eye, see green grass and sharp contrasts of an optic yellow or white ball bouncing accurately off the green grass.

TENSE:

The mind's eye of the driver swing is in the here and now. This is the most effective tense to be in. If other players are teeing off before you, you can be imaging your swing rather than watching anyone else swing.

Exceptions to a general rule of not watching others swing are perhaps when you are not in competition or if you focus in on some exact aspect of another players swing. Secondly, you may use some other players whole swing model, a Don January or a Tom Watson or even a Jim Furyk, if any of these swings are your focus model.

SPEED:

A golfer is supposed to mind's eye at full speed but an occasional frame by frame with a mind's eye freeze frame is alright too. A driver image can be mostly at full speed and can be accompanied by a hum or a whistle imbued with accelerating motion

The 3/4 speed swing can be modelled easily enough by the players own inspired model. Wristy pop-shots can be modelled and then struck with the same speed as the model. Some Tour players will repeat this type of delicate swing several times, even 8-12 times before they are ready. The same players are the best players around the greens.

COMPLETENESS:
A MIND'S EYE OF A SWING SHOULD COMPLETE ITSELF. For example, you should very much want to see your hands drive well past the ear on the follow through for a natural swing motion.

A **MIRROR** is helpful in completing this image. Lots of work on completeness can be done around home.

TIMING:
Most often the player can recall or call up a mind's eye just before the drive shot on the tee box. Sometimes, if the golfer is swinging with great tempo. The just the partial swing, the waggle or two, or the 'Bill Andrade' Swing Tip pre swing hold-the-follow-thru will do. The **TIMING** is an internal feel and does seem to vary day to day in golf and for that reason it appears that the pace for the

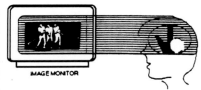

IMAGE MONITOR

day is important. Perhaps if you spend the a.m. rushing around, that same rush-pace is picked up by your internal timing sense and transferred to the swing.

ANIMATION:
The mind's eye images can use musical or animal like qualities. Only occasionally does a swing try to imitate a 'tiger ready to spring' but once in awhile it could as the player prepares to delay the contact with the ball ever so slightly.

You may find that some sort of animal tempo can accompany every swing or actual stroke.

TEMPO:
Accelerating motion for a driver swing is often accompanied by a slow 1-2-3 count and a faster count on the down swing into impact. Also, a six count slow 1-2-3 up and a faster, accelerating 4-5-6 to follow through has been much used.

If the player is sitting in a chair imagining their nice swing motion, then the onomatopoeic 'oomm pahh' is very handy to imitate pattern and muscle force tempo.

SMOOTHNESS:

A smoothness mind's eye cue is especially important to those players who tend to be a little mechanical or 'phasey' in how they draw the club to the top of the swing. It is especially important with drives, long irons and those long putts we face. A good mind's eye accompaniment is 'custard smooth' or the chef stirring the huge spoon in the oversized stainless steel mixing bowl idea.

Smoothness of swing is observed by other players. One believes that scratch handicap players and Tour players hold smoothness in very high esteem as a mind's eye.

It is believed that smoothness of swing builds consistency. Also, smoothness allows you to hit many, many practice balls without tiring. Watching Annika Sorenstam, Lisa Kiggens or Fred Couples types will improve your mind's eye of smoothness.

Watching them in person is much better than in any other way. Pick up of and absorption of these cues seems to be enhanced thereby.

MOVEMENT:

Is your mind's eye image moving? Most often try to feel that the mind's eye you are recalling or absorbing is moving. **See images in motion. You may hear the swish of club movement or feel the muscles relax as they move the club. Build on the energy of each of your former swings.**

POSITIVE - NEGATIVE:

A mind's eye of a driver swing should never be negative or based on the last swing if the last swing was not what you asked your mind's eye brain to deliver.

For example, if you have been taught to be able to hit a fade or a draw, but only rarely use those skill shots since you are perhaps, a straight line visualizer, then, review those skills before using them out on the course. In other words, make some decisions now and then which force preparation.

Of course most all images are positive in nature it seems. Use a reminds eye if you have to.

BODY REACTION:

Small muscle forces firing off often accompany your driver-mind's eye. Do you feel tingling, tightening or relaxation? Reinforce this feel by multiple viewing in our mind's eye.

IMAGE OR MIND'S EYE ENDURANCE:

This is the **KEY** of all the mind's eye skills. Especially as you drive on holes 14-18, you might **remind your image selector to keep on the job.** When the late Bobby Jones said that golfers tend to do a little mental 'daisy-picking' he wasn't kidding. After some checking up, it has been found that he was quite right.

Good amateurs and even Tour players often do not have the 'Mark O'Meara', 'Karrie Webb' finishing touch it seems, on the last few holes.

The names of players from the Tour who have endurance changes season after season, and that is one of the great challenges in understanding and developing performance consistency. Maintenance of a finishing touch is one of the unknown areas for Tour players at present....however, surely enough a good mind's eye program and a build up of tempo will help such maintaining of success.

One learns how important the mind's eye is on the last three holes when you play in the odd weekend 2 day event and manage to stay in contention. If you are in contention on the 16th tee box (even back a little) you want to play 16, 17 and 18 flawlessly because your opponent(s) might be able to play flawlessly as well. Once in a town Open event, my 2 good pars and one scrambling par held up for a rare 72 and a win for the author.

Later, on checking with the closest competitors, it was found that their last three holes truly determined the players final placing.

Most often after such an experience a players' mind's eye can be effective for the finishing holes since in imagery one builds on former successes. You can use the same systematic mind's eye on those finishing holes.

SUMMARY: THE BASIC EXPECTATIONS OF THE MIND'S EYE
The review of the 14 KEY expectations of the mind's eye includes the important drives of a typical golf game. In addition to applying these expectations to driving and your iron play, putting and all near green shots, you can apply them to special and trouble shots as well.

SUMMARY: THE BASICS
Most often you will want to turn your mind's eye on and leave it on for 18 holes in golf. Since golf can be quite frustrating, it is not unusual to get some streaks of good golf in which the mind's eye works well and sometimes the opposite.

If the Tour player or regular player make some sensible decisions, they will usually decide to get back to whatever was making their game tick along in the first place. It was perhaps a streak of good aiming.

PERFECTING TECHNIQUE: A KEY PRIOR TO MIND'S EYE
Almost always good golf is accompanied by fine course management or systematic play, good tactics, a good start and tempo of play. However, haphazard technique or unconfident technique can affect all players in golf. Consider some of the well known golf disasters. Even a Tour player can forget to turn on their mind's eye play, and score an 11 on one hole even though the same player won an event or two on Tour.

John Daly, playing very well these days, has had the odd big number and an even more famous incidence was recorded by John Schroeder at Muirfield Village when his 11 was followed by a 7 on a Par 3 when he whiffled three left hand attempts from under a tree when a branch hindered his golf movement.

At the **Olde Course** in St. Andrews town, the 17th hole lying just in front of the hotel has a drop off to a sand bunker that runs balls into it. The same hole has a paved roadway and stone fence included as a integral part of it. If you have played it, you will remember how critical the **AIM LINE** is on the drive (remember, a big old painted Rail shed). If you inadvertently set up a bad second shot situation, you will suffer a big number usually.

It was on this hole that a Tour player from Japan scored a 19 when he repeatedly went from green to bunker and back and forth.

On Schroeder's day at Muirfield, Ohio, he hit a perfect drive and a perfect sand blast to 1 ft. from the cup and a 1 ft. putt. In between he recorded penalty stroke drops (one p. stroke each), three rebound to a hazard, rebound off cart path into trouble, another unplayable lie, flubbed wedge, and sand blast. **IT IS DURING SUCH TIMES THAT A GOLFER SIMPLY SWINGS WITHOUT PREPLANNING IT SEEMS BUT OFTEN THE PLAYER WILL REMEMBER PLANNING EACH SHOT.** BUT IT STILL RESULTS IN A GOLF DISASTER TO BE SURE!

KEY TECHNIQUE MIND'S EYE NEEDED FOR WEDGE

*a mind's eye of controlled back swing
*a mind's eye of shape of the swing
especially steepness or lack of.

Golfers tend to dread the use of the half wedge in which approximately one-half of a full back swing and shoulder turn is used. The half wedge may require 40-75 yards of flight as opposed to a longer wedge distance.

Short wedges or wedges hit off of varying lies may require even more delicate fine tuning of the swing with varying back swing and steepness of take-away angles involved.

No other method seems possible than working on the practice tee with 35 yarders, 45 yarders, and 55 yarders and up. Soon you will form the necessary feel for the mind's eye needed. Simply being patient and practicing with various targets (real or imagined) at various lengths is among the few ways to confirm that your mind's eyes and internalized feel are correct. Usually hit only one at each but sometimes do repetitions.

Any player who uses deceleration of club speed will suffer some additional problem it seems. However, players like Annika Sorenstam seem wonderfully capable of this short shot and her club speed seems next door to decelerating.

So stress accurate mind's eye and matching swing length and speed. With classes I have used the phrase: 'shorter to longer and slow to faster' and it seems to help. However, it is a very personal skill to be sure.

It helps the golfer if they develop accurate mind's eyes and matching short back swings. These images feature short back swing to longer foreswing length or simple short to longer length and feel. The idea of short to longer and slow to faster applies to all golf swings since it is a **NATURAL KINESIOLOGICAL PRINCIPLE** for every player.

This assures that the player does not use a long back swing accompanied by a shorter follow-through (and the usual disastrous faster to slower swing tempo).

Tom Kite from Texas has said it very well when he pointed out that the reason most players have so much trouble with the partial wedge is that they tend to over swing on the back swing, which causes them to decelerate on the downswing. For this reason, the mind's eye must suggest acceleration or at least the avoidance of deceleration.

Besides using specific target practice, you might try swinging through as far as the back swing went back. This is extremely effective. It is suggested that players who want to look at the **TECHNIQUE**, read the back issues of *Golf Digest* to get some outstanding advice from one of the great players, Tom Kite.

TEXAS GOLF INSTRUCTORS AT THE PGA LEVEL HAVE RECENTLY DEVELOPED A SPECIALIZED SET OF LESSONS FOR WEDGE PLAY. When this author spent six moths attending TCU in Fort Worth, it included practicing and learning to use three wedges at the practice area at **old Glen Garden Golf Club** just up a hill from a worn out commercial neighborhood. There the lessons on wedge became my afternoon delight and challenge. There was a special area for wedge distance and lots of time to use our own shag bag and balls.

It was the **same club location that Ben Hogan grew up at** while caddying for Ed Stewart, a scratch amateur. Hogan learned the swing there it is said and that fact is confirmed by the older members and staff. So there was a sense of historical aura as I practiced. Hogans statue is up at the Colonial which is a little closer to the TCU campus. Hogan would sometimes lunch there it was said by the many caddies in the area.\

Also, pictures in the clubhouse attested that **'Iron Byron' Nelson and Sandra Palmer were at Glen Garden as well when they were young players.** Besides learning from a fine teaching Professional, one can also be taught to play Dominoes and cards almost each and every afternoon. **My teaching professional gave me a large amount of modeling as he would hit 50-60 wedge shots or more for me to pick up on and absorb for the mind's eye.**

Tom Kite, Lee Trevino, Al Geiberger and nearly all Japanese Tour players started carrying a third wedge some years ago and most bags on the LPGA Tour have 3 wedges in them.

The third wedge for more distance variety is in addition to the regular wedge and the sand wedge. The other wedge is adjusted in lie and loft so it can add a mid range distance with a full swing thus avoiding somewhat the dreaded one-half swing. Combined with accurate mind's eye imagery, the use of three wedges can produce some very accurate distance skills. Short game accuracy can cut down your game score. You may have to sacrifice one of your longer hitting clubs to keep your limit to the 14 required in the rules of golf.

Ask your golf professional for help. **He can measure the degrees of Lie and Loft and help you with a wedge(s) lesson since it is the most accurate of clubs outside of the putter.**

It is a well known dictate among teaching professionals that, particularly with the wedge, too short a backswing causes a jerk motion and too long a backswing usually causes deceleration. Both lead to inconsistent shots.

ART OF FIXING ON ONE OR TWO KEY MOVEMENTS

For golfers excessive thinking prevents good effective golf shots from developing. As explained earlier, the analyzer brain has a role in golf.

But that role is purely for analyzing the shot situation and golf intuition and not for 'lecturing' oneself about all that has to be remembered out on the golf course.

There is a parallel with using the mind's eye and technique improvement. Select only one or two key swing mind's eyes prior to each component. **The next game you might find that one simple mind's eye such as swing smoothness does the same effective job.** Remember to stretch out your muscles as a warm-up so that your imagery system can be allowed to work. In practicing one theme image at a time will suffice.

DAY TO DAY VARIATION IN THE MIND'S EYE IS OK

*Although you require a bank of technique mind's eye, narrow down the # selected.

For example, an instructor who is familiar, former Teacher of the Year, **Joanne Winter of Scottsdale, AZ.**, had our classes practice hit one shot with one mind's eye and another shot with a 2nd mind's eye. The same shots and two different images is the theme until some improvement surfaces.

After the lesson, the mind's eye act as reminders for further improvement. Your teacher and you can identify swing priority and what to work on.

In the same way, the Walt Disney World Golf School in Florida finishes a lesson by giving you a video of what they call 'Mickey Mouse' golf reminders to let you narrow down your swing improvement to a few **KEY** mind's eyes. Thus, you do not get overly global in your swing improvement program.

Fix on one or two KEY movements at a time. At the Disney School, they show you your swing on a large screen video to enhance your swing knowledge and you thus visualize your own swing against your new mind's eye pictures of the swing you are working toward having.

SWING SPEED AND THE MIND'S EYE
The basis for an effective mind's eye program for swing speed is to 'see' a set of pictures which include the timing component for the backswing, change of direction, and downswing to impact and follow thru.

Depending on your body-flexibility and the length of your bodies interconnected lever system, you allow just under 2.0 seconds for a full swing. So we speak of the 1.8 second swing as near ideal. A 1.2 swing to impact would have little chance of taking full advantage of a body's neuromuscular system and levers. A mind's eye includes a slow take away to a somewhat faster downswing with the slight delayed hit characteristic.

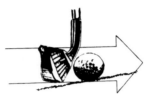

THE TIMING OF A TYPICAL GOOD GOLF SWING
The mind's eyes that lets you imitate your full golf swing are verbally cued or musically cued (whistle, hum or sung) via a 'slow' - 'thousand-one to the top' cue.

Swing pictures show about a full second for the club to get to the top. The KEY image and learning involve how deliberate a good swing really is from slow take away to stretch position at the top.

Movie pictures taken at 50 frames/second will take just over 90 frames to complete a full swing in any reputed tempo swinger like Fred Couples. Al Geiberger or Liselotte Neuman. So for your swing, take nearly a full second to take it to the top on any full swing including your shorter clubs.

To use swing images for most swing positions, do the following: stretch out your shoulder muscles and your body rotatory muscles and levers. Memorize some accurate swing mind's eye pictures. Put a stop watch or large face clock somewhere near you. Use a big sport timer clock.

Use a mirrored room or swing just outside of a set of glass doors or large windows. Use the mind's eyes to work on your slow take away and time out various takeaways until you settle on a speed that seems just right for your body situation.

THRU THE BALL MIND'S EYE
The take away will be next door to a lazy-leisurely swing as far as the feel is concerned. Practice this notion of moving the triangle (shoulders-arms-grip) or even pre set the wrist-levers to that 'hip level platform' we all are taught about these days, and then finish your smooth take away.

You do not need a club to do this movement, so do it throughout the day, at work, at school, or anywhere you can imitate the swing. Practice the change of direction too.

While not rushing, you are accelerating thru a the ball and not to the ball.

'STRETCH - MACHINE' EVEN AT OLDER AGE

Soon you will be acquiring a slow take away quite like a good Tour player or a 'tempo swinger'. Stretch as much as you can and use all kinds of images that act to remind your body-lever system that it can be a tremendous 'stretch-machine'. Stretching reacts well not matter what age, but not if you have not been regular with stretching sports or activities. In that case be gradual with a new stretch program.

Recently, deep massage programs or therapies have been linked to improving sport flexibility and stretching. A procedure for 'deep muscle flexibility' has been labelled 'rolfing' and you might investigate it and other stretch/flexibility teaching and programing in your locality.

Continue your mind's eye program on the practice tee. On hitting balls, you will find out what fine golfers have found. That 1.8 second leisurely swing tries to become a faster 'zip-zip' swing. Change your practice, if that happens to your swing, as follows:

1. Swing without a ball 10 times via only the mind's eye and good timing.

2. Your subconscious will gladly accept this CNS reminder of the slower pattern you seek.

3. Hit 5 balls or more with this same tempo swing.

Marvel at how far the ball goes now even with what you may think is so little effort. Now repeat this 10 times - mind's eye/no ball and 5+ hits over and over or until it starts becoming integrated with your natural swing. *THE ROLE OF THE MIND'S EYE IS WELL WORTH THE EFFORT.*

SPEED VARIATIONS IN THE GOLF SWING

Once you have a steady tempo in your swing, you will start to know if you swing your driver at 115+ a very fast swing speed in golf. This would be like a Lanny Watkins type (i.e. super fast). Or a lot slower, would be at 106+, perhaps silky smooth, like Patty Sheehan or Don January. Naturally, your mind's eye should be one you know is natural to your body levers. With a new light weight driver a 18 handicapper who swings too fast will likely hit a lot OUT OF BOUNDS so choose the swing speed that will let you score low also. YOU STILL WILL BE CAPABLE OF OMINOUS DISTANCE.

DETERMINING YOUR SWING SPEED

Without having to be tested on swing speed, electronically, it is

possible to accurately know your actual swing speed. The ball will land at 160+ yards (flight) if you swing at 80 mph; while you will land at 200+ yards you will have a swing speed of 100 mph (if you make good contact with a normal driver in regular wind conditions). So if you land the ball at 200, 210, 220, or 230 with little effort or what is called an 'effortless swing tempo' you are getting in the upper reaches of the Tour player distance on either the Women's or Mens Tours.

A three 'wood' (meaning laminate, titanium or any other lightweight alloy head) swings a little slower due to decreased length and less mass so expect a 5% decrease but more accuracy. Expect more distance with clubs well matched to your body muscle-lever type, as well.

Power varies somewhat as **when a Tour player such a Greg Norman comes off of shoulder surgery** and says his **power** is just coming back to prior levels or more, due to increased **muscle mass** from power weight lifting over several months, involving a **gain in body weight** of 5-8 lbs.

You can take all these factors into account including failure to hit the ball on the sweetspot of your driver in determining your mind's eye for swing speed and distance.

THE MIND'S EYE AND SWING SPEED VARYING

Gary Hallberg had become fairly well known on Tour. He won a consistent $16,000 per Tour event and has had Top ten and better finishes, which is considered ominous indeed. On one Tour event, he finished in 7th, won $19,000, in the Texas Open.

Since graduating from Wake Forest University, he has been a consistent performer. He has already won one 1sts. Hallberg is a 'playing editor' for *Golf Magazine*. Hallberg gives some solid advice as he combines imagery with swing speed variation (he talks of imagery, visualization and self talk) with swing speed variation.

Shotmaking is hitting more than ball spin with hook pattern and slice pattern, rather it is the ability to match swing speed to shot requirements according to Gary Hallberg. He suggests the rule of swinging at 80% of maximum power on all full swings (take power as meaning swing speed which it is not exactly). On the slow swing his uses 'quiet hands' mind's eye imagery on the top of the swing, before starting the club back down.

On the faster swing, he says that visualization is equally important. Just as noted in prior examples of time distortion in this book, he speaks of slower type shots and walking slowly up to the shot, talking 'slowly', using deeper breathes, focusing on target and imagining swing and ball trajectory.

Maybe the reader would like to look up some valuable Hallberg advice in his writing on Lob shot, slow Punch, and in-between speed shots in golf. Your mind's eye will appreciate this effort on your part.

STAY WITH SPEED LIMITS APPROPRIATE TO YOUR BODY LEVER SYSTEM

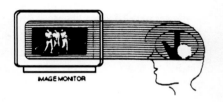

MY TECHNIQUE IS GOOD MIND'S EYE

It is critical that you provide your golf sub conscious with many mind's eye messages that point out you are a good golfer, especially TECHNIQUE wise in several of the following ways. AFFIRMATIONS or good messages acknowledging your mastery of elements of TECHNIQUE provide facilitating messages or talk that lets you improve without the feel that you are out of your comfort zone for shotmaking.

*see your swing obey basic laws of motion
*see a 'pause' as you stretch to the top
*see a clockface. Super impose your swing speed to the face.

*see your body as capable of total balance and held follow thru
*see the swing mind's eye that matches shot requirement
*see a reverse C body, even a little one
*see slow to faster
and....**see your TENACITY & TACTICS**

PRE GAME MIND'S EYE

Using a mind's eye of slow to faster tempo for your swing, you can have a personal range of speed for your swing. **All effective golf seems to be based on excellent control of tempo and feel for it. Imagine a slowly but forcefully increasing race car motion.** See a jet accelerate off of its launching pad off of a ship deck.

The last two hours at your job, try to do your work with totally controlled tempo. Just the idea will help your mind's eye brain in golf. You will see your work-effort improve by virtue of steady, consistent effort. Occasionally swing your arms or with a ruler swing them. Swing with great tempo in your visualization. Do a putt motion feeling that putter face-inset 'feel' that golf ball type.

Finally, when driving to the golf course stress steadily controlled acceleration via the gas pedal and steady braking to a stop. ARRIVE EARLY AND DO NOT BE IN A HURRY!

ALL PRE GAME MIND'S EYE PICTURES WILL PAY OFF WITH GOLF COURSE DIVIDENDS

WALTER HAGEN: MR. SLOW MOTION

Walter Hagen is known to have said that when he had a match to play, he would relax as soon as awakening. He said he did everything slow and easy! That went for striking the ball, stroking the shaving razor, getting dressed, and eating breakfast. He said he was practically slow motion. By the time he was required to Tee off, he felt he was ready since he was so used to taking his time that he felt it was impossible to hurry his swing.

Hale Irwin indicated that swing tempo is among the three things he constantly works on for consistency. The other two being: alignment and swing plane.

Jack Nicklaus taught himself to play slowly and with planned visualization to such an extent that according to Tom Watson, Ñicklaus actually allowed himself to play at a slightly faster pace later in his career. He apparently functioned at golf just as well.

Laura Davies, playing for Europe in the Solheim Cup matches could not play fast enough to suit her personal style of faster play. She evidently is not happy with regular pace play. Once when caddying for **Karen Davies**, our group caught up to Laura Davies group on the next Tee box out in South Carolina, and with the delay soon enough Laura laid down on the Tee and stretched out and got about 3 or 4 minutes of rest.

Of course, when the same thing happened to **Chris Tidland** from Oklahoma on the Tee box at Heritage Point in Canada, on the Canadian Tour, he took a pocket book out of his bag and read for a few minutes and then led a little discussion on current books that are an interesting read. **Tidland qualified to play in the Masters and apparently was pretty intimidated by it all, but came back to win a Canadian Tour event shortly after.**

Soon enough, both Davies and Tidland and their Tour groups were on their way and the Caddies had taken a surprise rest. **It is difficult to assess the effect of slow play on the various natural tempo of Tour players.**

EVEN TEMPO BACK AND THROUGH

A mind's eye that is especially effective for players who tend to take the club away nice and slow but who rush the downswing to the point of destroying timing and consequent power development, is a metranone-type activity which can hone the mind's eye for later use on the golf course. The metranone on top of a piano has a regular 'tic-toc tic-toc...' which suggests even tempo and seeing the swing as following even tempo going back as well as thru the ball.

*mind's eye your swing and follow an even tempo both back and thru the ball

Since the body picks up speed naturally when the club is swung back down (due to large power muscle coming in to action) the SUM OF SUCH MUSCLE FORCE EQUATES WITH SPEED.

But for some golfers it appears that it is much better to strive for even speed back and thru and let tempo take care of itself. An accelerating type of tempo that is. It is interesting to note that if you think of keeping an even speed, you will end up with enhanced swing rhythm. Jack Nicklaus agreed with this basic golf idea and has been known to state a belief "...is that, you imagine your swing is even in tempo back and through, but in actuality of course, speed is picked up on the downswing".

BOBBY JONES: A PERFECT MIND'S EYE CUE

When Bobby Jones used the expression the "hips moving beneath yourself", it provided a perfect cue for seeing and imitating the position shown in the last frames of a typical swing sequence image. Attempt to have a clear mind's eye of such positions as you move through the full swing. Do a quick check off in a mirror. Such a mind's eye will improve both your footwork and your ball strike posture along with your dynamic leg drive off your inner foot and leg muscles of your non-green side leg. AND OF COURSE YOU HIPS WILL MOVE 'BENEATH YOURSELF' AS JONES TERMED IT.

DIFFERENT CLUB LENGTH AND THE MIND'S EYE

Swing a full swing with a 3 iron, a 6 iron and then a 9 iron. Try to hear a distinct 'swish' with each club. Put exactly the same swing on each club. Swing each club several times.

Next, go and strike one ball with each club in succession. Relate this to your mind's eye as much as you can. You will feel the 9 iron deliver less speed with that some swing. THE SWING STAYS THE SAME AND THE CLUB PRODUCES SLIGHT SHOT VARIATION. LET THE CLUB WORK. BE A MASTER OF EQUAL EFFORT!

SWING STYLE AND THE MIND'S EYE

After you get used to swinging the golf club frequently and with even tempo during the off season (as well as in season) then you will start to 'see and feel' the swing as a simple motion. After your golf muscles stretch out, then swinging 150 times a day is easy and nothing more than a 12-18 minute. Even better spread out your practice to 30-40 swings at a time. *SO LITTLE TIME TO KEEP SUCH A WONDERFUL POSSESSION AS A DEPENDABLE, GOOD LOOKING SWING, WHICH IS 'IN TUNE' WITH YOU AND NATURE --- RATHER AMAZING TO BE SURE! RATHER EASY TO KEEP IN YOUR MIND'S EYE TOO.*

Knowing the accurate mind's eye images of your own swing will let you practice correctly and not let swing errors creep in. View your swing from various mirror angles and take pride in your ability to use a full shoulder turn flexible golf swing.

Your own swing style will build up and as **Robert Tyre 'Bobby Jones'** *so effectively said:* "When we speak of sound swing or of good form, we mean nothing more than the possessor of either has simplified the swing to the point where errors are less likely to creep in, and that (they) are able consistently to bring the club against the ball in the correct hitting position" (see Bibliography and Resources).

DYNAMIC POSTURE AND THE MIND'S EYE

THE MORE YOU STUDY AND LEARN ABOUT THE GOLF SWING, THE MORE YOU REALIZE THAT THE **key** TO THE GAME IS CONNECTED TO tempo-rhythm and posture and some power.

A KEY mind's eye is therefore required to imitate the posture in the dynamic movement of the swing.

To develop this dynamic posture use your swing in front of a mirror. From the belt up, curve your spine ever so gently. Mechanically, this inclined axis or slight reverse C preserves the correct natural ball striking angle of the clubface. As well it preserves the mechanics of the swing.

A SUMMARY OF TECHNIQUE MIND'S EYE REMINDERS

To Improve Your Golf Technique

1.   Do as much as possible to become so visually oriented that you can provide multiple mind's eyes to your image selector and your image monitor. Watch golf videos incessantly for example.

2.   Choose one or two mind's eyes at a time to work on in TECHNIQUE.

3.   Demand a lot of your mind's eye expectations (as outlined earlier).

4.   Work with your **PGA Instructor** where ever you are in the golf world, and develop a plan for the parts of your game and your swing that you should work on.

To Build Your Confidence

1.   Slowly and surely build a 'bank' of mind's eye images and your ability to imitate and duplicate a consistent swing will grow. Prepare for all shots including special shots and weather shots. **Your confidence will begin to skyrocket.** IMAGE THAT YOU ARE A WINNER AND YOU WILL BE A WINNER AT THE LEVEL YOU ARE WILLING TO WORK AT IN GOLF.

To Build Your Self-Efficacy and Beliefs

1.   The self conviction that you can improve is totally built upon the completeness with which you undertake a TACTICS, TECHNIQUE AND A TENACITY **mind's eye program.** *Under the right conditions there can be no holding you back.*

To Eliminate Bad Habits

1.   Bad habits in golf almost always occur when an environmental or mental 'trigger' provides a momentarily held bad mind's eye of you or your golf. Your selector brain has no choice but to use these bad habits. The only way to deal

with them is to cancel them before they do any damage.

Replace them with good and accurate images suitable for your swing and game. LOOK FOR THE SITUATIONS THAT YOUR BAD HABITS USUALLY TAKE PLACE IN. AMAZE YOURSELF THAT THIS WORKS VERY WELL FOR YOU!

To Prepare Interventions

1.   Intervene with positive self-talk and refer to your mind's eye as your friends that you have developed beforehand for the many situations of golf. **If the situation is absolutely new to you, try to see a mind's eye of a golf swing that is as close as possible to that which is required.** Depend on the simplest solution and immediately refer to your TENACITY plan for the one-score-eighteen-hole game as an entity notion.

To Develop Consistency of Performance

1.   There are many approaches to becoming consistent but in the main it accrues when you adopt a golf system which uses your abilities and shortcomings and then becomes a system to such an extent that confidence is a by product.

2.   For most golfers, personal-lifestyle consistency and patience lays a good foundation for consistency. CONSISTENCY ALMOST NEVER DEVELOPS OVERNIGHT OR EVEN AFTER A SUCCESSFUL SPORT CAREER IN ANOTHER SPORT.

SUMMARY:
KEY WORDS AND NOTIONS OF CHAPTER FOUR

*Accurate and suggestive **KEY** mind's eye images are outlined in this chapter.

*Accurate mind's eye images for skill inputs to the Image Monitor which feeds the Selector brain are included. The golf swing uses such Mind's Eyes for consistency and accuracy of the swing. Lower golf scores can result.

*The basic expectations for your **TECHNIQUE** mind's eyes such as vividness, color, self or other, tense, completeness, timing, speed, animation, tempo, smoothness, movement, positive-negative, body reaction, and mind's eye endurance are outlined.

***KEY** mind's eyes to assist the player improve wedge play are outlined.

*The art of fixing on one or two **KEY** body movements and not on several movements at one time is reviewed.

*Swing speed and how the mind's eye can tame speed are completed.

*The golfers follow through and the mind's eye are detailed.

*The basic **'MY TECHNIQUE IS GOOD'** notion is developed.

*Swing style and even tempo is explained and how to augment it is explained and related to the mind's eye system.

*Dynamic golf movements and the relationship to posture while swinging is developed.

*A SUMMARY OF KEY TECHNIQUE REMINDERS IS INCLUDED.

****

CHAPTER FOUR:

BIBLIOGRAPHY AND RESOURCES

Adams, Michael and T.J. Tomasi. To Play Better Golf. Journey Editions, Rutland, Vermont & Tokyo, Japan: Charles E. Tuttle, 1993

Geiberger, Al and L. Dennis. Tempo: Golf Master Key. New York: Simon and Schuster, 1980

Brown, Barbara. Supermind: The Ultimate Energy. New York: Harper and Row, 1980

Yokum, Guy and Brett Parker. Australian Golf Digest. "New Shafts: Adding Order to Chaos". 1994

Lucas, Geoffrey and Lloyd Boody. Congress of AIESEP. "Golf Improvement Intermediated by Imagery Training or Success Videotape Viewing". Finland: 1990

Jones, Robert. Bobby Jones On Golf. Garden City, N.Y.: Doubleday and Company, 1966

Nicklaus, Jack. The Lesson Tee. (Also see Total Golf Technique). London: Wm. Heinemann Ltd., 1972

Hallberg, Gary. Golf Magazine. "Speed Shots: Developing Your Shotmaking", 8.1984

Kite, Tom. Golf Digest. "Dreaded Half Wedge". July, 1982

Watson, Tom and Nick Seitz. Getting Up and Down. Random House 1983

CHAPTER 5: TENACITY IMAGERY FOR TARGETTERS AND AIMERS

Objectives: The chapter illustrates the methods and benefits of being tough with your self demands and standards that you accept of yourself in golf. Also included are: mind's eye examples in tenacity from simple to complex in golf; the standards and self demands you accept; principles; tenacity not courage notions; pressure off ideas; and toughening up for golf ready situations.

The idea that the subconscious does not recognize sickness (where possible); unsuitable decisions; someone who upsets your equilibrium on purpose to make you better (dissonance); arousal and tenacity in sport; programs for success; concentration; relaxed body/relaxed mind; 'easy' images; and the best...the **mini peak experience** in sport, golf and family and life.

****

Every golfer sees themselves as playing strongly for several holes every golf game. Exceptional players on Tour carry their good golf for near eighteen holes. It is almost always pointed out in the books and magazines of Golf that superior players are tough (inner) playing golfers. They may play in a controlled way that may seem 'trancelike' to spectators. However it is usually thought of as being in a zone or in a channel of concentration. The mind's eye can provide simple reminders such as when a player places their hands onto their golf cap or visor in a channel shape, as if they are blocking out the sun's rays.

It is nice peak to be in and it is usually not disturbed at all. Some players can go in and out of this zone but they usually go 'out' only briefly. Some stay in the zone fearing it will diffuse. Irregardless it is TENACITY AT A PEAK.

****

PURPOSE OF MIND'S EYE EXERCISE

This form of exercise with the mind's eye provides standards of desire in your golf game. For example, are you tough enough with yourself in a variety of demanding golf situations? The images that you exercise aid you in doing the 'right' thing and can lower your golf score. Maybe! Mind control combines with self discipline in imagery **TENACITY**.

Specifically, it is used to carry out the tougher shots faced in the game of golf.

There are several ways in which the regular golfer can tune up **TENACITY** and the mind's eye to play superior golf. Tenacious golf gives pleasure as well as better golf to the golfer. Just look at how **Mark Calcavecchia** has been tenacious near the end of a Tour event and has become associated with finishing strongly and just look at how he loves to hug his two children as they scurry across the 18th green to meet him. Just look at how **Betsy King** loves to finish a Tour event with **TENACITY** and then earn that jump into the water in memory of such a time, after being tenacious for the final 18 hole of a Tour event. Why she even likes to drag her caddy into the water too. **I guess that kind of TENACITY is a very special skill in sport, but in golf it is even more so. Of course, Mark O'Meara and Annika Sorenstam are tenacious also, in addition to countless others.**

If you can play TACTICS style golf for ten or more holes, you may be able to so play for 15 holes and later perhaps for all 18 holes and you will become well known at your club or on Tour as *a tenacious player.*

You are tough enough and self disciplined as you play against the golf course. If you use Technique mind's eye golf, then you also are getting the maximum out of your present golf swing. That also contributes to your golf toughness!

There are several ways to improve your golf score even more and these are all by way of mind control type golf. Your control ability is tested by the demands and golf situations which you place in the way of your success in golf.

Most golfers can improve dramatically on the greens and one of the more productive ways of proving this is by being tenacious with the 3 basic images which are required to finish off properly on the greens.

TENACITY IMAGERY ON THE GREENS
Three part system

*See a ball-track into the hole
(the middle of the hole.)

*See, Feel, and Practice the
stroke to put the ball on track.

*See yourself as being Tenacious
enough to duplicate the stroke when
over the actual PUTT.

The main way to use Tenacity exercise for putting is to repeat the three parts over the ball on every putt you face. From 30' down to the 18" put never fail to use the three part system.

On recent **LPGA** and **PGA** weekend Tour events in Florida and in Tucson, both the winner and the 2nd place player **missed short putts**--one an 18" and one a 10-12" putt. If you had witnessed the extra time **Dana Dormann** spent on putting on the LPGA Tour, you might not have believed she could miss any short putt, nor **Michael Bradley** for that matter who appears to be very systematic in all of his golf play.

See all the short putts going into the exact middle of the hole and take full advantage of your subconscious brain's ability to deliver a one-putt on each green. **Your subconscious will accept such an idea and will not question your goal of making each putt.** Making sure that each putt has enough roll to make it slightly past the cup is the result of consistency and feel which you have developed on the putting green. During winter practice putt to a 10' line and not past an 11' line and calculate a % for each 10 tries and set up a game with your own best record and your consistent high % as your two goals. Practice for feel at home on that smooth carpet. Vary your distance systematically.

SOME SAMPLE IMAGES FOR THREE PART TENACITY PUTTING

When you use three part TENACITY mind's eye for putting, select your own images. As you select the 'track' or line to the middle of the hole, you might visualize a continuous track of balls to the hole (as if you are seeing a instant replay of a line of balls moving to the hole). A row of tees, highway lane markers in miniature, a bright yellow snake, or a door made with golf tees that shows where the ball must pass over. Try it as dusk approaches at night in the dark. Try it with the eyes closed. Substitute or exchange balata and surlyn balls in a random order so you don't know which one you are striking next and your feel will get very acute. Try a putter with an inset face if you have not used this style of putter face.

Another good idea is to use two spike nails and a yellow string suspended above the line of the putt. This provides a real image as a permanent one. Try several putts with the string up and then several with the string line taken away. You can also put a line directly on the green with an edge or marker leaving only a slight mark line. Chalk a line down by using a carpenters chalk line snapped onto the green and simply wear it off from frequent use. I guess it goes without saying, to try all distances as you work through these excellent exercises.

Normally, I repeat the **'track' visualization** at least three times prior to the actual stroke on the ball. **This takes only a split second to finish.** Base your actual path to the hole on what you know of the speed of roll on that green and the idea that speed influences 'break' (amount of sideways tendency of the grass or grain).

Be very hesitant about giving the hole away, as they say. Of course, look at the grass itself and the slope and general contour of the green., Look for the ocean side or the mountain side tendency, if any exists. **Find out the type of grass you are on and see when it was last cut and how sunshine effects how fast it grows in the afternoon.**

TENACITY on the green includes being tough enough to read and 'track' every time. Your stroke is rehearsed via the mind's eye to assure that the stroke feels 'square' and firm through the ball. Recently, I have discovered for myself that short strokes are the best warm up strokes for accomplishing 4 or 5 'squared up' strokes in a row.

Use an electronic putt analyzer for checking putting strokes 'squareness' or simply check it against a baseboard and you will prove to yourself that a short stroke is a true stroke (and the kind which will deliver on the golf course).

DELIVER ON THE GOLF COURSE

The reason that the golfer has to be so tenacious about the warm up strokes on each green, is that only 'square' strokes and center of gravity contact (that is middle of the golf ball) will produce a roll that follows the track. Your weight must be good as well. **One of the most frequent compliments that you hear on Tour or in top play, is that someone put a good roll on that putt.**

One image which has been effective for the stroke is an ***arrowhead*** image where the mind's eye is of an ***arrowhead*** over top of the ball. See that 'arrowhead' move back and forward through the center of the ball and even try to see the ball moving along that ***arrowhead*** path, while still maximizing your view of the line to the hole.

The third and last TENACITY Image for putting is probably the hardest to depend upon. The golfer must absolutely 'see' a good vivid mind's eye of an ***ARROWHEAD*** on the actual putt. Of course, that is the key.

The image is clear and the player simply duplicates what they just practiced as they do the 'real' putt. The ***ARROWHEAD*** must contact the C. of G. of the ball and thus the putter concentrates on the ball as the primary focus of the eyes. At this stage do not look at the hole, look at the ball or one blade of grass. If you have superior vision then some players say that they see both the hole (the path) and the ball. Again, spend maximum time viewing line.

SUMMARY: TRY FOR 28 PUTTS OR LESS* (HOT SHOT GOAL = 26) OR TRY FOR 1.5 STROKE AVERAGE FOR GREENS WHICH YOU HAVE REACHED IN REGULATION

To SUM up, the player must see that they follow the 3 part mind's eye system for each putt.

The system becomes automatic within the subconscious brain. Be self demanding with this mind's eye system and your scores will reflect the same. Only by visualizing successfully each time will your putting totals drop to where they have to be to be a 'player' who has low putting statistics.

The golfer should also develop a TENACITY routine for all those other golf situations where shot preparation can be subject to being lazy or to poor preparation. Trap shots, greenside shots, even tee shots will sometimes be in this category. Your brains' subconscious is particularly accommodative to mind's eye routines. By using **TENACITY,** you can respond to the pressure that golf can put on you. By anticipating and practicing for pressure, you soon deal with pressure in an easy and comfortable way.

*Usually the winner has 110 or less putts (or 106 for Shigeki) although recently 109 putts won but there was a 102, 103 and thru 104's. Chris Couch won at New Orleans with a 109 and Mi Hyum Kim had 112 putts on "quirky" greens with Janice Moodie and Christina Kim having 111 putts (at Reunion, Fl.)

PRESSURE IS 'CONTROLLABLE' IN GOLF

One of the advantages of TENACITY IMAGERY is that it can work for all golfers from occasional players right to the Tour player. Jack Nicklaus said that pressure is part of a golfer's life and has added that pressure is the FUN of the game. Tiger Woods also tells about fun golf.

RESPOND TO ALL GOLF CHALLENGES

Most athletes view pressure as the key challenge of their sport and take time to devise, rehearse and visualize responses to pressure. They are responding to a challenge and this response is seen as the fun part of the game. Here, they see the sense in a challenge well met.
TENACITY IS A 'HANGING IN THERE' BEHAVIOR
*SEE TENACITY AS A LOW KEY
HANGING IN THERE BEHAVIOR
FOR EACH GOLF GAME

*SEE THAT **PATIENCE IS ALMOST
ALWAYS REWARDED IN SPORT**

Some Tour players also hold several course records and they have stressed that in almost every course record case, the first part of their game in which they set the record was unspectacular but steady with some streaks of birdies, or an eagle in there. See yourself as being the same, hang in there, and get a game face on, as they say, and get TEMPO AND RHYTHM going for you as you get on a roll or gain momentum in one way or another ESTABLISH A FLOW.

Don't take any risks that result in a larger number score on a hole. Stay on the roll. The only game in which I shot below 70, came on a day when I was playing between below average and terrible, until I reached the greens. At the greens, my chips and one putts were uncanny. When I did not play the hole in the standard way or 'classic' way, I came away with a par regardless. The first nine was played in even par (at tough Windermere, Edmonton where I was a member at) but my patience on the back nine came so easily that I got 3 birdies without much effort at all.

The last holes were especially fruitful that day. Hanging in there imagery is very helpful for your everyday style of play. THERE IS A MOMENTUM IN GOLF AND YOUR TENACITY WILL LET YOU GET FAMILIAR WITH THAT MOMENTUM.

Hanging in there TENACITY IMAGERY is also effective because disturbances are accepted as normal or as part of the game. This aides concentration. If the regular player suffers by trying to concentrate or if the Tour player is on edge about their putting then they should have prepared themselves with relaxed images of hanging in there type just mentioned. SEE A CLEAR IMAGE OF YOURSELF AS A PERSISTOR. Perhaps players like a historical Ben Hogan and a modern day V.J. Singh might not agree, but I see players like 'VJ' as being a little too perfectionist! The late Ben Hogan was once a perfectionist also, but he worked to a more realistic style later in his career, it was said.

V.J. Singh has by now shown that his own style of perfectionism can produce winning streaks of unbeatable Tour play. So it is likely that his style will have an interesting part of Tour golf's future. His mind's eye inventory may be immense.

CONCENTRATION HAS TO BE A NICE BY-PRODUCT

Most sport performance experts would agree that it is impossible to 'try' to concentrate. Instead, try something else and soon enough concentration will return. Imagery tends to help in this dilemma since such procedures tend to build concentration as if by accident.

This is where the beginning golfer has all kinds of trouble since trying to remember all about the swing is a fruitless task, whereas using the mind's eye establishes a tempo or a flow. Perhaps the beginner has picked up that concept in another activity or sport or even elsewhere.

WEDGES OVER HEDGES

One exercise that is used in golf classes is called 'hitting wedges over hedges' which forces you learn to use the loft built into wedge clubs. This exercise is a simulation of a pressure situation in golf. The idea to give the player 10 attempts at hitting rapidly rising shots from within a few feet of the 'hedge' and see how many shots clear the top.

To hit 'wedges over hedges' you must have both **TECHNIQUE MIND'S EYE SKILLS and TENACITY**. Open the clubface, use lots of early wrist action, develop a steep arc of swing, and pre set the hands back at address.

Soon you can hit 10 of 10 up and over 'hedges'. You will be developing a TENACITY system or routine, much like those routines you will want to have to take out on the golf course with you. Soon the pressure simulation is FUN. Maybe you will notice that the visualization allowed you that little extra time to get your head together for the situation. This is very common in golf.

THERE ARE MANY WAYS TO DEVISE PRESSURE SIMULATIONS THAT ARE CHALLENGING, FUN AND REALISTIC WAYS TO LOWER ONES SCORES OUT ON THE GOLF COURSE. CONCENTRATION IS A NICE BY PRODUCT.

IMAGERY AFTER THE PRESSURE IS OFF

Often times in golf, you play best when your mind is relaxed. You will find countless examples of that in golf. For example, if a golf match ends at the 15th hole, you almost always play some great golf after that even though you may be the loser and perhaps seemed to have little momentum going for your game. While playing badly, you may tell your mind's eye to show some pictures of relaxing and play "I don't care golf" (for example, you may have another golf cap in your bag which you associate with 'cool scoring golf' or low numbers golf). Put that cap on. Play cool. Your play blossoms. If you play 2 or 3 extra holes late in the afternoon, just for practice, you will see that your play blossoms.

Why do you play especially effectively at these times? Most often you

play well at these times because your muscles are relaxed and your mind is not demanding shots that you are incapable of delivering. Since golf is a pressure game, you must learn to be relaxed and have a mind's eye system or other play system in these circumstances. It is precisely because you have not practiced for pressure that you succumb to pressure. Remember how we cannot 'turn' concentration on since we start it with little events.

BOB GOALBY: SKINS GAME IS TENACITY

Turning on concentration is evident in special golf events such as in 'skins' golf games and the like. "Skins' is a term that means a small or a large pot of winnings for the best score on a hole. For example, each Saturday morning we meet early at the Club and put in say, $5 each, for the skins pot or a birdie pot. At about noon, when each of the 'skins' players is back in, we sit around and divide up the pot money. Perhaps just 3 players win a skin and each skin pays, say, $28 or so. It is a great deal of fun and a big thrill to win. Usually you have to birdie a difficult to birdie hole to win a 'skin'. Most clubs put up an 'Eclectic board' which keeps track of the # of birdies over the whole golf season for each interested player. This is where the idea of the 'skins' big money games in Tour type golf came from. One other term is 'carryover' which means the 'skin' which is not won carries to the next hole and makes the 'skin' twice or three or four times as valuable.

Turning on concentration is occasionally exemplified in a skins game.

Once while I was watching **Tom Watson**, a favorite player of mine, he showed an amazing concentration skill. He was playing 'skins' at Desert Highlands in Arizona. The players group consisted of Watson, Palmer, Nicklaus and Player who were all in their prime as far as scoring golf goes. The jackpot of money was not won and the prize carried over more than once. Because the players were all so good, there was a large prize by the 9th hole.

No golfer could make the crucial putt and the pressure built up dramatically and steadily. The four players did a lot of joking and laughing as the match continued.

'Skins' format is usually a lot of fun. In one memorable scene Watson was shown laughing and joking at one moment and suddenly shifting back to concentrating the next moment. It was such a distinct switch over that it could be easily enough seen that concentration can be turned on and off. *This distinct skill is available to the learned athlete.*

Watson prevailed that day and made a dramatic putt to pocket the $0.150 million dollars, a nice pot for the time. The next day, Nicklaus won an even larger 'skin'. The television commentator for the event, Bob Goalby, used a graphic which illustrated that the four 'skins' golfers had won 41 major events between them and 39% of the majors in recent history. **Goalby singled out mental toughness as the key reason for that rather startling statement.**

Previously in golf, it seemed that TENACITY WAS AN UNUSUAL SKILL which only superior golfers possessed. Such is not the case any longer. In the future, many athletes and golfers will be capable of golf-tenacity.

YOU WILL BE TOO!

IMAGERY BASICS FOR TENACITY IN GOLF

*I see myself as being tough and tenacious in situations such as:
1. **Where I really need good putts**
2. **Where I need a good sand shot**
3. **Where a difficult shot is required**

I IMAGINE MYSELF AS BEING A TENACIOUS GOLFER JUST WHEN I NEED IT THE MOST!
****

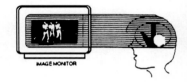

TENACITY IMAGERY AND GOLF AS AN 18 HOLE ENTITY

*See a Mind's Eye and get the feeling that golf is an 18 hole game and entity. See lots of 2's, 3's, and 4's on your score card. Include 5's or 6's if that is a good level of play for you.

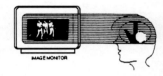

Totaling up your golf score after 9 holes only creates a dangerous mind delusion. It is just like a self fulfilling prophecy setting up in golf. Instead, you should see golf as an 18 hole entity in which only one number counts. The other 'score board' you should use in golf relates solely to how good a job you are doing of controlling your mind and playing up to your personal potential in golf. Be tenacious enough to see these as the only scores that count.

18 HOLE ENTITY: SCORE CAN AND DOES TAKE CARE OF ITSELF

For example, a player does not care to have score added up after nine holes since they know exactly where the score stands relative to par in any case. As they say, know where you are 'off par'. Remember that the main thing about getting out of your own 'comfort zone' in golf is when you say to yourself that your nine hole score is too good and you create pressure on yourself. **Instead of letting your mind feel that pressure, you can use low pressure** *hanging in there images*. **Some days, I will not know what my score is even after 18 holes until it is added up, since I may have forgotten if I am on a par 70, 71 or 72 or even 73 golf course.**

In Florida, one often plays on and gets to like the short par 59, 60 or 62 courses which often do not include par 5's. Forget your score and play *even - fours* or try *under - fours* for scoring.

Those are the most satisfying days in golf because score doesn't matter and score usually takes care of itself (and you know you did ok). **IN GOLF THAT'S FOR SURE!**

TENACITY AND ACCEPTING YOUR GAME SCORE

*Imagine yourself talking about your game and your

score and say the numbers freely. Good or not so good be the 'owner' of it and proud of it since you are the only one who can change it. It will change if you do your mind's eye and make some adjustments. DON'T WIMP OUT.

Some golf courses play extremely tough, some weather conditions make scoring difficult and some tournament golf courses keep scores very high it seems.

Often times, after a competition, you are surprised by how mediocre appearing scores hold up quite well against the competition. Remember that only one number counts, so be proud of it. ***Only you know how many 'great' demands you made of your self and only you know your golf is on the right path to development.***

Improvement will happen if you believe, if you visualize and if you work at it and get some support from your 'significant others'. Below I am going to explain some miniature 'tragedies' which are only that when they are not overcome. ***It is as if they are just little roadblocks in a players way before better days.***

Once I wrote a letter to Tom Watson and packaged the letter up with a copy of a book I had just published on performing in golf, taped up the package, put air mail and the required stickers on the package ***and never mailed it.***

TOM WATSON ACCEPTS GAME SCORE

Since Tom Watson was and probably is my favorite player and it was just the start of the period, when it was said, he was going through hell with his putting stroke, I thought my type of golf improvement might help his putting or his putting mind set. But as I said I never mailed it and I have not had the opportunity to caddy for him, meet him, or interview him as of yet. ***Clearly he could improve and would improve was my thought. However, in retrospect it took a long, long time for his improvement to surface.***

To me, Tom Watson's golf is still amazing and now, some years later he seems in contention again for a top 25 or top 10 finish almost any Tour event week. Remembering just how difficult it is to win a Tour event at any time.

ONLY YOU KNOW:
1. HOW MAY GREATS DEMANDS YOU TAKE ON;
2. YOUR FULFILLMENT OF SUCH DEMANDS.

As stated previously, only you know how many 'great' demands you have made of yourself in golf and only you know your golf is on the right path to development. Sometimes by losing your temper or not invoking TENACITY, you score 2, 3, or 4 or more strokes higher than you should have on a hole. On most occasions, if you would have just been smart enough to 'take that score', you could have been a contender or even a leader or near-leader in the competition.

PLAYING IN QUALIFYING ROUNDS

Just recently I entered the Canadian Senior's Match play Championship which was contested at a windy and difficult golf course named Paradise Canyon, which had been developed by a former NHL hockey player by the name of Vic Stasiuk (from the famous hockey forward line of Bronco Horvath and Johnny Bucyk with the Boston Bruins).

Every morning that whole spring and summer, I practiced a lot to prepare for this tournament. I had scored well that winter while playing in Arizona as well as some rounds at Mission Hills and over in South Carolina. I caddied a lot that winter and spring and had some powerful mind's eye images that seemed to set my game up for effective scoring. My game is usually lacking in **natural scoring**, if such a skill as natural scoring even exists in golf. In other words, scoring does not come easily for me especially early in the game.

Coupled with that I had picked up a mind's eye procedure which I thought was the very best, that turned out to be a bad one for my game. A few weeks before my big Qualifying rounds at Paradise Canyon, I caddied in a group with a player from Oklahoma State University golf team who was now on the Canadian Tour and was the leading scorer going into the final round. He always took two full out practice swings on each hole where he used driver and then he hit a long and straight drive. **I was very impressed and took on a new mind's eye system in driving. What a bad decision!**

For the whole week of my big event, I took two full practice swings and didn't realize that they were too long for my best swing. So all week my drives got poorer and poorer on the course, yet on the practice range they seemed excellent for distance. The wind came up and I got worse, not better at driving the ball, like I usually would do in adverse conditions. Not only that but it is a violation of mind's eye golf.

I lost my confidence and didn't adjust and kept right on with my mind's eye procedure. Later, I reminded myself that my best driving was when I shortened the backswing and came to a great follow through position and held the position. NOT WHEN I LENGTHENED OUT THE SWING. My best driving occurred with a squared up follow through combined with a shorter take away as a mind's eye image just before teeing off and a slow motion, momentarily held mind's eye. I should have been using that mind's eye, which I called the 'Billy Andrade golf tip' image. I had almost always used such a mind's eye when I try to compete in golf. Currently, television golf analysts keep stressing a momentarily held follow through, which is always an accompanying skill when a shot is a good one.

I REALIZED ONLY LATER THAT AN IMAGE HAS TO BE CAREFULLY SOUGHT OUT FOR ITS APPLICABILITY. HOWEVER, AT THE TIME, THE OKLAHOMA STATE IMAGE USED BY CHRIS TIDLAND SEEMED VERY RIGHT TO ME, **AND IT SURE**

WAS NOT. SO I REALLY FAILED MISERABLY AND FELT LIKE MY ABILITY TO COMPETE IN GOLF WAS JUST A MYTH, IN MY MIND. **My short game and especially my putting was fine yet overall, without driving the ball well, golf scoring can be a disaster.**

TENACITY IMAGERY AND SYSTEMATIC GOLF

*Imagine that you believe
in systematic 18 hole golf

IMAGE SELECTOR

WHAT IS SYSTEMATIC GOLF? The good and the mediocre.

Systematic golf is NOT golf tactics or golf course management. Walter Hagen believed in what I call systematic golf. Ben Hogan also was systematic yet believed that he only struck a few great shots every game. Actually Hogan said usually he only struck one good shot a game, his standards were so high especially in his early years of Tour play. I think it is exactly the same as Tiger Woods saying he felt like every putt could go in and yet he is prepared to accept all results. As if it will happen.

SYSTEMATIC GOLF is the mental ability to accept the good with the bad in golf. Systematic golf proposes that you see yourself as doing several good golf things out on the course each game and that you accept a few bad things as normal (that is, you have planned for them and have a plan as if to accept them). As in any system, you accept a variety of reactions to situations. I suppose, as in theory systems you have loops and re-routings of a game plan.

The key thing about SYSTEMATIC GOLF is that over 18 holes almost all things even out. See yourself getting some pars, some birdies, and some bogies. If the bogies are balanced somewhat by the birdies and you get several steady pars, you will be posting a good score.

Most Tour players believe that they will experience good putting days. These days will come along to boost their round or the whole Tour event.

*During the midst of a bad hole,
you must imagine golf is systematic.

PRACTICE AND PREPARE WITH THIS GOLF SCENARIO

Simulate that here you are in the midst of a bad hole and you feel yourself losing control and building self-tension and some anger. You must immediately use a mind's eye of calmness, coolness and SYSTEMATIC GOLF. **Immediately refer back to another situation from your golf past in which imagery and systematic golf thinking kept you in control.**

Attempt this even if you strike your ball from one sand trap to another sand trap or if you sense a four putt coming along. A four putt is not all that unusual if the first putt goes much too far on some very hard greens. **Do not accept the bad situation.**

Instead, make your belief in systematic golf and pre preparation a vividly imagined one. **SEE YOURSELF AS GETTING OUT OF THE BAD HOLE SITUATION BY USING THE MIND'S EYE.**

TENACITY IMAGERY AS AN INTERVENTION FOR GOLF

*Prepare some interventions for the following:
*weird recovery shots
*not enough practice or pregame preparation
*a big match
*unhappy about swing
*rush or patience

There are several ways that you can prepare effective TENACITY mind's eye images for situations in golf. If you face a weird shot, that is, a shot you have never faced before, try to see that you have faced that shot in a somewhat similar way before; if you have not had time to warm up and practice before a game, then rehearse visually and make sure your body is stretched out and ready; if it is a big match you face, get your TACTICS mind's eyes rehearsed for playing the course and not the opponent and do the 'no rush mind's eye' seeing a calm self in all your golf. If you are impatient, see yourself fishing or relaxing in a favorite spot like a mountain meadow or the Florida Keys.

Try to transfer this pleasant image to golf. Try to cultivate enough imagery that you feel in control and confident. Exercise these mind's eye images as if you were an 'imagexerciser' in golf.

TENACITY IMAGERY FOR THE SICK, UNHEALTHY OR UNFIT YOU

*It is true that your subconscious knows nothing about your health

A successful mind's eye program requires overall commitment and some small accomplishments in health, fitness and flexibility. A golf fitness program appears to assist both the requirements of the golf swing and the overall self-preparation and psyche of the golfer-athlete. However, golf tenacity need not be reduced by sickness or temporary unhealthy conditions since the subconscious brain is never evaluative.

Tommy Aaron, Terry-Jo Myers, Paul Azinger and many Tour players have had their tenacity tested by health conditions. Aaron, who won the Masters, considered it remarkable that his health gave him an excuse for bad play, yet he persisted and visualized his health. He suggested that his sprained back may have caused his game to go downhill since then. FOR IMAGERY IT IS BEST TO USE HEALTHY IMAGES AND ONES WHICH FRESHEN YOUR GOLF GAME, DESPITE THE PAIN WHICH OTHERS DO NOT KNOW OF AS WELL AS YOUR OWN LONG SUFFERING.

YOUR SUBCONSCIOUS BRAIN DOES NOT KNOW SICKNESS

Debbie Meisterlin, a successful Tour player of the 1980's, had a history of health problems going back for seven years. In an interview with the Denver Post, she mentioned tiredness and her tendency to psychosomatic thinking which reduced her ability to cope with pressure situations. Meisterlin was still on Tour four years later however. Unfortunately, there are many health problems on Tour.
PLAYERS SUCH AS MEISTERLIN, MEYERS AND AARON HAVE TO MAKE SURE THAT HEALTH AND FITNESS ARE WORKING FOR THEM AND NOT AGAINST THEIR PERFORMANCE.
Recovery from recent surgery has slowed down some notable players' performance but has not halted their overall career objectives in golf it seems.

TENACITY IMAGERY AND COMMON DISTRACTIONS

*See an image of a level of
CONCENTRATION which is not
bothered by outside noise.

All golfers have experienced days when unexpected noise never bothers their concentration at all. They have also experienced days when the same disturbance brings a 'scowl' and some disruption. **A TENACITY image of imperturbability is quite advantageous to the Tour player.**
Concentration should be capable of accepting a variety of situations. Writer P.G. Woodhouse used to say golfers could be disturbed easily by 'an uproar of butterflies in an adjoining meadow' as sufficient to upset them.
Once when Gary Player, Tom Weiskopf and Johnny Miller were playing a Tour practice round, a spectator took some ill advised movies from behind the roped area. Most disturbances are of course, during a swing. Two players reacted calmly but one remarked that the noise was like 'banging rocks together back there'.
During the LPGA one season, a spectator with a small camera decided to snap a shot of Jan Stephenson doing a sand shot at a critical time in a Tour event at Moon Valley in Phoenix. Jan's caddy asked the spectator to please not take another shot on the actual sand shot. The spectator went right ahead and snapped away and the player was pretty unhappy since she was in contention. Her shot didn't come off well.

The caddy reached over the rope and snatched the camera and did a dance all over it. The headline in the local paper the next morning read 'Caddy does Jitterbug on Spectator's Camera'.

It does not seem likely that such examples of disturbances are sufficient to upset a focused golfer but they do. It seems that Tour players have to include the skill of some defensive mechanisms for this part of Tour golf.

*Always see yourself as having
self-performance standards
in addition to score standards

IMAGE SELECTOR

It has been the theme of this text to recommend that any golfer should include at least two measures of success in self judging golf performance. Namely, the 18 hole score measure plus some basic performance self measure. A third measure is the social value of golf since it can realistically be viewed as a justification for participation in this game. **Score is not the only measure of success.**

Stress caused by competition is three-pronged according to sport social-psychologists. Interpersonal factors are important and healthy golfers know their 'within-feelings' as well as their 'externally judged performance'. Martens found out that players are more accurate and realistic in appraising stress in coaches, than coaches are in appraising players' stress. **This is not surprising and golfers can often handle their own stress well.**

The type of sport is important in this situation since a high achiever might thrive on an individual sport such as golf whereas a highly stressed person might be better off in a team sport environment.

A well regarded social-psychologist, Tara Scanlan, has put the won-loss and stress situation nicely by mentioning, "as long as victory is the principle or only goal defining success, defeat must be defined as failure and will be stressful". Scanlan advises that it is critically important to put won loss results into proper perspective no matter what the game may be. Realistic performance goals are the key to this competitive factor. **TENACITY IMAGERY should also stress maximum tenacity but a multiple view of success and lack of success. As pointed out in this text, there are multiple factors related to sport success. Mastery of self and game tactics are as important as other factors.**

MAXIMUM TENACITY WITH MULTIPLE VIEWS OF SUCCESS

Another fine example may be to use a year of a period of time to recover game success as if you are taking a year off to focus or retune health and game skill. Fred Couples and Helen Alfredson are Tour players who have used such a procedure. **FURTHER MAJOR SUCCESS CAME TO BOTH PLAYERS ON TOUR.**

TENACITY AND LEVEL OF CONCENTRATION

*The golfer athlete should use a mind's
eye of extended concentration or
super concentration

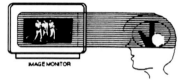

As a golfer, you will desire to be able to concentrate for extended periods of play with a good level of ordinary concentration. At times, you may find that CONCENTRATION is easier than usual and that your golf game and you are in a period of SUPER CONCENTRATION. On the other hand, you may have permitted outside disturbances and lack of focused awareness to destroy concentration to an extent that may be difficult to recover.

As a sport-scientist, I take the commitment to encourage the golfer to develop along a path which permits maximum golf development.

Perhaps you can only see a mind's eye of your significant others as evaluating your golf strictly on the basis of score (your family, your teachers, friends, and key others). What others see in your golf can create problems for you and your golf. Instead, see an image of some inner values or feeling that suggest what you are doing in golf is right for you.

When you accomplish your golf goals, do you see some 'inner beauty', do you see the 'wealth of potential you possess' or are you aware of the hidden 'ultimate athlete' in you?

Kenneth Ravizza has coined such expressions as he has studied and described the experience of sport, including what has been called the peak performance in sport. Another expression has come to my mind and I have used the term, the 'mini peak experience' for golf, for describing the experience of concentration.

*The aware golfer 'sees' the peaks
in golf and knows how to imitate that
peak of the best golf

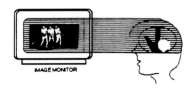

Ravizza, a University based philosopher-psychologist in human movement and health care has examined the nature of the peak experience in sport. The athlete gets involved in three aspects of performing. The first aspect predominates and the third aspect may be rare.

The aspects of the Peak experience are:

1. Focused awareness

2. Complete control of self and environment

3. Transcendence of self

(Ravizza 1, 2, 3)

To utilize or experience focused awareness, the golfer must be able to exclude external 'variables'. External variables negatively effect performance. For example, a golfer coming from the office or work may lack the ability to submerge or forget the concerns of the day. It is difficult to get rid of the feeling that one should, sometimes, still be at the office or at work rather than be on the golf course.

Later the player moves into the level of experience called control-over-self/ environment. This level can be highly self satisfying and may consist of the following mind's eye images.

*See an image of self-control and tactical control over your golf environment

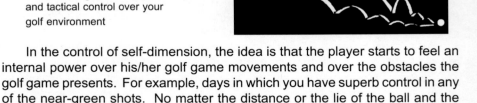

In the control of self-dimension, the idea is that the player starts to feel an internal power over his/her golf game movements and over the obstacles the golf game presents. For example, days in which you have superb control in any of the near-green shots. No matter the distance or the lie of the ball and the contour over which the ball must travel, the player exhibits high levels of self-control and high game environment control. A good imagery plan and mind's eye skill will likely improve you in this dimension.

THE ABOVE IS WHAT IS LABELLED THE GOLF MINI PEAK EXPERIENCE AND IT HAS A LOVELY FEEL TO IT.

PERFECTION AND LOSS OF FEAR MIND'S EYE

In this dimension, you are never trying to avoid mistakes at the conscious level. They just do not occur (mistakes in golf that is).

Dimension 3 is called Transcendence of self and entails a 'oneness' of feeling of the golfer, your golf equipment and your effort and the golf course demands themselves.

My background indicates that a player can indeed come to this level. For example, if the player is completing the last few holes of a tournament which they may win, they play with such a 'oneness'. It is said that you are going all-out and are very intense, or channeled and focused. A total harmony is said to be reached. It is known that cyclists, skiers, rowers and swimmers and GOLFERS have talked about reaching this level.

Ravizza quoted a skier's experience description of a full peak experience as in the following quote: (Ravizza, p. 459)

"...Everything was so perfect, everything was so right, that it couldn't be any other way. The closest thing I can say about it was that there seemed to be tracks in the snow that my skills were made to fit in...it was no longer me and the hill, but it was both of us. It was just right. I BELONGED THERE."

HOLE IS A WASHTUB IDEA IN GOLF

Michael Murphy in his text *(The Psychic Side of Sport)* described a peak experience by golfer Jack Fleck. When Fleck 'upset' Ben Hogan in the US open,

Fleck stated from the 5th hole on the hole started looking very large ("as big as a washtub") so he started feeling very good about his putter and become convinced he couldn't miss (p. 42, Murphy).

It was said that he just tried to keep his feeling and he continued to play well and won the OPEN (not The Open, but the US Open that is).

The performance by Fleck, it is agreed, was like a Tour player in a virtuoso performance. Later the present author saw Jack Fleck in a Senior Tour event he was still a fine putter and a smallish, compact swinging player.

ENLARGED GOLF HOLE MIND'S EYE IN GOLF

Large hole images can help some putters but a track line mind's eye is just as dependable it seems in mind's eye golf. The **British Scientific experiment Series into golf** did not confirm that the use of a larger golf hole enhanced scoring for occasional golfers. Instead, do mind's eye imagery of the regular sized hole using the middle of the hole or the sides in certain situations. Read and understand what David Stockton's text (**Putt to Win**) has to advise on the topic of the hole itself and aiming.

If the Greenskeeper or cup-setter has been careless in setting the cups for the day and the cups are too high or the hole cutter tool is dull and the cups are set in a shoddy manner, that also can (negatively) effect the players mind's eye of the golf hole. **If you are playing early in the morning and you meet the Greenskeeper or their cup-setter on the course, make sure you congratulate them or at least remark about the cups being well set, or nice to putt to. Cutting holes takes some real skills, especially in the vertical cutting domain and the golfer should help them along where feasible.** If the plastic of the top of the cup is set too high, the ball will actually bounce out instead of drop in nicely. One day recently, at the City owned Ft. Myers Country Club public course, the ball actually bounced out up to five times for the players in our foursome.

TOTAL HARMONY OR PEAK EXPERIENCE GOLF DIFFICULTIES

The peak experience for golfers is not as likely to occur due to the fact that there is an analysis phase for most shots (left brain).

Nor is it possible to surrender visual thinking in golf as is often reported in the golf peak experience. Dimension 2 (Ravizza) called a feeling of power over self and the golf players environment may be an ideal experience-awareness state for a player to be in.

I felt as if my golf play and myself were in **a golf mini peak experience when I won the one and only Open golf tournament of my life.** My team had won team sport championships in basketball, ice hockey and football but to win in individual sport was a new experience. The peak experience in sport was as unique as a near death experience has been. Many golfers remember one or both of these vital life experiences.

In golf, the *Vulcan Open* was won with an 80-72 for a two round 152, not very impressive I realize. **However it was more the way in which it happened, as stressed in this text wherein the golfer interfaces and interacts with the**  **ball environment and the course and course play interface.** When an opening round 80 is eleven strokes back of some opening round player's score of 69, then you are immediately the 'chaser' and not the 'chased' or 'protector' of the lead. So, I was in the third group out on day 2 and early in the Round, for some reason the idea that the eleven lead would evaporate for the leader came easily to me. A lot of the golf course was laid out with side by side fairways and my irons on my 2nd shots landed pretty close to the cup and the leaders group saw our groups play and some of those near-pin shots. **'No problem at all', was my mind set. My club selection got very easy very early. Some putts dropped and I remember hanging in there golf, once or twice.**

They say to win, play well early in the round, especially the last round for those in contention (for example, in the **TPC at Sawgrass**, it was believed that any of over 24 players might win the event and as the TPC turned out the winner, Justin Leonard really asserted himself only at the start of the final nine, about the same time David Frost, Tom Lehman, Mark Calcavecchia, Len Mattiace, Scott Hoch, Lee Westwood, Glen Day (earlier) and other players did so). Tiger Woods was right on when he said that any player who made the qualifying score might win the event.

Jerry Potter, a USA Today Columnist, ferreted out a telling commentary by Tom Lehman, who ended up 2nd which equals huge money at the TPC ($350 t) when Potter reported on Monday morning's column that there was a lesson in Justin Leonard's performance (quotes) **"if you just hang in there and give yourself a chance, you don't know what will happen on the weekend".**

Also, Jerry Potter reported Lehman saying "he's very determined and poised. He's very mature"...and regarding his distance, his putting stroke and his chances at the Masters, the comment was exciting for Leonard' fans and supporters. **Lehman thinks he has the game, although not a Tour long hitter, but,..."when you have his putting stroke it doesn't matter how far you hit it".**

Anyway, I got the focused awareness, the control of self and the lead player came back very badly from his opening 69. I remember trying to play especially well on the last three holes so that I could transcend any golf-self that plays poorly on the last three holes, which is a frequent occurrence in competitive golf and the sport of curling also it seems. Transcendence of self occurred on 15, 16, 17 and 18 and my score was 72, to my delight and surprise.

FEELING SOME POWER OVER YOUR GOLF

My role as 'chaser' was successful and I remember the award with an envelope stuffed full of $20 bills (it seemed stuffed full, at the time!). Later, I remember pure EUPHORIA on the drive home, luckily by myself so my JOY could keep punctuating itself with smiles and laughter of winning and doing something unusual in sport competition for **the self. Later it occurred to me that the leader in golf does just the opposite of the three aspects of the peak experience or the peak comes too early.**

For example, in the aforementioned TPC at Sawgrass, Lee Janzen was totally in control up to and including round 3 and the opinion was that he would not be denied a win in this event. Yet in the final round absolutely nothing went the way he planned it seemed.

Three other great commentaries and great events that I was following in sport that weekend surely enough solidified my thinking about the peak experience in sport and in golf and basketball.

I remember **Pat Hurst** being very careful about what she would say when questioned by the Media over at the LPGA golf event at Mission Hills. She won the Major. **She kept focused, kept a total control over her self and her golf environment as she possibly could and would not be led into any premature analysis of how she would feel about the potential win or the potential jump into the water.** I had been there when Betsy King jumped in after winning that event the year before and remember the pressures of that event and the 'billions' of women spectators and golf lovers there at Mission Hills.

Another event, in the NCAA Championship finals in basketball, was the down keying of pressure that **Rick Majerus**, the **Utah** University's basketball coach, kept as the focus to allow his worker-bee team to use such focused awareness and some transcendence of self as their peak experience occurred. When he told his team to only pack enough for one game by one game' just as coach **Tubby Smith** and **Kentucky** was likely preparing or advising his team. Coach Smith talked of good hard nosed basketball, clean ball, and getting back to the basics and fundamentals. Maybe pure athleticism or even fatigue would decide the outcome but obviously many of the players' play transcended the self.

Even over two gruesome and joyful weeks of their sport and in addition how **Tennessee's** coach **Pat Summitt,** in the NCAA final, could focus team members even on an attempt at a 3rd consecutive National Title.

It seemed to me that Chamique, Tamika and Serneka and their teammates were as focused as **Louisiana Tech** and Alisa, Monica, Tamicha, Amanda and LaQuan and their teammates, but coach **Leon Barmore** seemed to be cautious with his comments about team offense and the **peak experience** that was just as potentially there for the Lady Techsters members.

Perhaps in team sport, the peak experience notion in total, and its having to surrender visual thinking is not nearly as available. **Perhaps the dynamics of the interface is not like golf, at least the non match play type of golf we are focusing mostly upon in this part of TENACITY SPORT.**

MASLOW INTRODUCED 'IT' BEFORE SPORT (Peak Performance and Humanity)

When **Abraham Maslow** became the focus of our psychology of personality studies in University classes in the late 1950's and later became the humanistic psychologist that we all admired, his ideas brought many joys and some applications to health and sport.

Maslow had introduced the idea of the peak experience prior to its application to sport and lifestyle/health thinking. Because scientists, philosophers and theologians from cultures throughout the world had **designated life experiences** that stood out from the usual ebb and flow of daily life, the notion of a different or peak experience developed.

Maslow became well known in humanistic circles, as it is said. Besides studying the healthy personality, he described **moments of total unity, inner strength** and wholeness of being. He described **high happiness** and fulfillment. One term was 'towards a psychology of **being**' and many of my golf related analyses touch from this thinking I have to believe.

TENACITY AND A 'FLOW' EXPERIENCE IN GOLF
While golf concentration can be thought of as partial or total excursion into peak experience, the idea of working into 'game tempo' has been stressed in this book.

***See yourself as a flow golfer--
see a merging of your golf actions
with the golf course itself**

Imagery of tempo makes it possible for you to gather momentum for a game tempo to start, or to get into the 'flow' of the game itself. IN GOLF, it may be more difficult to conceive of 'flow' than it may be in a ball type game. When **Czikszentmihalyi** described the 'flow' experience of play, he meant the following: *In golf, a player would experience flow as a merging of golf actions with golf course awareness; they would experience the loss of personal ego (for example, you would play without knowledge of what your handicap is, you don't have to be a 22 handicap, perhaps); the player would center on higher attention and see detail; the golfer would be in high control of personal action such as personal control of emotional outbursts; the golfer would control the sport environment instead of the environment causing shot problems and the player would control the demands for game action so they would not 'slash' at any shot in a non planned manner.*

In 'flow' golf clear feedback will occur as for example, knowing their score through playing well and not through adding up by math, and the rewards of playing well would feel intrinsic.

No external rewards would help. That is, for the player to say they played well would be good enough even though someone might think they didn't score to their usual level of play. This is the way of viewing and feeling flow.

These examples and descriptions of flow points out a way of decreasing the players dependence on the external world and peoples opinion. The golfer is into the game, as it is said.

A TENACITY MIND'S EYE OF THE PLAYER AS A SHOTMAKER

*Imagine you are a shotmaker
who can get the most out of every
club in your golf bag.

When my boyhood buddies and I caddied as 13 year olds at the richest private club in Edmonton (Alberta), we looked forwards to Fridays. On Fridays, the members didn't play golf. So on Fridays, we caddies golfed. I remember golfing in all kinds of challenging ways. Most often we played with 2 or 3 clubs and that was all. Some days, we borrowed left handed clubs and played lefty.

Some days we went all out, and had a driver, two irons and a putter. I remember big Louie Galamau hitting a 2 iron so far that I envied his skill. We played in the dark and learned to hit it in the dark quite well. **Little did we know that we were learning 'shotmaking'.**

Once Tom Watson received an "Ask To Watson" letter from a puzzled 15 year old junior player. The 15 year old had played a game with a 5 wood, a 6 iron and a putter and shot a better score, an 80, than he usually shot. He was puzzled so asked why. The answer was: "You forced yourself to play each shot carefully, to ask yourself how you wanted to make the ball fly, and how you would hit it to achieve that result. Asking and answering those questions are the **essence of concentration.** It taught you to be a SHOTMAKER" (Golf Digest series).

SHOTMAKING IS ENHANCED WITH THE MIND'S EYE &....

SHOTMAKING IS EXPERIENCE WITH A GOLF CLUB IN MANY SITUATIONS

On Fridays when we played with four clubs, we also taught ourselves to play each shot carefully and figured out how we would have to hit it to achieve certain results.

Many golfers play with what is essentially three clubs, a driver, a wedge and a putter. They feel that they should hit a wedge 150 yards and they force their hand position. They force the wedge to do shots which the 7-9 iron is designed for. They will not have much success in tournaments. **SHOTMAKING that is not.** Just lately, a clubmaker told me that many wedges have the loft angle of a six or seven iron and that is the reason.

Gary Player from South Africa, the home of many of todays' great players, said that while at home resting up or practicing, he would go to his home club and hit 6 irons off the teebox to create situations where he could use all the clubs in his bag. He felt that on Tour, the tendency was to underuse some clubs. He also was against forcing a club and encouraged shot variety with all clubs.

TENACITY IMAGERY OF DAYDREAMING YOUR WAY IN GOLF

***See yourself reacting to important
shots in a calm manner
*Rehearse with a mind's eye
every chance you have**

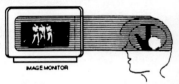

When Sharron Morran was LPGA golf's Rookie of the Year and when she left the Tour ten years later, she gave golfers some memorable advice, when she penned an article for Golf Magazine. Basically, she recommended that free time or daydreaming occasions be used for visualization. She suggested especially that women play more golf and use any extra time for specific golf improvement, such as reacting to bad shot situations, facing important shots, and focusing on golf shot execution.

As well, she stressed playing well via the mind's eye in rehearsals for club championships and amateur tournaments. She talked of using those free moments that all of us have to prepare for better golf, among other bits of sound advice.

TENACITY MIND'S EYE AND STRESS FACTORS IN GOLF

***See yourself as a reducer by
shutting off outside distractions**

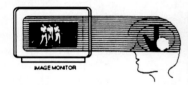

Athletic performance is related to the amount of stress the athlete-golfer is under. The relationship between performance and stress is well known in sport science and has been labelled the INVERTED U RELATIONSHIP.

WHAT IT IS MEANT TO ILLUSTRATE IS THAT TOO LITTLE STRESS IS ASSOCIATED WITH POOR PERFORMING AND TOO MUCH STRESS IS ALSO ASSOCIATED WITH POOR PERFORMING. If you visualize a U turned upside down, then the proper amount of stress is roughly half way around the U or up at the 12 noon position. Somewhere there, depending on your personality type is your zone. It will indicated the degree of arousal with which to play golf. Perhaps a moderate amount of stress is productive of good golf scores but a relaxed state for mind's eye images to function indicates a lower inverted U position might be better.

Under this relationship, you would not expect to perform well if you were under great stress at work, in your personal life relations, or perhaps with your golf swing.

Likely, you will conform to the relationship and need some arousal to play well. Strangely, in golf, it is very clear that a Tour players day for performance may require a modified inverted U relationship. Earlier, we have discussed the final day of play of **Lee Janzen, Justin Leonard and Pat Hurst and the author,** and are puzzled over just what happens on the final day of a golf event. Certainly, persistence and the 'hanging in there' type of golf seems vital to superior play.

Some other cases illustrate the general nature of the inverted U relationship for golf.

Patty Sheehan exemplifies a consistent inverted U. She says she gets her life in top running order, for her meaning solid routines and time management skill and application, along with health and fitness. Perhaps then, she has a knack of playing with the appropriate level of inverted U. However, I remember that on the practice area during a Tournament last year, she stated that a new set of clubs where overwhelming her regular distance and giving her some adjustment concerns.

Lee Trevino is the same as Sheehan, Sorenstorm and Woods, in that as he says he plays best when he is at home doing the regular at home lifestyle. He likes to play on Tour with a moderate stress and not in a state of high stress or running around and is well known to seem to show 'relaxation cues' whether out on the course, giving a clinic, repairing a club, or joking around. He won for the 28th time on the Senior Tour which is amazingly enough, more wins than his incredible 27 on regular Tour. He keeps his cool for the inverted U, plays with pride in wind and competition, and obviously loves being in the winning way in golf. Since he plays for few mistakes, he has the 'hanging in there' concept in his golf and he feels winning has several consistencies in itself.

PUZZLING EXCEPTIONS TO THE INVERTED U

Certain Tour players have played better under severe stress levels and may have learned to reduce anxiety overload in their own way. Amount of stress being talked about here would leave most of us a long ways from even being on the golf course, let alone competing and winning a Tour event. Rod Funseth is one of my favorite WEDGE players of all time, along with Asao Aoki, Laura Davies, Scott Hoch, and Jim Furyk.

Rod Funseth played a Senior Tour event in Calgary and I followed him nearly exclusively to watch his Wedge play. His wedge action was a little like Furyks, as I remember and his results were near perfection. Funseth won or finished near the top in several events during those years. He also finished very well on the Senior Tour. Unfortunately, before the next season, he received bad medical news. A medical checkup put him under severe stress yet he decided to return to the Tour the next year.

There are four main ways of reducing pre competition anxiety and apparently Rod Funseth was able to reduce his concern by returning his anxiety to a manageable level in the inverted U. **AMAZINGLY ROD FUNSETH VERY NEARLY EQUALLED HIS FINE BEST YEAR PERFORMANCE OF THE YEAR BEFORE.**

Equally illustrative is the sagas of Jerry McGee, John Daly and Helen Alfredsson. Tour player Jerry McGee was involved in a nagging court case over a Tour sponsor contract and had related phone calls and demands on his time. He joked that he had to finish in the Top 5 to pay his phone bills. Although he said he was very tight inside and woke 5-6 times from his sleep, he became a top Tour event finisher during that time, especially in two Tour events. He won the Kemper a few days before the court case appearance and then won a second time at the PGA Hartford, at a time when he was under immense pressure.

A key to such problematic circumstance may be that managing stress is best done when you recognize your own stress-anxiety level and start finding some keys to reducing it. We all try to do so, and perhaps golfers have time to take action and use mind's eye pictures in seeing a normalized situation allowing good golf.

FORGET YOUR CELL PHONE ON THE GOLF COURSE
Having to make a lot of phone calls has taken on a different meaning in our society. Maybe Jerry McGee was the forerunner of golfers who can handle many phone calls. Recently, I played with a golfer who used his cell phone to check up on Real Estate advertising and some incoming calls while out on the golf course. He would putt out and then use his phone. He knew nothing about the inverted U and its relationship to golf performance.

My cell phone using golf foursome member did not often play with our morning group of early riser-relaxed players. He felt he had to tell us quite a lot about his low handicap and was, in general, a very busy person. That day he was a little inconsistent in his score. The other players were not very keen about his mix of business phone calls and being out on the golf course.

So far it has not been shown that cell phone usage in a golf course environment has impacted the relationship between good golf and anxiety. It is obviously different for high performing golf play than casual golf play.

AROUSAL LEVEL TOO HIGH IN ATHLETES
A recent study has shown that nearly 40% of top college football players attempt to compete with such a high arousal level that their maximal performance is reduced. When you shut off outside distractions you allow your competition plans and your concentration to be maximized, but some athletes cannot do that.

You also may reduce your anxiety by regular exercise and by a time out procedure, during which you could use a series of positive or stress reducing images and bench sitting, rest inducing or relaxing procedures. For basketball, football and hockey that would be rather easy.

TENACITY MIND'S EYE RENDERED USELESS IN GOLF
There are times when a player in golf or any athlete lets outside occurrences upset their ability to concentrate and a mind's eye system might become a shambles as well. Once you get into that position, you can attempt some get-back-on track procedures. As you gain experience, you will hardly ever allow such circumstances develop, but once I wasn't very experienced about hiring a caddy.

There are many ways of rendering mind's eye pictures useless and here is one of the worst caused by a bad decision to change a normal procedure in a set system.

After posting a score of 76 in the first round of a two round Qualifier held the **Eden Course Amateur at St. Andrews,** Scotland one summer, I decided after the game to take a caddy for the next day. A fourteen year old boy from Glasgow was hanging around the caddy area, back at the side of the Royal and Ancient Clubhouse and I thought I would hire him on. He wasn't a golfer but he was a footballer on holiday in the town of St. Andrews. When I hired him on, I told him all he would have to do is carry a light golf bag and that would be all he would have to do.

I met my caddy the next morning, showed him an easy way to carry the bag and off we went, this time on **the New Course,** which I knew.

By the end of four holes my golf was not settled down but I had got my caddy performing reasonably well. By the 8th hole he was getting tired he said, and I said 'oh, oh'! He couldn't get the knack of his job and he had troubles carrying the bag and walking briskly, which is pretty usual in Scotland. Slowly enough I was getting upset and losing my mental game. On the 10th one of the players in my group, complained that my caddy was moving around during his shots.

Unfortunately for me, I never did straighten out my caddy's work and my golf was poor that round. I didn't have the heart to dismiss my caddy part way through the round as I should have. Good caddying does take a long time to learn and I had let that fact slip by me. I didn't visualize a solution either.

RE ESTABLISHING THE MIND'S EYE AND CONCENTRATION

There certainly is a point beyond which a golf round cannot be salvaged. Normally it takes 3 or 4 holes to regain a lost plan for the game. Eight or nine holes may already have been played so that it can be two-thirds of the game before you reestablish your good golf. Some players feel they cannot recover the round, but hanging in there is vital.

Psychologists feel that it is important to get back as quickly as possible to a basic. One basic. For example, hit one good shot and then use the same mind's eye or routine to make it two in a row. In other words, reestablish a routine and get some small of momentum working for you.

Tiger Woods is working hard on this part of golf at the present time. Fred Couples and Jim Colbert have made that part of golf work for them, as below.

The basis of consistency is to get back on plan. Easily enough said. The player needs to pre-rehearse what is called an intervention or a few interventions. It is a little pre plan for just such a set of circumstances. Expect that the loss of concentration leading to a few flat holes is normal. It is an unwanted part of golf and therefore do not be surprised by such a situation.

Earlier, the plan Fred Couples used to get back on track was a situation review and a long term plan with slow regaining of full health for golf. His plan was well known to the golfing public and he lived out his plan.

Jim Colbert got back on his plan for being highly competitive, like he is in golf, as follows.

RETOOLING A COMPETITIVE EDGE

When Jim Colbert was a high ranking Senior Tour player he was right on top of the Senior Tour week after week. However, after double surgery and rehabilitation, he said his loss of concentration for his golf was from the lack of **'adrenaline kicking in for him'** on the golf course. He worked on that aspect.

Recently, Colbert and several Senior Tour players have gone through rough times as they try to recover their games after surgery. Arnold Palmer is another prostrate cancer victim. Amazingly enough, many do recover their scoring touch.

Not only is the Senior Tour a medical disaster of sorts, on the regular PGA Tour at the TPC Steve Elkington from Australia could not defend due to sinus surgery, and in addition a list of injuries to Tour players read: shoulder-out; back-out; back-out; shoulder-out; rib-out; and flu-out. On the LPGA Tour Helen Alfredsson played for a year during recover from major injury. Her driving distance had fallen back and her reputation of being one of the longest hitters was in question, when I caddied in her group last year. She has won on Tour again. Unfortunately, Colbert is not all the way back to his goal and many of us are with him in spirit, for his quest.

Regarding Jim Colbert, the golf columnist Jerry Potter of USA Today, commented on the competitive edge and the mind - body connection in golf via Jim Colbert's lament, when Colbert said "I was great as long as the adrenaline was kicking in, I played two and one half good rounds (i.e. two rounds of 65 and another good nine holes...) but after that nine I knew I couldn't win when the adrenaline quit. My mind wanted to keep going but my body wouldn't do it". In the last weeks Jim Colberts scores have been moving up the Senior Tour leader boards again.

It seems the Senior Tour golf, especially, has put a whole new clarification on mental golf and healthy golf, yet here we see the physical health element to be of supreme importance in golf.

EASY CONCENTRATION FROM EASY MIND'S EYE

Another key to reestablishing the game plan and the mind control is the golfer requires to try for 'easy' concentration and 'easy' imagery. Let imagery and concentration build through a natural momentum.

Attempting too hard to concentrate and visualizing 'too hard' makes it impossible to get back on track. This is the concept of soft concentration. The basic notion is to let things happen naturally, freeing the mind to lapse, refocus and concentrate again. As has been noted by Dorothy Harris, "it is essential to eliminate constant strain to concentrate". This applies to the problem of reasserting concentration in golf and this is TENACITY.

SUMMARY
KEY WORDS AND NOTIONS OF CHAPTER FIVE

*Mind control combines with self discipline in mind's eye tenacity.

*There are three basic mind's eyes required to finish off effective putting on the greens.

*By anticipating and practicing for pressure, you soon enough deal with pressure in an easy and comfortable way.

*Many psychologists agree that it is impossible to try to concentrate. Instead, try something else and concentration will return.

*Practice simulations of pressure.

*At the present time in Tour golf and in top Amateur and club play tenacity can be learned.

*Systematic golf is the ability to accept the good with the bad in situational golf and the key is that within 18 holes almost all things even out.

*Make your belief in systematic golf and in preparation a vividly imagined set of mind's eye ones.

*A golf player should always see themselves as having several self performance standards in golf in addition to game score.

*The aware golfer 'sees' the mini peak experience in golf and knows how to imitate such an experience. It is rare.

*Imagery of tempo makes it possible to gather momentum for the game play of golf.

*The basis of consistency in golf includes a systematic way of getting back on plan. All Tour players and all golfers frequently use such procedures.

*Senior golf has provided further clarification of the mind-body-healthy body connection in golf. Injuries in Tour play golf are frequent and require tenacity procedures.

****

CHAPTER FIVE
BIBLIOGRAPHY AND RESOURCES

Martens, R., Rivkin, F., and Burton, D., "Who predicts anxiety better: Coaches or Athletes?" In Psychology of Motor Behavior and Sport. Champaign, Illinois: H. Kinetics Publishers, 1979.

Scanian, T., Competitive Stress (Chapter 9) In Psych. Foundations of Sport., H. Kinetic Publishers, 1984.

Ravizza, K., Qualities of the Peak Experience in Sport (Chapter 32) above Op Cit.

Potter, J., USA Today. "Colbert's competitve edge as healthy as ever". Nov., 1997.

Lucas, G., Boody L., Golf Improvement: Intermediated by Imagery Training or Success Videotape Viewing. Finland: Congress of AIESEP, 1990.

Murphy, M., White, R., The Psychic Side of Sport: Reading, Maine: Addison-Wesley, 1978.

Maslow, A., Toward a Psychology of Being. (2nd), N.Y.: Van Nostrand Reinhold. 1968.

Czikszentmihalyi, M., Journal of Humanistic Psychology, "Play and Intrinsic Rewards". 15. 1977.

(Resource: Beyond Boredom and Anxiety., San Francisco: Jossey Bass Publishers, 1975).

Watson, T., Golf Digest. "Tom Watson talks to Juniors"., April 1978.

Potter, J., USA Today. "5-shot deficit didn't faze Players Champ, Leonard". March, 1998.

Associated Press. "Janzen, Ozaki lead at the TPC". March, 1998.

Morran, Sharron. Golf Digest. "Ladies: Daydream your way to lower scores". 1978.

Harris, D., Harris, B., Sport Psychology: Mental Skills for Physical People. N.Y.: Leisure Press, 1984.

Staff and wlre reports. USA Today. "Trevino claims 28th Senior win at Dominion". Mar. 1998

CHAPTER 6 THE TOUR PLAYER AIMER: OUR MODEL

Objectives: The chapter includes the various ways in which TOUR players and golf course architects and designers use aiming as a central focus in their play and in their work. Objectives also are included for: persisting with focused golf behavior, focused golf situation and weather, succeeding in lowering golf scores versus odds when golf course design may overwhelm the golfer; focusing on the task at hand; focus on the swing task to succeed with the shot; recovering focus; and using new golf course design and golf skills to your advantage in practice and practicing in the right place. Included is getting a bag on Tour: A Commentary on Caddying; Golf course architecture and golf skill; wins and finding a way to win; Finding a way at the JC Penney Classic; A way to win by systematic controlled play; Ways to win: Pattern likely; and two summaries titled: Shooting 59's (and 69's, 79's and 89's); the likely Pattern; Qualifying time and again: One Tour test. Summary & Bibliography.

TOUR STATISTICS AND AIMING IN GOLF
Some players pay proper attention to Tour statistics and we tend to see aiming go along with Tour money winning success and top ten finishes.

Even when we see that top Tour players are not always top ten putters (since there are many great putters)...we do see that driving distance and the number of birdies scored has a high correlation with success.

Birdies are more so the result of good putting and good chipping in or chipping close and so too are eagles connected with good putting. In addition, the statistic labelled **all around** is vital to the top ten finishes and overall ranking it seems.

PGA Tour statistics for the LPGA Tour and the PGA Tour after several events for the same year showed top ten men in **driving distance** and **all around** most frequently. However, just one top ten male player was in **greens in regulation** and none were found in putting leaders. At the same time for LPGA, top ten players fully 40% were in **birdie leaders** and in **driving distance** while 20% were in **greens in regulation** and none were in top ten **putting.**

However, it is universally conceded that in top golf putting is a vital key to top fifty and top 100 performances. Since top players hit their key shots close to the hole, most often they are likely the players that get on hot putting streaks most timely and most often.

Sometimes statistics don't tell true and complete stories. In the putting statistic that seems to be so. For example, Barb Sherbak-Bunkowsky, a formerly fine player on Tour, is in the top five in putting and chipping but is having her worst year by far in winnings earned and in overall placement. Once when I caddied in her foursome at a Myrtle Beach Tour event, I noticed how often she hit woods other than her driver from both the fairways and the tees, and often ended in sand or close to many greens. From these places Barb would chip or blast in to the hole or very close to the hole almost every time.

Yet another player on the LPGA Tour with unproductive statistics is Karen Davies of Wales and Florida. She is an incredibly effective sand and greenside player and practices this part of the game endlessly and effectively and appears in top ten or top twenty statistics in putting. Yet she doesn't often get into top birdies made statistics and thus in not usually a ranked player. She along with many other players floundered at Tour Qualifying school recently. For sure, the all around play statistic cannot be under valued in Tour golf. Tour players cannot be unsure of their play since it impacts their confidence.

At the Dinah Shore Nabisco LPGA event, one of the majors in women's golf, Scherbak-Bunkowsky seemed out of contention after a bad first round yet shot her best round in a long spell in round two, a fine 66 and made the cut by one stroke. She remained in the top ten in putting for the whole season.

There are several unusual situations in Tour statistics that show some difficulty in finding a clear picture of just what performance really counts. There are, however some unmistakable and important statistical connections as this section highlights.

In addition, putting stats reward good chipping (statistically) so that birdies made is a true indication on both Tours of **fine all around play and fine putting.** Some formats of play such as the Ryder Cup, seem to show more clearly when good putting is meaningful and effective, since the players go all out for low score on each and every hole in Ryder Cup type play.

WHAT THE FINAL CHAPTER INCLUDES: WHY?

This chapter includes persisting with focused golf behavior and the skills for persisting out on the golf course, which the above statistic shows to be necessary for winning golf.

The chapter looks into the Tour Players who currently use aiming, even in adverse weather conditions to bridge the gap to become winners on Tour. For sure, there seems to be claims made for additional attention to aiming on and around the greens. Even top players have improved their aiming immediately prior to winning. Consistency and the ways to win and finding ways to win is included because of its extreme importance. A pattern is outlined which may be effective. **Aiming features in this chapter** include sharpening visualization skill that is, reading shot requirements accurately; focusing on the situation that you are in; focusing on the swing task that is at hand; refocusing and using golf course architecture and design to advantage in your game and in your golf practice.

The Tour player also is coming to know certain concept words that the amateur golfer should know about and should apply to golf: such as representation of location, visual selection, shot shape, visual learning from inside and outside the sport, and a new term I am introducing for golf, ATSV which means 'always transferring specific visual information' in an effort to gain better mind's eye imagery for golf. The reason for this part of the chapter is growth in the technology of the game, yet keeping the game as simple as possible.

PERSISTING WITH FOCUSED GOLF BEHAVIOR
The whole idea of using and choosing focused golf behavior can be broken down to two mind functions we all use. Perhaps we do not pay enough attention to these two notions.

First is conscious brain decisions from our rational side which we all make. Second, is the **mind's eye brain function** which we do not always use. That brain, the right brain, is apt to use intuition and insight and combine with the subconscious to focus on golf behavior that can be very effective. You will probably **remember the big advantage** here, that is that the subconscious is not evaluative and can accept all of our mind's eye decisions that we send it. **If we have seen it once with our mind's eye, we can see it again and do repeated fine golf shots.** Perhaps we can become **fine all around golfers,** the most important statistics of all for better golf.

Again, we remember that we can use this to our real advantage in golf. This is a key which I have tried to consistently stress. This key advantage is not easily taken out on the golf course, all of the time. It seems to me that not all Tour players or Amateur players can take advantage or consistently use visualization. Yet its advantage is there for us to play better golf with. **And consistently with!**

GIVING OUR RIGHT BRAIN A CHANCE
What the above means is that we had better share accurate information with our rain and then ask for performance by our lower brain prior to hitting a golf shot. For example, if the last message you decided on is a bad message for golf such

IMAGE SELECTOR

as what will happen to my score if I hit into the water when trying to clear the water with an approach shot, then you may hit short if the last mind's eye is of that. Learn to back off mentally and restart by using a positive mind's eye image for your shots. When I wrote my earlier book titled **Imagery of Golf: *Visualizing Your Way to a Better Game,*** used an illustration involving a Tour player and a Tour caddy.

Kathy Hite, a former Tour player knows how to refocus when her subconscious brain is enticed and endangered by bad golf information. She was once on her way to an event record 65 when a caddy lost his cool and asked about what would happen to their score if they played the ball into the water. It was said later that she was cool enough to **back off and refocus** and remind her caddy of the correct time to discuss score. **She apparently sent another message with a correct mind's eye and hit a good shot, nearly hitting the flag and almost hitting the ball in the hole and birdieing it.**

ANOTHER EXAMPLE OF GIVING THE BRAIN A CHANCE

Although you do not see Tour players back off and redo their mental preparation for a shot very often, I came across another example which took place on Tour last Spring at Muriiells Inlet, Myrtle Beach S.C. **Such backing**  **off and redoing is not easily done it seems but it is straight forward enough for any Tour player who is gaining more experience each day. Perhaps todays Tour players mentally back off often in their systems and we do not see them do so.**

Nancy Harvey, a late blooming LPGA Tour player form Saskatchewan and Arizona, was tied for a Tour event lead at 6 under par with **Laura Davies** and so was paired with Davies for both round 3 and round 4 at the **Susan G. Komens** (a foundation charity for breast cancer research and awareness).

Nancy Harvey, up to this current LPGA season, usually would not have been paired so highly but was doing fine and was on the way to being a top notch "A" player out on Tour. Perhaps Harvey was somewhat nervous but it did not seem so.

The 18th hole is a wicked water hole left all along the fairway and beyond the green. Laura Davies was a way too far right into the trees. In fact her ball rolled under a volunteer's rolled up rain gear that was set against a tree. So that a ruling was needed and a delay was taking place. There was a medium long delay before the official came by because of the large gallery.

Nancy Harvey in the meantime, was forced to wait beside her perfect drive on this tough hole and be patient. She talked to her caddy to avoid any excessive bad mind's eye images to be formulated. Here we have the classic example of too much time and bad image time as well.

As bad luck would have it for Harvey, all the spectators were on the path on the right side keeping company with Laura and waiting and hoping to see a spectacular shot. After she got a ruling, which was a favorable one, a free drop, she still had a difficult shot.

As it turned out, Davies, a very fast player, hit right away and got off a spectacular effort to the edge of the green but not really near the hole. The gallery went berserk anyway and cheered and yelled like they do anywhere for Laura.

To her enduring credit, Nancy seemed to slow down and reprogram herself in some way while someone in the crowd started quieting the spectators. Then Harvey pulled off a beautiful shot to right next to the hole.

In all the time delay, was excruciatingly a long one and a redoing of a mental system had to be a good mental golf skill, in this example.

PERSISTING WITH FOCUSED GOLF BEHAVIOR II

As it turns out, Nancy Harvey again is paired with Laura Davies at 7 under par. She has little trouble scoring decently again and almost finishing in the top ten in the Tour event. Both players cool off in their putting and lose to hard charging **Annika Sorenstam** who battles Australian **Karrie Webb** and Prince Edward Island (Canada) **Lorie Kane,** another late developer, who seems in contention in almost every Tour event and into the next Tour season. Kane makes many birdies and putts well but the Press seems to think that P.E.I., is some unheard of city called Pie, Canada. Soon enough she gets some added respect it seems and TSN has its facts very straight. Later Kane finishes outright second in the Tour Players event

Later in the LPGA Tour season, Nancy Harvey who as it turns out has been trying for success on Tour for nine years turns in an awesome 2nd place finish and wins over $50,000 for one event.

The press plays on the fact that she did not win outright first but they do not seem to understand that confidence builds up surely and then even more surely, along with true mental ability in golf. Her earnings reach an astronomical figure for her of nearly $350,000 in winnings. **She seems to follow the statistics referred to above of making lots of birdies and strong all around play that seems so necessary to Tour success.**

Here is an example not that different from that which low **scoring Amateurs and Tour players** need from their golf performance brains. It contains a system of play and focused golf behavior that can be surely enough depended upon.

By playing consistent golf and scoring well in all rounds, she finds herself in contention in nearly every event. Persistence such as she now exhibits is evident in many Tour players. Young successes and late comers are more frequent on Tour it seems.

REVIEW: CANCEL OUT BAD GOLF IMAGES

THE SUBCONSCIOUS NEEDS ACCURATE AND SUITABLE INFORMATION FROM THE RATIONAL CONSCIOUS SIDE OF THE BRAIN, THE RIGHT SIDE WHICH GOLFERS SHOULD CALL THE PERFORMANCE SELECTOR SIDE OF THE BRAIN. THE MORE THE GOLFER CAN DO TO MAKE THEIR SUBCONSCIOUS OR MIND'S EYE IMAGES WORK FOR GOLF SCORE ATTAINMENT, THE MORE THEY WILL BE IN CONTROL. SUCH THINGS AS DISTANCE AWAY FROM MOUNDS, GRASSY HILLS AND BIG LONG SAND BUNKERS AND GREENS WHICH REQUIRE GREAT READS.

THE BETTER WILL BE THE AGREEMENT OF PERFORMANCE BRAIN WITH IMAGERY BRAIN. WHAT IS THE USE OF DOING A VERY PICTURESQUE ACCURATE IMAGE OF PUTT LINE OR SEEING AND ANALYZING A GREAT DIVOT LINE TO AN EXACT SPOT ON A GREEN, IF IT IS BASED ON UNSUITABLE INFORMATION SENT TO THE SKILL SELECTOR AND SKILL PERFORMER PART OF THE BRAIN IN THE FIRST PLACE.

ACADEMY OF GOLF: LAKEWAY, TEXAS

Once while the present author was giving a talk at the Academy of Golf PGA Workshop at the Hills of Lakeway,

Austin, Texas, the speaker for the afternoon was David Pelz.

Pelz is an engineer and former Tour golfer who turned to full time golf research and writing. This colleague had done some fascinating research all aimed at improving putting and the conditions around putting. He made a mechanical putting man which could putt extremely well with a repeatable pendulum swinging motion. He showed us how it worked with its mechanical arms. The robot like mechanical man even lookes slightly like a golfer. He named his man Mr. Perfy P. Putter.

As well Pelz used moulds and plaster of paris to study shoe footprints on the putting green to ascertain the wear and tear on the greens. **He called the worn out circle of grass around each pin the *Doughnut Effect.***

THE **Doughnut Effect** WAS THE GOLF SHOE SPIKE RING AROUND THE HOLE. THIS RING DEVELOPED EACH MORNING OF A TOUR TOURNAMENT ON THE PUTTING GREEN AND LATER NEAR EACH HOLE ON THE GOLF COURSE. SOME PLAYERS FELT IT CAUSED DETERIORATION IN PUTTING ACCURACY. SO DAVID PELZ MEASURED THE ACTUAL RING AND FOUND OUT THAT THE WORN OUT GRASS DID SURELY ENOUGH EFFECT BALL ROLL.

During my talk on mental golf and mind's eye imagery, I carefully laid out the function of the mind's eye image for the more rational conscious brain, the brain that functions in our decisions on the golf course. I talked and we discussed endless examples occurring on the golf course.

I think that Dave Pelz was fascinated and made the connection right away with his putting science. All six of the presenters at the Academy agreed that this aspect of mental golf needed a lot more resources like books and videos for the golfer and the professional PGA instructor. Mind's eye self success videotapes and research were to come later as explained elsewhere in the present book.

David Pelz has since then utilized the idea of the need for the conscious mind agreeing with the subconscious performer mind even when a Tour player reads a green. **He talks about the sign that the two minds are closing the gap, that is, working in harmony for better golf.** This was the main idea expressed in *IMAGES FOR GOLF: Visualizing Your Way to Better Golf, now titled the New Images for Golf.*

DAVE PELZ MAY BE CREDITED WITH STARTING A REVOLUTION IN BETTER PUTTING WITH ALL HIS WORK AND CERTAINLY HAS SHOWN THAT PUTTING AND READING GREENS IS A MUCH MORE UNCERTAIN GOLF SKILL THAN ORIGINALLY THOUGHT TO BE. LOOK UP THE COVER STORY WRITTEN BY DAVE PELZ (WITH JAMES A FRANK) IN *GOLF MAGAZINE*. IN ADDITION YOU MAY WISH TO ORDER A PELZ VIDEOTAPE TITLED *THE AMAZING TRUTH ABOUT PUTTING.* CURRENTLY, TOUR PLAYERS ARE OFTEN OF THE OPINION THAT FEEL AND TOUCH FOR DISTANCE ON THE GREENS IS THE MOST IMPORTANT ASPECT OF GOOD PUTTING. **PELZ'S MAIN MESSAGE** IS THAT READING PUTTS IS THE MAIN AREA FOR PUTTING IMPROVEMENT SO THE TOUR PLAYERS DO NOT NECESSARILY AGREE. MOST OF THEIR

TIME ON THE GREENS IS FOR PUTTING TOUCH, IT SEEMS.

THE ACADEMY AND BIOMECHANICS

The Academy of Golf at Austin, Texas was the location of our golf science and golf swing improvement week and included an outstanding talk by Dr. Joe Inman on a PH.D. done in the biomechanics of the golf swing. **It is said to have been the work which revolutionized the way teachers think about the golf swing.** The work was done by this researcher and PGA Professional while he was teaching at famous old Medina Golf Course in Chicago. The PGA later encouraged this model.

He simplified and revolutionized the understanding and the teaching of the golf swing and soon after that, most teaching professionals simplified their instruction. In fact, this simplified biomechanical model of the golf swing is by now the main model for instruction for most instructional leaders and workshops within the PGA.

THE BODY'S HINGES AND LEVERS ARE USED IN A SIMPLE AND EFFICIENT MANNER IN THE SWING. IF THE MAIN LEVERS ARE THE ARMS, THEY ARE TO HANG DOWN IN A NATURALLY HINGED POSTURE AND THE BODY NEVER ASSUMES ANY UNNATURAL POSITIONS OF MOVEMENT. ONE CAN SEE IT EASILY IN THE MANNER IN WHICH ARMS HANG FOR PUTTING, IN THE CURRENT TOUR PLAYERS PUTTING MECHANICS.

I remember what he said about mind's eye imagery and visualization, something like this paraphrase. The golf world awaits and deserves great info on the newer field of golf imagery and the mind's eye. He indicated that precise and simple biomechanical images can become the norm for accurate computer models for the golfer of the future. Let your body assume natural and not forced positions. **Use computer generated models for the cues of hinging and leveraging.** Several other teaching professional and Tour players agreed that the golf world deserved better materials in this field and it was then that someone suggested that more books and resources were needed in mind's eye golf. Perhaps a three book series, or what is called a trilogy series of books for the field of **golf education.**

PRACTICING IN THE RIGHT PLACE OR IN AN IMAGINED LOCATION

When we where at the Academy in Texas, we saw and used a facility which was like no other one to learn and practice at. We were told that the design was by Jack Nicklaus Associates and it was the Director, Michael Adams who brought us together.

THE ACADEMY IS A GEM, BEING 500 YARDS LONG AND HAVING TEE BOXES, GREENS AND TRAP SITUATIONS AT EACH END SO THAT WIND

VARIATION COULD BE USED IN PRACTICE. THE RANGE WAS SURROUNDED BY THREE GOLF HOLES. A PAR 3, PAR 4 AND A PAR 5. THOSE WERE IN TURN SURROUNDED BY NICELY STYLED VICTORIAN CONDO AND RENTAL HOUSING UNITS, WHICH IN TURN HAD THREE FULL SIZE GOLF COURSES ON THE PERIMETER. THE HILLS OF LAKEWAY TENNIS ACADEMY WAS OFF TO ONE END. TAME DEER AND LOTS OF SMALL LAKES, ONE BIG LAKE AND WATERFALLS CARESSED THE GOLF COURSES.

EACH OF THE THREE PRACTICE HOLES HAD THREE TEE OFF LOCATIONS. SO THAT WE OFTEN PLAYED THE EQUIVALENT OF NINE HOLES BY HITTING THREE TEE SHOTS ALL THE WAY AROUND.

The Tour players practicing there would often be found hitting repetition shots in to these greens from the sides of the fairways. **This provided a variety of wedge distance practice, a vital component of better golf.** Of course, the three full size courses could be played on later in the afternoon.

IF YOU CAN GO THERE BY ALL AND BY ALL MEANS DO SO. ENCOURAGE YOUR GOLF PROFESSIONAL TO GO WITH YOU, AS THERE ARE MANY PGA PROFESSIONALS IN ATTENDANCE THERE. ONE OF MY FORMER GOLF PROFESSIONALS WAS THERE. CLAYTON ROBB, OF PINEBROOK (CALGARY), A COURSE DESIGNED AFTER A PYRAMID SHAPED LOS ANGELES CLUBHOUSE WAS IN ATTENDANCE. ROBB IS AN EXCELLENT PGA INSTRUCTOR AND ORGANIZER OF HUGE GOLF SCHOOLS. THE READER COULD TAKE IN A GOLF SCHOOL SESSION OR STAY A WEEK. PRESENTLY MR. BILL MORETTI IS THE DIRECTOR THERE AND HE HAD GIVEN THE PUTTING IMPROVEMENT SESSIONS.

Practicing in the same location as the Tour players and aspiring Tour player is very favorable to your golf game. A huge transfer effect is gained by being exposed to hundreds of ball striking examples among golf swings.

Mike Adams, the former Director, has moved to the Florida PGA Academy location. Currently I have neither taught there or seen the location. Mike Adams is a former Tour player whose putting was not up to the balance of his ball striking, he says. So he set out to be one of the finest instructors of golf that he could become. He has made it. **He is known throughout the American based golf world as MR. SWING DOCTOR, while being rated among the 100 best teachers by Golf Magazine.**

WHILE CADDYING ON LPGA TOUR, I HEARD HIS NAME MENTIONED BY PLAYERS QUITE OFTEN, EVEN ALMOST URGENTLY IT SEEMED. TOUR PLAYERS OFTEN SEEK OUT SUPERIOR TEACHERS. HIS NAME IS MENTIONED ON THE FORMER NIKE TOUR AND THE CANADIAN TOUR, BOTH CONSIDERED TO BE FINE PLAYER DEVELOPMENT TOURS. **It is said that LPGA Tour players' teachers are not as well known as are the teachers of the mens Tour but recently several articles in US golf magazines have given credit to top LPGA coaches and teachers.**

IMAGE SELECTOR OR MIND'S EYE TOUR PLAYERS
Greg Norman, Ernie Els and Nick Faldo are sources of image selector or

mind's eye images. Their swings have been posed in three swing positions on the cover and inside of a great new golf book by Mike Adams and T.J. Tomasi titled *PLAY BETTER GOLF.*

The book was published in Japan and in Boston USA. Each of us needs a **"BIBLE" of swing images** for our swing selector brain and this is a very good choice. The book has 300 color swing images with distinct photographic excellence by photographer Mark Feldman.

 TEMPO

Swing sequences such as these are a fine choice for you. Use these for your own practice and your own golf rehearsal studio. This is the concept room that a good mind's eye player uses. The studio can be your favorite room you use for golf or even can be imaginary.

You could use such an studio for visualization exercises and for viewing such videos as golf ones or even better, your own self success videotapes of you making 10 or 20 putts in succession or other impressive green side or trap shots that you have had videotaped and edited such as we did for our Academy research study with Tour aspirant golfers.

THE IMAGES OF NORMAN, ELS AND FALDO AND THOSE OF ALICE MILLER AND BARB THOMAS CAN BE USED FOR YOUR SWING SELECTOR IMAGES TO DEVELOP ALL THE LITTLE POSTURE AND SWING NUANCES FOR THE PUTT-CHIP, PITCH, BUMP AND RUN AND LOB SHOT. IT WILL PROVE A GREAT BENEFIT FOR IMAGE REHEARSAL FOR YOUR SWING. **ALSO IT IS A BIG HELP FOR TRAJECTORY AND AIM CONTROL SPOKEN OF OFTEN IN THIS PRESENT BOOK.** YOU NEED IT FOR YOUR IMPROVING ABILITY TO USE HIGH TRAJECTORY AND LOW TRAJECTORY GREENSIDE SHOTS. THE FINE BOOK REFERRED TO ABOVE AND TITLED TO *PLAY BETTER GOLF* IS DEVOTED EXCLUSIVELY TO RIGHT SIDED SWINGS AND MOSTLY TO MENS SWINGS. HOWEVER, I HAVE NEVER FOUND A BETTER BOOK FOR ANYONES GOLF AND BOOKSTORES AND GOLF BOOK SECTIONS WOULD BE POOR INDEED WITHOUT THIS RARE BOOK. ORDERING INFORMATION CAN BE FOUND AT THE REAR OF THIS BOOK. WHAT FOLLOWS GIVES A LITTLE MORE INFORMATION ON **PLAY BETTER GOLF.**

BOTH **BARB THOMAS** AND **ALICE MILLER** ARE INCLUDED IN STAR SWINGS AND MUCH CAN BE ABSORBED INTO ONES IMAGE SELECTOR BRAIN REGARDING THE MODERN SWING WHICH IS DEFINED BY MIKE ADAMS AS INCLUDING **LIGHT POSITION** EARLY IN THE BACKSWING (ALL ABOUT EARLY WRIST SET AS A PLATFORM, SAID TO BE A BIOMECHANICALLY NATURAL POSITION, AS OPPOSED TOT HE FORMER CLASSIC SWING POSITION).

THE BARB THOMAS SWING SEQUENCE SHOWS THIS **"THOROUGHLY MODERN GOLF SWING"** AS THE AUTHORS PUT IT. WITH THE HELP OF MIKE ADAMS, BARB THOMAS, NOT YET A HOUSEHOLD NAME IN GOLF, IS REPRESENTATIVE OF A NEW TYPE OF LPGA PLAYER.

SHE WON THE HAWAIIAN LADIES OPEN AND HAD POSTED FIVE TOP

TWENTY FINISHES. YOU ALSO MAY HAVE NOTICED ANOTHER THOMAS, THAT IS SUE THOMAS FROM TEXAS WHO IS ALSO AN UP AND COMING PLAYER WHEN I CADDIED FOR HER. I LEARNED ABOUT SYSTEMATIC GAME PLAY AND TREMENDOUS CARE WITH GAME MANAGEMENT, WHICH IS ALSO A CHARACTERISTIC OF MODERN TOUR PLAY.

ALICE MILLER IS A TALL PLAYER WITH A POWERFUL LEFT-HAND GRIP AND FAST HIP ACTION. DURING THE MID 1980'S, WE WATCHED HER FINE PLAY. SHE WON SEVEN TOUR EVENTS DURING THAT STRETCH. SHE BECAME A BOUNCE BACK PLAYER OF THE YEAR WINNING AT TOLEDO, USA.

EARLIER, SHE WON THE PRESTIGIOUS NABISCO DINAH SHORE, AND LPGA TOUR MAJOR. IT IS A PLEASURE TO WATCH HER FINISH POSITION, THE CLUB FINISHING WELL BEHIND HER. THIS POSITION IS SAID TO BE A SURE SIGN OF A FULL RELEASE IN THE GOLF SWING.

All in all these images, including Adams and Tomasi' own swings show swing sequences and result in a brilliant and easy to understand text of advanced golf skills.

It is notable that **Kathryn Maloney** was the project manager for this fine mind's eye image book in golf. She is a LPGA teaching professional at Ironhorse in West Palm Beach, Florida. A copy can be bought at any Atlantic Bookhouse or other fine bookstore. Use the ordering number ISBN# 1-885203-35-7.

THE SWING DOCTOR AND INTERNAL IMAGERY

In discussions with the author **Mike Adams,** he says he calls for strong internal imagery or mind's eye images in absorbing golf skills. Adams gives over 3000 lessons per year and his teachings are well accepted it seems.

FOCUSSED GOLF BEHAVIOR

Mike Read, a Veteran Tour player, is one golfer who seems to focus on aim and aim applications of the golf course. Read is surely an accurate player in Tour Statistics and out on the golf course. It is said he is the Tours **"straight man"**. He is known to hit more greens and he sets up his green striking accuracy by hitting a lot of fairways and by hitting position shots.

Since Mike Read didn't consider himself a long ball hitter, he focused on aiming to the extent that Tour buddies started calling him **"RADAR"**. He says he tries for accuracy with every club, not just driving. He also counts on his **advanced visualization techniques.**

OFTEN TOUR PLAYERS MAY MISALIGN AND MAY NOT KNOW IT, AS DAVE PELZ CONTENDS FOR PUTTING ALIGNMENT. SO THAT MIKE READ HAS UTILIZED A WELL AGREED TECHNIQUE ON TOUR OF CHECKING AIM LINE WITH A CLUB AT HIP AND AT KNEES AND AT SHOULDER IN PARTICULAR. DESPITE WHAT SOME MODERN GOLF TEACHERS SAY ABOUT NOT USING

A CLUB ON THE GRASS TO CHECK FOOT ALIGNMENT, IT IS STILL VERY COMMON ON TOUR TO SEE A CLUB TO SHOW AIM LINE BUT NOT TO NECESSARILY SET TOE LINE. THAT IS BECAUSE FOOT ALIGNMENT VARIES DEPENDING ON THE SHOT YOU ARE PERFORMING.

Another Tour technique used, especially with a wedge is to put two clubs down on the grass to form a channel to pass the clubface of the wedge through as you practice swing.

Another LPGA player uses a board such as the 2" by 2" range dividers to hit along side of. Again this is for wedge exactness hit line. An up and coming player on the Canadian development Tour at the Telus event Calgary, Alberta uses the club itself for improving alignment and striking.

He aims the club while holding it a hip level and passes the club slowly through the exact position twice or so. Then he hits what turns out to be a super accurate shot to a target flag.

This type of practice can be repeated lots and lots and then returned to during long practice sessions. It definitely develops mind's eye pictures that are easily transferred to the real game.

We find **Mike Read** stressing on old reliable check off that still is the best. He picks a spot a few feet ahead of his ball position on the exact line to the green or the layup. He then uses this shortline to aim the clubface. Then he sets his body on line. This aim technique goes very well.

On of Mike Reads rule for accuracy is to never try to hit the ball straight. Instead, use a slight draw or slight fade to widen your target area. Of course Read never aims at trouble. Instead, he is safe in two ways he says. Just recently some scores in from the Texas Open shows that Mike Read is up to his steady par + game and then some! **On the par 72 LaCantera course (San Antonio) his scores go 70, 69, 72 and 62! No kidding.** Hal Sutton nudges Justin Leonard and Jay Haas for 1st, but there is Mike Read tied with Steve Lowery, Andrew Magee, and Loren Roberts for clear 3rd and $66,938. Maybe Mike Read believes in my contention that 59's and 60-62's are probable in Tour Golf (see the end pages of the Chapter). Mike Weir, an up and coming Canadian goes 70, 70, 70, 70. My oh my!

OFTEN I HAVE MENTIONED IN BOTH THIS PRESENT BOOK AND IN THE NEW IMAGES FOR GOLF: *The Fundamentals of Visualizing and Scoring (ISBN 09 692902-4-1) ($16.95 U.S.)* THAT VISUALIZING THE SHAPE OF THE FLIGHT OF YOUR NEXT SHOT IS FREQUENTLY DONE ON TOUR. HOWEVER, IT IS ALSO UNCANNY THAT WHEN YOU SEE THE BALL LAND AND ROLL TO THE HOLE IN THE MIND'S EYE, YOU OFTEN GAIN BETTER RESULTS. MIKE READ ONCE MADE AN INTERESTING AND CONFIRMING STATEMENT WHEN HE WROTE: "IF I NEED TO GET THE BALL REALLY CLOSE TO THE HOLE OR TO A SPECIFIC PLACEMENT ON THE FAIRWAY, I VISUALIZE THE RESULT. FUNNY HOW EASY IT IS TO GET THE BALL CLOSE EVERY TIME" (SEE BIBLIOGRAPHY).

VISUALIZATION DOES TAKE PRACTICE FOR GOLF
VISUALIZATION DOES TAKE PRACTICE AND SO THE PRESENT BOOK INCLUDES THE BEST 17 PRACTICE EXERCISES KNOWN AND DEVELOPED BY THIS AUTHOR. THEY CAN BE PRACTICED WITH THE HELP OF THE APPENDIX SECTION OF THIS BOOK. AFTER GETTING TO BE VERY GOOD AT GOLF VISUALIZING YOU MAY BE READY TO GET ON GETTING A SET OF SELF SUCCESS VIDEOTAPES, EXPLAINED ELSEWHERE IN THIS BOOK.

OBSERVING BALL SHOT SHAPE FROM BOTH ENDS OF THE SHOT HAS BEEN AN IDEA I ENCOURAGED PREVIOUSLY IN THIS BOOK. MIKE READ IS ON TOUR PLAYER WHO BREAKS VISUALIZATION DOWN TO **THREE PHASES:** THE BEGINNING, THE MIDDLE AND THE END OF EACH AND EVERY SHOT HE MAKES ON TOUR.

MIKE READ BELIEVES IT MAKES SENSE TO DO A MIND'S EYE OF THE BALL LEAVING THE CLUBFACE IN THE INTENDED LINE. HE ALSO INCLUDES THE BALL IN-FLIGHT (SHOT SHAPE) AND THE LANDING AND ROLL TO THE TARGET. THE AUTHOR LIKES TO VISUALIZE THE BALL BEING COMPRESSED AND THEN EXPLODING OFF THE CLUBFACE WITH ADDED ENERGY OF RESHAPING ITSELF. GOOD GOLFERS KNOW THAT 80 AND 90 COMPRESSION GOLF BALLS ARE BETTER FOR THIS IMAGE. THOSE COMPRESSION GOLF BALLS HAVE BEEN PROVEN TO RESHAPE DURING THE CLUB-BALL CONTACT PHASE. THIS WAS SHOWN BY STUDIES DONE BY THE BRITISH SCIENTIFIC SERIES OF EXPERIMENTS IN GOLF.

PHIL MIKKELSON HAS USED THE EXPRESSION OF A BALL COMING VERY HOT OFF THE CLUB FACE OF THE DRIVER HE IS DEMONSTRATING. THIS IS AN EFFECTIVE VISUALIZATION APPLICATION FOR GOLFERS WHO WANT THIS FEELING. ANOTHER GREAT IMAGE IS GAINED BY ASSOCIATING A POWERFUL FOLLOW THROUGH WITH GOOD COMPRESSION. THIS MAKES SURE YOUR GOLF MECHANICS ARE MODERN MECHANICS.

VISUALIZATION IS INDIVIDUALISTIC
Visualization is all about sharpening your golf game and staying within the game which works best for you. In that sense, visualizing with mind's eye images is a very tailored skill. It is a skill that can be honed for the elements of weather as well as the specific situation you find yourself in.

FOCUS VERSUS ELEMENTS OF SITUATION AND WEATHER
EARLIER IN THIS BOOK, THE AUTHOR FOCUSED ON FRED COUPLES WHEN HE WON A PGA TOURNAMENT IN HAWAII. APPARENTLY THE WIND WAS PRETTY SEVERE ESPECIALLY ON DAY 3 AND DAY 4 OF THE TOUR EVENT. **FRED COUPLES CREDITED HIS CONTROL OF SHOT SHAPE AND SPECIFICALLY KEEPING THE BALL BELOW THE WIND FOR HIS DOING REALLY WELL.** HE WON THE TOURNAMENT. RECENTLY HE DID EXACTLY THE SAME STRATEGY BY HITTING MOST OF THE NARROW FAIRWAYS WHEN THE RYDER CUP WAS

HELD FOR THE FIRST TIME IN SPAIN.

TO ME, **FRED COUPLES STRIKES THE BALL ENORMOUS DISTANCES AND HE ALSO REALLY KNOWS WHAT TO DO AROUND THE GREENS.** RECENT TOUR STATISTICS SHOW THAT COUPLES IS NEAR THE TOP IN DISTANCE OF DRIVES AND THAT COMBINES NICELY WITH SHOT SHAPE CONTROL.

KEEPING THE BALL BELOW THE WIND MAY BE A CONFUSING TOPIC TO SOME READERS AND GOLFERS. NOT BEING SURE ABOUT THIS SKILL, I WAS LUCKY ENOUGH TO TALK TO A FULL TIME METEOROLOGIST FROM THE NATIONAL WEATHER SERVICE RECENTLY WHO EXPLAINED AND USED WEATHER PATTERNS ON A TELEVISION MONITOR TO ILLUSTRATE THAT **WIND ALOFT CAN BE EXPECTED TO BE OF VARIOUS INTENSITIES AND DIRECTIONS. DIRECTION OF WIND ALOFT CAN ALSO CHANGE DUE TO VARIOUS FACTORS AFFECTING WEATHER.** In fact, the Weather Bureau Service had a sponsors tent at the Tour event to help spectators understand the elements of weather.

Recently, I caddied in a Canadian Tour event at a golf course called Wolf Creek (Ponoka) which each year demands incredible attention from the Tour players. The course is called **the Wolf** and is built in the sand dunes and creek country of the great plains of the Canadian West.

The course literally eats up the unwary or the momentarily unwary Tour player. The wind and black clouds were all about as usual for the late spring, early summer time of the year. The wind and the cloud movement was extremely fickle and even considered dangerous by the Texas, South Carolina and Florida Tour players on this Tour. It appeared that a tornado was headed right our way as we listened for the horn to call us off the course. However, the bad front veered off suddenly and headed away from us at great speed and we managed to finish the day.

My player for the week was a former USA College golfer and a left handed who generally hit the ball low and for medium distances. Jay Williamson and his new wife and Caddy were also in our group. Jay was the PGA Tour Buick event champion and was playing the Canadian Tour and some Nike events as he attempted to get back on the regular Tour. Williamson had a great open and positive attitude and a great way of setting up to the ball which was solid-solid in the wind.

My player also had a reputation for playing well around and on the greens. He was a **grinder in sport and earned everything he gained in golf. He seems to be a strong prospect since he is persistent in golf behavior.**

Instead of practicing on the driving range with most everyone else, **Marty Scoles** from the West Coast prefers preparing on a golf course location. **Naturally, I thought this was a great idea since mind's eye images are found most readily on real golf courses.** We headed to the South Nine (a third nine hole Wolf Creek location) which is considered so difficult that the players voted against using it for the Tour event. It is also longer and that fact is good for practice. There he hit lots of drives and hit into the greens from several angles. Then he hit green side shots but mostly he putted from every angle and distance.

THE TOPIC OF HITTING BELOW THE WIND CAME UP SO HE PRACTICED HITTING FROM VARIOUS ANGLES TO THE TARGET SIDES OF THE GREEN. THIS LOCATION FOR PRACTICE IS SUPERIOR FOR MIND'S EYE PRACTICE, TO BE SURE.

THE DIFFERENCE BETWEEN SHOTS THAT STAY BELOW THE WIND AND HIGH TRAJECTORY SHOTS WAS EVIDENCED BY THE FLUTTERING NATURE OF BALL SHOT SHAPE. HIGHER SHOTS WOULD DEFINITELY FLUTTER OVER OR AROUND THE GREEN AND LOSE CONTROL. LOWER SHOTS WOULD NOT FLUTTER. WIND IS IN LAYERS, AS IT WERE AND IS CONSTANTLY CHANGING IN BAD WEATHER. SO THE SKILL OF SHOT SHAPE CONTROL BECOMES VITAL TO TOUR SUCCESS.

That week our player-caddy team used all the weather clues including tree tops and cloud movement and every other navigation-sailing technique we could remember. The wind was frequently two clubs or more and shot requirements varied a great amount the whole week.

Alas, golf however is a confusing game for the Tour player, let alone the Amateur competitor, all of our special preparation did not pay dividends in good scores. We kept struggling. My player discovered a crack in the shaft of Great Big Bertha late in the week and the officials approved a change in shaft and driver on the 11th tee box. I sprinted to the parking lot to make the change and we got a shot of confidence it seemed. Then Marty Scoles hit the drives noticeably better and in the planned placements but it did little to help us since the Tour event was too far along. **All scores were high in these conditions. Jay Williamson was quite awesome in the weather and got a Top Ten finish. In the next tour event, my player scored effectively. And he continued to do so! Jay Williamson went on to Tour Q qualifying and was in the top 35 after the fifth day that next season.**

GETTING A BAG ON THE CADDY TOUR: Some Comments

Caddies who want to get a bag as often as they can on the Nike Tour or the Canadian Tour, LPGA or Florida Tour, should be aware of the following. Those player development Tours offer excellent levels of play according to media, golf experts and former or current commissioners of those Tours. Both the conditions for work and the chances of working for a developing or a winning player vary a great deal and work is not always available.

There are many reasons. However a long list of Tour event players on the big Tours come from the development Tours. Development Tour players are very International in composition and the experience gained caddying there is good but not the same as the big Tour events.

Caddying can be very time consuming and with practice and travel and course scouting can be a seven day a week job. Often on Sunday, we would drive, say from Palm Desert, California to Sacramento to see the next Tour Course and still

be ready for work bright and alert on Monday morning.

THE SALARY IS UNDERSTOOD BEFORE THE WEEK STARTS AND A VETERAN CADDY USUALLY GETS A SMALL PERCENT OF TOP TEN AND TOP FIVE OR THREE FINISHES. USUALLY THE SALARY CAN BE $350 TO $450 A WEEK IF AGREED ON BEFOREHAND. THE ROOKIE CADDY SHOULD BE WARY, HOWEVER IT IS BEST TO GET ADVICE FROM SOME OF THE MOST EXPERIENCED CADDIES AND THEY ARE THERE AT MOST TOURS. WRITE THE AUTHOR OR SENT AN ELECTRONIC LETTER TO THE E-MAIL ADDRESS (lucasgeoffondallas@shaw.ca) IF YOU HAVE SOME EXPERIENCES AND QUESTIONS ON CADDYING TO SHARE AND ASK ABOUT. THE AUTHOR WILL E-MAIL OR WRITE BACK.

OTHER COMMENTS ON CADDYING

The Tour is also an immensely interesting place to work and to play golf by association. Once in awhile and seemingly at the most unexpected times a Tour player wins something really big and a hard earned bonus can be paid to the caddy. Perhaps the Tour player makes a new course record score or takes a big jump in Tour placement. This happened at the Nabisco Dinah Shore tour event.

All in all it is a hard life and the standards are very high but the companionship and friends gained is worth it all by itself. Not to mention the travel and the good conversation and times back at the motels or in the restaurants. The broader caddy community is unique to be sure and the caddies sometimes help each other through severe times. Almost everyone on Tour is a high quality person and that applies to the players, as well as the caddies, the caddy masters, the local caddies and the Pro shop and club storage staffs.

Naturally the Tour players are highly tuned to success and often can suffer through non success or near success. The caddy has to be tough minded and patient and encouraging just at the right times. Mostly they have to be ready to do the basic job. The caddy, even the long standing ones, can expect abuse from the few Tour players who dish out their wrath at not winning.

BASICALLY, I AGREE WITH THE WELL AND OFTEN STATED IDEA THAT THE TOUR PLAYER TAKES ALL THE CREDIT WHEN THE PLAYER WINS AND THE CADDY COMES IN FOR SOME EXTRA AND SEVERE CRITICISM WHEN THE PLAYER DOES BADLY.

IT IS EASY ENOUGH TO GET FIRED ON TOUR AS MANY CADDIES CAN RELATE TO, EVEN IF THE TOUR PLAYER IS MERELY SAVING MONEY BY HIRING A LOCAL CADDY FOR A DAY OR TWO AND HAS NO LEGITIMATE REASON FOR FIRING YOU. IT IS THE NATURE OF THE GAME. THERE IS NO UNION AND THE PGA OFFICE WILL ONLY CASH CHEQUES FOR YOU, NOT LISTEN TO ANY GRIEVANCES OF ANY SORT.

Even before taking on a job, other caddies can inform you of your chances of getting fired by a particular player. Some players have a big reputation in this regard. However, this circumstance only applies to the struggling Tour player or the so called B player, that is a player who usually has to re qualify each Tour season.

Remember, you have to know exactly what you are doing out on Tour as a job, the distances and the winds, the procedures, the rules, when and where to be with the bag, when to set it down and the like, and the trust level you have with the player. Sometimes the spectators are a special problem for the Caddy if a camera clicker is insistent and too close by.

MANY CADDIES REALIZE JUST WHAT A UNIQUE CAREER CADDYING IS. IT IS A CAREER AND A VERY SERIOUS ONE AT THAT. CADDIES HAVE COMMITTEES AND ARE MAKING STRIDES WITH SPONSORS. THERE IS A GREAT DEAL OF LEARNING AND DADS SHOULD NOT FORCE A 12 YEAR OLD TO TRY TO GET A BAG ON TOUR (THE 12-15 YEAR OLDS SHOULD BE CADDYING AT A PRIVATE CLUB OR A SMALLER TOURNAMENT), WHICH IS, AS **LEE TREVINO SAYS,** A WONDERFUL PLACE TO LEARN A LOT AND STAY OUT OF TROUBLE.

IN CADDYING, THERE IS AN INCREDIBLE AMOUNT OF CIRCUMSTANCE WERE A TRUST RELATIONSHIP CAN START TO FORMULATE. THAT IS WHY MANY FORMER COLLEGE PLAYERS LIKE LINDA RANKIN AND OTHERS INITIATE CADDY PROGRAMS AND TOUR PLAYERS LIKE LEE TREVINO, CHI CHI RODRIQUES, CHICK EVANS, WALTER HAGEN, GENE SARAZEN, TONY LEMA AND OF COURSE, BEN HOGAN, AND OTHERS ADVOCATE CADDYING FOR YOUTH. THEY ARE FORMER CADDIES THEMSELVES. **THEY POINT OUT YOUTH CADDIES ARE BETTER OFF IN A GOLF LOCATION AND WITH INFLUENCES THAT A COUNTRY CLUB CAN PROVIDE.**

When I caddied at Edmonton Mayfair between age 12 and 16, I learned about caddying and caddied for almost every successful businessman and every American oil and gas man that lived there. Who ever could forget all that a good scratch or 2 handicapper can teach you. Or the famous Texas, Oklahoma or Mississippi football Professionals who also were scratch golfers (like Rolland Prather, Jackie Parker, Frankie Anderson and the future coach of the Minnesota Vikings, Neil Armstong, who all took caddies). Maybe that is why I later became a high school and junior football head coach. And I got such a basic grounding in golf and golfing fundamentals.

 THE EDDIE THOMASES, THE SNAP LAWSONS, THE DAVIE JONES, THE LLOYD LOVESETHS, THE LLOYD GREERS, THE LAURIE SCOTTS, THE DON SPRAGUES AND YES, EVEN THE BILL SAFFOLDS (WHO COULDN'T PLAY BUT SURE KNEW HIS WAY AROUND THE MONEY GAMES AND APPARENTLY, THE OIL PATCH) ARE THE ONES WHOSE **SPIRIT FOR LIFE AND FOR GOLF** WAS AND IS INSATIABLE. EVERY GOLFER IN THOSE DAYS HAD A HUGE GOLF BAG TO GO WITH THEIR GOOD GAME AND EFFECTIVE SELF CONTROL AND SELF DISCIPLINE. EDMONTON MAYFAIR AND EDMONTON WINDERMERE ARE TWO GREAT GOLFING LAYOUTS.

ALSO, CADDYING SURELY IS IDEAL FOR A YOUTH BADLY IN NEED OF STRUCTURE AND DIRECTION IN LIFE. Later my son, **James**, would get the same direction and structure in his life by being a quarterback in a highly organized school football program, that just happened to be head coached by an American CFL head coaches son, Todd Williams, who would later go to a US College football job.

LEE TREVINO SAYS SUCH ADULT DIRECTION FOR A YOUNG CADDY LEARNER IS EVEN MORE NECESSARY IN TODAY'S SOCIETY. LIKE MANY OTHERS AND MANY FORMER COLLEGE PLAYERS IN THE USA AND IN EUROPE, I, MYSELF, WANT TO SEE CADDYING FOR YOUTH REESTABLISHED IN CONJUNCTION WITH GOOD JUNIOR GOLF PROGRAMS AT EACH GOLF CLUB. TRY JUNIOR GOLF COORDINATION AT YOUR CLUB IF YOU WANT A GOOD EXPERIENCE AND TRY TO HAVE CADDYING IN THAT PROGRAM AS WELL.

IN LATER YEARS, IT WAS VERY EASY TO REESTABLISH THE TRUST SUCH A MAN PUT IN YOU THE CADDY. SURELY IT HELPS IN CONTACTING SUCH PEOPLE. THE PGA TRAINED PROFESSIONALS TAUGHT US A GREAT DEAL ABOUT CADDYING AND ABOUT TEACHING LESSONS AND RULES AND WE LATER WORKED OUR WAY UP TO CLUB CLEANERS AND SHOP HELP.

Where else would I have got to carry the golf bag of **Joe Louis, the famous USA boxer,** if I was not a caddy. He came to Edmonton Mayfair in 1954 when I was age 14 and the Caddy Master came to the back of the Caddy shack, where we were all playing a game of **peggy** (a game like cricket) in the forest field we had worn out. **He looked at all the caddies and then he pointed at me and told me to take the bag of the guest who would tee off shortly.**

Joe Louis, nearing the end of his illustrious boxing career shot a fine 80 at tough Mayfair and I carried his big bag all the way. He gave me a good fee for those days and the balls he used and naturally, it was an unforgettable experience, since he talked to me off by ourselves once in a while. In the Pro Ams on Wednesday, on Tour, some of the Amateurs, who are Celebrities of one sort or another, take caddies so the experience of extra caddying is sometimes still available.

I REMEMBER CADDYING IN A CELEBRITY GROUP WHEN MICHELLE MCGANN WAS OUR TOUR PLAYER. ACTUALLY, IT WAS A NICE GROUP OF BANKERS AND BOARD MEMBERS. **I LEARNED THAT MICHELLE WASN'T JUST THE HAT LADY AT ALL AND STARTED TO SEE WHY SHE IS THE BEST SPONSOR SELECTION ON THE LPGA TOUR.** SHE IS TRULY A NATURAL PERSON AND IS A BIG HITTER AND GOOD AROUND THE GREENS. **NOW I KNOW WHY SHE HAS BECOME A WINNER ON TOUR, WHEN SHE WAS ONCE A NICE PERSON WHO WONDERED WHEN SHE WOULD WIN.** THAT WAS A GOOD FIVE HOUR EXPERIENCE.

ONCE I CADDIED FOR THE ANHEUSER BUSCH GROUP FOR SENIOR EXECUTIVE VP **CAROL KELLEHER** AND HAD A GREAT TIME AND LOTS OF LAUGHS WITH HER, HER

GROUP AND ONE OF THE MOST PERSISTENT AND PESKY TOUR PROS AROUND AND LEARNED A FEW NEW THINGS. CAROL WAS GREAT AND KNEW HOW TO SUBLY REMIND OUR TOUR PLAYER THAT SHE SHOULD BE HELPING HER GROUP ON THE GREENS AND NOT TO LET HER MIND WANDER OFF.

WITHIN THAT LPGA TOUR SEASON, CAROL APPARENTLY GOT AN OFFER TO TAKE ON AN **EXECUTIVE POSITION AT THE LPGA TOUR** OFFICE. I READ IN THE PAPER THAT SHE DID ACCEPT THE JOB AND I FOR ONE THINK THE LPGA WILL BENEFIT WITH CAROL KELLEHER ON THE JOB.

MAKING CONNECTIONS IS ALWAYS A VERY IMPORTANT PART OF LIFE IN MANY PEOPLES OPINION AND THAT IS ONE OF THE ASPECTS OF CADDYING THAT IS SO FINE.

SOME CADDIES ARE IMPROVING THE LOT OF OTHER CADDIES BUT BASICALLY YOU HAVE GOT TO LOOK OUT FOR YOURSELF ON TOUR. **THERE ARE CADDIES THAT ARE MAKING PROGRESS WITH SPONSORS AND BEING PARTIALLY SPONSORED AND SOME WORK FOR CAREER BENEFITS.** MAYBE IT IS BEST TO SAY, HOWEVER, THERE IS A LONG, LONG WAY AHEAD FOR CADDY WELFARE TO IMPROVE ON. THERE ARE MANY CADDIES WITH MORE THAN 10 YEARS EXPERIENCE ON TOUR AND SOME WITH OVER 20 YEARS AND SOME OF THEM ARE VITAL LEADERS AND ROLE MODELS AMONG CADDIES. THERE ARE SEVERAL WOMEN CADDIES, SOME SENIOR AGED CADDIES AND EVEN SOME LIFE PARTNER CADDIES WHO BOTH WORK ON TOUR. LOTS OF PLAYERS' RELATIVES AND FAMILY ALSO WORK ON TOUR.

****

SUCCEED VERSUS GOLF COURSE DESIGN

A great hole for an illustration of playing against certain elements of course design is the 15th hole at Augusta, scene of the US Masters. In fact the whole last corner of the golf course in illustrative it is said. That corner is called "ahmen corner" which the dictionary says means either an exclamation used to attract attention or a word used after a prayer to express agreement. Surely it is both.

Playing well near the end of the game is immensely important it seems. Holes 15, 16, 17, and 18 often do result in a change in how a player finishes a Tour event. The rank within a Tour event changes round by round. Often it changes drastically and almost any Tour event illustrates this drama.

CRAIG STADLER WON THE 1982 MASTERS AND LATER HE WROTE AN ARTICLE ON STRATEGY FOR GOLF MAGAZINE. HE SAID 15 WAS THE LAST REAL BIRDIE HOLE AND ADDED THAT ON THE 15TH BOX HE WAS SURE HIS 2 STROKE LEAD OVER **DAN POHL** COULD BE INCREASED TO 3 OR EVEN 4 SHOTS. BUT THAT DIDN'T HAPPEN!

ACCORDING TO **CRAIG STADLER,** PLAYERS SEE THEMSELVES AS PLAYING THE 15TH AT AUGUSTA VERY BOLDLY. **THEIR SUBCONSCIOUS**

AND THEIR CONSCIOUS MINDS TEND TO AGREE AND THEY VISUALIZE A MIND'S EYE OF BOLD PLAY FOR THE HOLE. REMEMBERING THAT OUR SUBCONSCIOUS MIND IS NOT EVALUATIVE, WE CAN SEE WHY THIS COULD HAPPEN. NORMALLY WITH A TWO SHOT LEAD STRATEGY, WOULD NOT CALL FOR BOLD PLAY AT 15TH SINCE 16 - 18 HOLES ARE ALL THREE TOUGH HOLES. THOSE HOLES WILL BE REWARDED BY GOOD SOLID GOLF, NOT BOLD GOLF.

SEVE BALLESTEROS WAS BOLD AT 15 IN 1986 AND HIT THE WATER AND EVENTUALLY LOST THE MASTERS. THAT PAR 5 TRIANGULATED GREEN 15TH THEN **HELPED JACK NICKLAUS NAIL DOWN A RECORD SIXTH MASTERS,** IT WAS SAID.

IN CRAIG STADLERS MASTERS WIN, HE MANAGED A PAR AT 15 EVEN THOUGH IT FELT LIKE LOSING A STROKE HE SAID. OF COURSE, IN RETROSPECT, WE SEE WHY STADLER AND BALLESTEROS AND OTHER MASTERS' PLAYERS COULD BE TOO BOLD AT 15 OR AT KEY FINISHING HOLES SINCE THEY SEE OPPORTUNITY TO NAIL DOWN VICTORY.

FINDING A WAY TO WIN

THE PLAY OF **JUSTIN LEONARD, DAVID DUVAL, STUART APPLEBY AND PHIL MICKELSON** SUGGESTS **A NEW PATTERN OF FINDING A WAY TO WIN.** IT SEEMS THEY **ALTERNATE CONSERVATIVE PLAY WITH BOLD PLAY** AND LOOK FOR KEY OPPORTUNITIES TO PLAY AND SCORE WELL.

THE ALTERNATING OF BOLD PLAY WITH REGULAR PLAY IS NOT SUCH A CLEAR PATTERN IN THE LPGA AMONG WOMEN PLAYERS WHERE FEARLESS PLAY GIVES WAY TO CONSISTENT AND ACCURATE PLAY WITH OMINOUSLY GOOD PUTTING.

Take what the course will offer you and that which the subconscious accepts. Base it on a clear conscious decision. Nailing down victory could be a mythical notion in sport performance, perhaps it does not exist, but finding a way to win in a tight finish situation in a team sport and in individual sport is a revered skill among players and teams, and even spectators and the media and certainly the coaches.

When a player is in a zone of winning play, the mind is clearly making acceptable decisions while aiming and targeting becomes peripheral it seems, if only briefly.

TIGER WOODS METHOD OF FINDING A WAY TO WIN IS SOMEWHAT DIFFERENT. IT APPEARS THAT HE EITHER DOMINATES OR FALLS OFF THE PACE AND MAY HAVE TROUBLE COMING BACK INTO CONTENTION. ACCORDINGLY. LEE TREVINO STATED THAT TIGER WOODS PLAY IS OFTEN SUPERIOR BUT HIS DEALING WITH BADLY POSITIONED FIRST SHOTS OR SECOND SHOTS IS SUBJECT TO FURTHER LEARNING BY THE YOUNG PLAYER. I THINK AS AUTHOR THAT WOODS PLAY STYLE WILL CHANGE TO A MORE SYSTEMATIC PLAY STYLE REFERRED TO ABOVE FOR LEONARD, DUVAL, APPLEBY AND MICKELSON.

SOON ENOUGH, HE WILL LEARN TO COME BACK TO LEAD LATER IN

A TOUR EVENT I WOULD EXPECT.

ACCORDING TO **BOB HARIG,** A ST. PETERSBURG TIMES STAFF WRITER, WOODS HAD PROMISED TO LEARN FROM MISTAKES OF HIS RENOWNED INITIAL GOLF YEAR. **TIGER** HAS SAID HE EXPECTS MORE OF HIMSELF AND THAT HIS **GOALS** ARE "PRETTY MUCH UP IN THE **STRATOSPHERE.** I LIKE TO PUSH THE ENVELOPE, TO GO WHERE NOBODY HAS GONE BEFORE".

WITH HIS GOAL OF PLAYING LESS EVENTS, HE MAY PROVE THAT HE CAN PLAY EVEN MORE EFFECTIVELY IN THE FUTURE. IS IT POSSIBLE THAT HE CAN SURPASS SUCH GOLF FEATS AS WINNING FOUR EVENTS, INCLUDING A MAJOR AND BEING THE 1ST EVER PLAYER TO SURPASS $2 MILLION IN TOUR EARNINGS?

IT IS NOW BEING SAID THAT THE **UNDER AGE 30 CROWD OF TOUR PLAYERS IN THE PGA CAN FULLY CONQUER BOTH MENTAL AND PHYSICAL DEMANDS OF TOUR WINNING GOLF.** THAT CROWD INCLUDES ERNIE ELS, ALREADY A TWO TIME US OPEN WINNER AND JUSTIN LEONARD, THE BRITISH OPEN CHAMPION, AND PHIL MICKELSON, STEWART CINK, PAUL STANKOWSKI AND STUART APPLEBY AND OTHERS.

MICKELSON APPEARS TO BE IN CLASS BY HIMSELF WITH 11 PGA WINS AND DAVIS LOVE III IS A WINNER OF A MAJOR.

IT IS EQUALLY OBVIOUS THAT THE **LPGA** HAS A NEW CROWD OF UNDER 30 PLAYERS THAT HAVE MENTAL AND PHYSICAL GOLF WINNING SKILLS. **ANNIKA SORENSTAM** AT AGE 27 HAD WON TWO PLAYER OF THE YEARS IN SUCCESSION AND HAD 6 TOUR WINS. ALONG WITH **KARRIE WEBB** WHO HAD 3 WINS IN ONE YEAR AND HAS LOWERED THE SCORING AVERAGE ON THE LPGA TOUR AND WON THE VARE TROPHY OF DOING SO.

THE YOUNG LPGA WINNERS AND RUNNER UPS IN MAJORS ALSO INCLUDES **LORENA OCHOA, PAULA CREAMER, CRISTIE KERR,** AND NEW SENSATIONS, **MARISA BAENA, NATALIE GULBIS, AND JEON LANG AND OTHERS.**

FINDING A WAY TO WIN: A TORTURE TEST OF THE UNPREPARED GOLF PSYCHE.

The Masters, The British Open, US Open, European Open and other National Opens are considered to be annual torture tests of the unprepared psyche, according to **Cam Cole, a modern day sports writer.** He says The Open, writing from **Troon, Scotland,** is all about how to handle the elements of weather and psychology.

However, while sometimes the golf course does overwhelm the golfer, sometimes a player's performance threatens to overcome the reputation of the golf course. That happened when **John Daly** made some of the holes vulnerable on the Olde Course at St. Andrews, Scotland in his memorable Open

victory when **Antonio Rocco** mishit and flubbed a finishing shot on the 18th hole and then survived by holing out in dramatic fashion to go to a playoff with Daly.

SOON AFTER SUCH A PERFORMANCE, THE COURSE DESIGN IS CHANGED IN SUBTLE AND NOT SO SUBTLE WAYS. PERHAPS THE TEE BOXES ARE LENGTHENED AND EVEN CHANGED, THE ROUGH IS GROWN UPWARDS A FEW INCHES ON AN ALREADY NARROW FAIRWAY, OR A PAR 5 IS CHANGED TO A PAR 4.

DURING A RECENT BRITISH OPEN, THE COURSE OF PLAY, ROYAL TROON LINKS, OUTSIDE OF GLASGOW, WAS REDUCED TO A PAR 71 FOR THE OPEN. THIS MOVE, DEEMED REASONABLE BY THE OPEN COMMITTEE AND THE LOCAL TROON BOARD WAS NOT TOO PROUD A ONE TO MAKE, ACCORDING TO THE ON THE SCENE REPORT BY CAM COLE.

AIMING AND TARGETING AND THE SPECTATORS

As aiming and targeting skills continue to become more and more prominent among golf skill so does the golfing publics awareness of the beauties and baffles in the challenge to play well on these courses. A course redesign by an architect group may cause a renowned golf course to be continued to be held in awe by the golfing public.

Even magazines such as automobile travel club journals and other travel magazines feature golf travel articles which portray golf course design. As Ian Cruickshank wrote in AMA Travel Getaways, "all across the Nation, golfers are getting twitchy anticipating that premier design golf course".

A COURSE LOCATED ON HAWAII'S BEAUTIFUL KOHALA COAST, A NICKLAUS GROUP DESIGN CALLED **HUALALAI,** IS SAID TO BE FRAMED BY THE PACIFIC OCEAN AND IS ALL ABOUT **VISUAL CONTRAST,** WITH TUFTS OF GREEN GRASS SPEARING THROUGH BLACK LAVA ROCK.

ON HUALALAI, ONE OF THE PAR 3'S IS DESCRIBED AS A SLIVER OF GREEN AWASH IN A MIX OF SAND, ROCK AND WATER. ONE CAN SPOT DOLPHINS AND OTHER WHALES SUCH AS HUMPBACKS PLAYING IN THE OCEAN. **AIMING SKILL MUST HOWEVER STILL PREVAIL EVEN OR ESPECIALLY ON SUCH A DESIGNER COURSE.**

GOLF COURSE DESIGN AND GOLF SKILL

FOR A DESIGN GOLF EXPERIENCE, ONE CAN PLAY THE FLORIDA DISNEY WORLD MAGNOLIA, PALM AND LAKE BUENA VISTA COURSES WHERE 99 HOLES AWAIT THE GOLFER EVEN AT A NOT TOO RIDICULOUS COST OF PLAY.

DESIGN ICONS TOM FAZIO AND PETER DYE LAID OUT THE BEST OF THESE GOLF COURSES, WHICH WIND THROUGH WETLANDS, DENSE FORESTS AND MOSS HAMMOCKS AND ARE HOME TO DEER, WILD TURKEYS AND HIGH NESTING OSPREYS.

COURSE FAVORITES

A PETE DYE COURSE AT MISSION HILLS (NABISCO DINAH SHORE) IN PALM DESERT, WAS MY RECENT FAVORITE ALONG WITH A TARGET COURSE ON THE OCEANGRASS AND OCEANSIDE SAND HILLS NEAR KITTY HAWK, NORTH CAROLINA CALLED NAGS HEAD. IN THESE SAND HILLS, WHERE WILBUR AND ORVILLE WRIGHT TOOK MOST OF THEIR SUCCESSFUL INAUGURAL AIRPLANE FLIGHTS.

COURSE TYPES AND GOLF SKILL

THE **BOULDER COURSES** IN THE VALLEY OF THE SUN IN CAREFREE, ARIZONA, THE HIGH SONORAN DESERT ALSO ARE BEING CALLED **TARGET COURSES**  BECAUSE THE PLAYER IS REQUIRED TO STRIKE PURE SHOTS FROM ONE STRETCH OF GRASS TO ANOTHER AND FROM ONE TO ANOTHER TARGET. **THERE IS LITTLE CREATIVE GOLF PLAYED ON SUCH A COURSE.** DESIGN IS REALLY QUITE MODEST ON COURSES SUCH AS THESE IT HAS BEEN SAID.

IN SOME LOCATIONS, THE PLAYER GETS THREE VERY DIFFERENT STYLES OF COURSE DESIGN AT ONE LOCATION, SUCH AS A **DUNES COURSE ON A DESERT LOCATION, A LAKES AND WATER HAZARD** STYLE COURSE AND AN **ARROYO TYPES COURSE** WINDING THROUGH DRIED OUT RIVERBEDS AND FLOOD PLAIN. HUGE SAGUARO CACTUS DOT MANY ARIZONA LANDSCAPES. THEY ARE OFTEN SAID TO APPEAR HUMAN LOOKING DUE TO A BRANCH SYSTEM OF GROWTH AND ARE PROTECTED BY LAW AND AVOIDED BY GOLFERS.

TIGER WOODS PLAYED THE AFOREMENTIONED FLORIDA LANDMARK COURSES REFERRED TO ABOVE AND WON AT WALT DISNEY WORLD IN THE OLDSMOBILE CLASSIC. **THEY SAY TIGER WILL ATTEMPT TO KEEP UP TO JACK NICKLAUS' RECORD OF THREE IN A ROW CLASSIC WINS WHEN THAT EVENT IS PLAYED AGAIN. IT IS ALSO SAID THAT THE DISNEY COURSES ARE FAVORITES AMONG TOUR PLAYERS BECAUSE THE GREENS REWARD FAIRLY AND CONSISTENTLY.** THE TOUR PLAYERS LIKE THEM.

DISNEY WORLD ALSO OFFERS FINE INSTRUCTIONAL PROGRAMS THAT ARE SENT ALONG WITH YOU ON VIDEOTAPE WITH A BAG TAG SERVING AS A SKILLS REMINDER. IT IS EFFECTIVE TO USE A LESSON VIDEOTAPE SOME YEARS LATER. SOME BIG SWING CHANGE SHOULD NOT BE FORGOTTEN BUT SHOULD BE REVIEWED AND RETAINED IN YOUR MIND'S EYE IMAGE SYSTEM. RECENTLY, I FOUND MY DISNEY LESSON VIDEOTAPE FROM EIGHT YEARS AGO TO BE USEFUL TO **REFRESH KEY MIND'S EYE IMAGES.**

COURSE DESIGN CONTINUES TO STRESS WELL SELECTED MIND'S EYE IMAGES OF ACCURACY. FOR EXAMPLE, THE NICKLAUS NORTH COURSE AT WHISTLER VILLAGE (OUTSIDE VANCOUVER, BC) MAY NOT BE AS PUNISHING AS SOME OF THE 150 EARLIER NICKLAUS DESIGNS, BUT

THE MANAGER THERE MENTIONS THAT EACH HOLE REQUIRES ACCURACY AND THINKING THROUGH OF EACH SHOT. **VISUAL IMAGE ACCURACY IS IMPORTANT AT THIS COURSE, THE GOLF COURSE WITH NICKLAUS NAME IN ITS OFFICIAL COURSE TITLE. COURSES SUCH AS THE ONE AT WHISTLER OFFERS THE GOLFER A CREATIVE AND OFTEN, A MIND'S EYE CHALLENGE.**

SWEET WINS BY FINDING A WAY TO WIN

Raymond Floyd and his son Ray Jr., have a string of sweet wins that will forever be unique in golf. Ray Floyd has used visualization in golf and mind's eye images to win previously on Tour and aiming is an obvious focus of his golf play. Recently the Floyds team were the only Champions of the father/son Tour Challenge at Vero Beach in Florida. **That was because after their repeat win they had won the event three times successively since in inception.**

Floyd has won four majors and has 35 Tour wins, yet jokes that he has had to accomplish about 15 comebacks in his golf career. It is his swing itself that we see him applying imagery repeatability to it seems.

While it is unusual for a Tour player to shoot below 60 when excellent Father and Son golfers combine in a Best Ball, they can sometimes do so. Both a sweet win and finding a way to win was accomplished by the Floyds in scoring 62 followed by 58 at Vero Beach.

More recently, there were three 58's and several 59's in the two Tour Pro's Best Ball at the M L Shootout at Naples, Florida.

CONSISTENCY AND THE WAY TO FIND TO WIN

CONSISTENCY SEEMS TO BE ONE KEY TO SWEET WINS OR UNEXPECTED WINS ON TOUR. WHEN **NICK PRICE** WON AT SUN CITY, SOUTH AFRICA IN THE MILLION DOLLAR CHALLENGE, THE ZIMBABWE GOLFER  SCORED 71 FOLLOWED BY **THREE STRAIGHT ROUNDS OF 68, 68, 68.**

Nick Price uses a mind's eye image and kinesthetic feel of level shoulders in his putting to create just the correct impact angle and feel with his putter and that gives him the consistency he seeks and we see him using.

That level shoulder idea for putting seems to be an easy one to work with when you try it out on the golf course or the putting green. Level shoulders in putting can be easily observed to give you feedback.

AIMING IN PUTTING EQUALS BIRDIES ON TOUR AND UNLESS A TOUR PLAYER STARTS GETTING BIRDIES, THEY MAY NOT GAIN MOMENTUM IN A ROUND OF GOLF. NICK PRICE WORKS VERY HARD ON THAT IDEA. MANY TOUR PLAYERS SHOULD. SOME TOUR PLAYERS HAVE TOLD ME THAT BIRDIES WILL COME IF A TOUR PLAYER IS PATIENT, YET TOUR STATISTICS DO NOT SUPPORT THAT IDEA.

FINDING A WAY TO WIN AT THE JC PENNEY CLASSIC

According to the Tampa Times Newspaper, the Tour win recorded at the JC Penney Team event Classic at Tarpon Springs was sweet indeed for the team of Amy Fruhwith and Clarence Rose, especially for Amy. After never winning on the LPGA Tour for five seasons, she gained a 3rd place finish at the Nabisco Dinah Shore and seven top 10 finishes. The team of Rose and Fruhwith won $188,000 each. This added nicely to Amy's previous winnings of $200,000.

Clarence Rose made a lot of great putts and went at the pins frequently in the event. Perhaps finding a way to win can be related to Amy's post Sunday interview comments: **"I LEARNED THAT I REALLY NEED TO WORK ON MY PUTTING AND CLARENCE MADE A LOT OF GREAT, GREAT PUTTS. SHE ALSO SAID... FOR ME IT WAS GREAT TO WATCH THE GUYS PLAY, I THINK THEY HAVE A DIFFERENT GAME, TO LEARN SOME OF THEIR TOUGHNESS, THEY HAVE NO FEAR, THEY JUST GO FOR THE PINS AND IT IS GOOD TO SEE THAT".**

Ways to win by systematic controlled play and consistency seems to have a pattern to it, at least a tendency seems to be emerging I believe. No always but usually aiming well in putting seems to emerge combined with a great deal of patience but not a patience with few if any birdies or eagles at all in a round of Tour golf.

One exception seems to be a Tour round with 14 or more pars. Such scores as are put up frequently by Nick Faldo, Annika Sorenstam, Liselotte Neuman, Colin Montgomery and other steady Tour players.

Amateurs often report hitting a lot of greens in a round but often do not report low scores despite this.

A hint may be added to further explain this pattern of finding a way to win. Dan Forsman from the Tour explained that the nature of the game is that one day you may hit one or two crisp irons in a round (meaning next to the Pin) and those crisply aimed hits build a confidence and then that round gets going better.

IT SEEMS AS IF A TOUR PLAYER OR A TOUR TEAM STARTS THE FINAL DAYS PLAY IN THE LEAD, THEN IT APPEARS THAT TO GET THE WIN, THEY HAVE TO GET THAT ROUND GOING WITH SOME PIN KNOCKING IRONS OR GREAT PUTTING.

It seems that pattern is not unusual although the leader or leaders often do not win. Some tour players do not like to be in the lead, preferring to emerge with the lead on the final day, yet some do thrive when in the lead but the day of the big lead on the PGA Tour at least seems long in the past. Perhaps the mind's eye set of image goals is very important here in this situation for finding a way to win.

WAYS TO WIN AND THE PATTERN LIKELY

@CRISP HITS EARLY
@MAKE SOME KEY PUTTS
@AVOID THE UNUSUAL
@BUILD CONFIDENCE
@PATIENCE BUT NOT WAITING
@PRACTICE AFTER A LOW ROUND OR A HIGH ROUND
@USE KINESTHETIC AND MIND'S EYE PICTURES
@EXTRA WORK ON PUTTING
@READ PUTTS VERY WELL

@SEE A MIND'S EYE OF A SCORE BELOW 59*

In sport players should always see a mind's eye of scoring well. For example, hockey players visualize 4 or more goals in each game and Tour golfers can visualize a score of 59. The most important idea in this book is that your mind's eye pictures are believable, that is, the subconscious is not rational. Besides that Tour players can shoot 59's or come close to it and still believe in consistency. Fully six+Tour players have recorded a score of 60 and either three or four 59's have been recorded. In addition, with the advent of more and more two player or team events, we have seen several more scores that are in the 58-60 range. Wow, eh!

(**Just about the time that this book went to printers, another 59 (and 2 more 60's) had been recorded. **Notah Begay** from the Mid Plains USA, then Stanford, then the Canadian & Nike Tour did the 59. A phenomenal accomplishment to be sure! Notah is one of those friendly Tour players, but most notable is his **hard work ethic** and his use of the **video to create analysis and mind's eye experience.** So he will play more such satisfaction. Often when others leave the practice tee, Notah will remain with his two video camera set up and I sometimes stayed out to watch his practice style and chat with him. Eventually, he may join Tiger on the big Tour as Notah's scores on the Nike Tour are improving some weeks.) By now, Notah Begay has left the NIKE/Nationwide and Canuck Tour and plays with the Big Boys PGA Tour.

WAYS TO WIN BY SYSTEMATIC CONTROLLED PLAY II

When **Dan Forsman** played the recent JC Penney team event with **Catriona Matthew**, they started off the final round tied with the team of **Meg Mallon and Steve Pate.**

Forsman hit a crisp, pin knocking shot on 17 when his great 3 iron from 222 yards stopped just 5' behind the hole.

Later Amy Fruhwith hit an equally crisp shot from 175 yards to 5' from the hole. The final day was an alternate hit so as it turned out Clarence Rose converted Amy's shot but Forsman and Matthew didn't match that putt on the 17th hole when they had a chance to pull into a tie in the JC Penney event.

Stewart Cink and Emilee Klein came from back in the field by birdieing 3 of 4 of the first four holes to perhaps illustrate getting on a roll, a roll of 'crisp pin-

knocking-make-putt-build-CONFIDENCE' in a Tour event. They shot the best score of the final day, a 65, a seven birdie one bogie round of golf.

Interestingly, we had watched **Klein and Cink** practice extra hard after the Saturday's third round was complete. Cink is enormous physically and is another Tour player who hits the ball out of sight it seems. Later I found out that Cink was rookie of the year on the PGA Tour. **Many times I have seen extra practice on Saturday lead to Sunday success on the Tour. Extra practice any day is not unusual on Tour however.**

NICK PRICE: PUT IT ALL TOGETHER IN WAYS TO WIN

After a recent Million Dollar Challenge, Nick Price is said to have lived out **every golfers dream.** He sunk a 12' putt to keep the win after having pulled past the leader, **Phil Mickelson.** He also held off final birdie putts on 18 by **Ernie Els and by Davis Love III.**

Sometimes the leader appears to struggle in Tour events where a great amount rides on making crucial putts. The *Australian Golf Digest* magazine Editor thinks so highly of Nick Price's golf that the magazine printed Price's ideas on placing fundamentals together especially the fundamentals that can be very worthwhile out on the golf course.

The Australian magazine offered a four part *BONUS BOOKLET* that came with the monthly Golf Digest, Price's was the final booklet. The third one was on **Aim and Alignment by Hank Johnson.** They say that these Booklets are golf cart sized ("buggy sized") guides to Better Golf. The booklet on Grip by **Peter Kostis** was useful review information I had found.

Aiming is more and more being considered a basic by golf writers and perhaps this is only because Tour players seem to be capable of knocking down pins with their shots more and more frequently. All golfers place aiming as a very revered skill it seems.

DARTS & GOLF BALLS GOING EXACTLY INTO THE HOLE

The golf illustration graphic used in this book which shows the ball going exactly into the hole and knocking down the pin may be a more realistic one than at first appearance. Why should not golf be thought of as dart playing and dart board gaming when it is an idea our golf subconscious can accept, even repeatedly. *LATELY, I HAVE FALLEN INTO ADMIRING AND BUYING AND USING DART BOARDS AND DART SHOOTING AND AM BACK PLAYING BILLIARDS.* Surprisingly, darts and billiards help aiming in golf I am finding.

A SUMMARY: SHOOTING 59's IN GOLF

In the summary chart above titled **WAYS TO WIN AND THE PATTERN LIKELY,** the idea that seeing a mind's eye picture of scoring 59 or less is part of the pattern.

By all means accept this notion and see a mind's eye image of a 59 even as an amateur, especially once you really know how to hold a club, to stand to the ball, to take dead aim, and to put the key golf movements together.

It is my understanding that the Swedish golf coaching staff holds that a scoring goal of 59 in not unreasonable for their developing national team players, who often go on a USA universities and colleges for further golf scoring and playing honing of playing skills.

When **Annika Sorenstam** tried to be a tennis player, she probably had clear goals for that sport. When this Swedish born Tour leader is seen going back to the practice tee, along with a set of Laser binoculars for more target practice even after a sensational appearing round of golf, then it seems to me a **very sensible mind's eye picture** to see 59's on the scoreboard. Even if both 59's and 60's are very rare scores for a golf game on a regular golf course, at the present time.

Many players appear to have elevated golf to a further level of scoring objectives for the game.

Just as shooting a 69 is a reasonable mind's eye visualization for a single digit amateur golfer, a 59 is a proper goal for a Tour player. It is also a proper goal to hold a 79, 89, or 99 (or 109) in front of the mind's eye "camera" of your golf mind.

A realized dream can be that 69 that you once shot and that once came rather easily to you. Those same dreams can be really through visualization in golf. When Colin Montgomery and other great modern Tour players come in with an eagle and seven birdies, they are not far off 60 and 59.

Perhaps the time for this way of thinking about golf scoring has arrived. Mind's eye pictures can convey important advice to us in golf. YES INDEED!! AND PERHAPS THE NEXT REAL CHALLENGE IN GOLF TOO...WHICH MAY BE TO HARNESS ENDURANCE IN MIND'S EYE AND MENTAL GOLF. SO FAR, THIS PART OF GOLF LIES UNDEVELOPED.

ANOTHER SUMMARY: QUALIFYING TIME AGAIN, ONE TOUR TEST

When Scott Verplank had to return to PGA qualifying to attempt to earn a PGA Tour card, he seemed to have an incredibly clear plan, perhaps a visualized one, for playing all six rounds in December in Florida. This Tour Test is the time in which all parts of a Tour players **preparation must flow together and the mental element is of primary importance.**

Playing at the location for the Tour Q school in Grenelefe Resort in Haines City, Florida, he shot 66, 64, 67 and then continued on with three more solid rounds only one of which was even a 70 or 71. That is some consistent performance of Scott Verplank.

Coming back to the Tour with great aiming golf also was **Blaine McCallister** of Texas. He was the player who had a lot of Tour success after having a memorable putting battle with another Tour player, **Richard Zokol,** in the Canadian Amateur. McCallister shot 413 at Tour Q school and

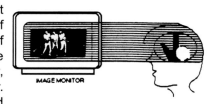

IMAGE MONITOR

Stephen Ames and Lee Porter had fine 416's. Zokol thrilled his fans with some great golf at the GVO, the **GREATER VANCOUVER OPEN,** a Tour regular event these days. As if by some futuristic plan, **Zokol and McCallister** would be again in another big event. **The Texas Open as if to commemorate the remarkable Canadian Amateur battle of past years.**

All told 35 players and ties got Tour cards for the regular mens PGA Tour. The last score in was 423 which is an average score of 70.5 for the six rounds.

This is consistency indeed, especially versus the incredibly small difference in the next 70 qualifiers. These scores were between 424 and 431 for six rounds a stroke average of 71.83 on the same Grenelefe course. Par is 432.

All 70 players got Nike Tour cards full time and for consistency it seems that shooting below 70 either two or three times is necessary in this level of consistent mind's eye play. Their other rounds are ones that stay in the low 70's.

It came as little surprise that one of the Tour qualifiers for the year was South African and Arizona's **Mark Wurtz** who carded 69, 66, 67 and three other good scores at Grenelefe. Wurtz came off the Canadian Tour and was the most impressive scorer in the foursome in which I caddied at rugged Heritage Pointe (Calgary) and its big time wind challenge in the Telus Alberta Open series, this past summer.

Like Sorenstam, Mark Wurtz and other new Tour players get their aiming ability from practice specifically intended for golf but also have other sports in their past history. Like Greg Norman, perhaps these Tour players ascribe to, or are models of the **Ways to Win pattern,** I have written about and the emerging mind's eye aiming play of the best of these golfers.

GO FORE IT! ENJOY YOUR GOLF AND PLAY BETTER GOLF!

E-mail & Information & Updates: lucasgeoffondallas@shaw.ca
Database. Any large book supplier website: www.Bookmasters.com
or simply mail order by E-mail.

CHAPTER SIX

<u>BIBLIOGRAPHY AND RESOURCES</u>

Editorial Staff, Australian Golf Digest. "The Basics: Buggy Styled Guide to Better Golf", 1994

Lucas, Geoffrey. "The New Images for Golf: The Fundamentals of Visualizing and Scoring", AZ., Victoria.Golf Technology Calgary

Tour '97: An Official publication of the PGA Tour. Published by Golf Magazine, 1997

Mike Adams and PJ Tomasi, Play Better Golf. Rutland, Vermont: C.E. Tuttle, 1993

Golf for Women. "Mini Tours", and "Whistler Beckons", IX #6,5,6. 1997

Golf Week. Orlando, Fl. 2006

Rubenstein, Lorne. Links: An Exploration into the Mind, Heart and Soul of Golf. Rocklin, California: Prima publishing 95677 and Toronto: Random House of Canada 1993

Cole, Cam. Edmonton Journal. "A Leaner, Meaner Troon". July, 1997

Harig, Bob. St. Petersburg Times. "Tiger Raises the Bar". Jan., 1998

Read, Mike. Golf Magazine. "Accuracy: All I Know". April 1989

About Golf Research and Books (page 170)

Lucas had the idea that his 21 hour *Introductory Golf* classes and his 21 hour *Advance Golf* classes should involve visualizing via one memorized visual image before each golf shot, even for occasional golfers. He chose some key golf mind's eye images from the Jack Nicklaus golf comic book format and found that his experimental group hit 5 irons a full 8' closer to target. But beginners could not do it. Only once or twice a week golfers training in class could. Beginners had too much 'reminder type' thinking in their golf so they said that was why they could not improve right away. Soon enough he knew what brain overload was in golf and he reported the same to the Los Angeles pre Olympic Scientific Congress.

While it was pretty difficult to control all variables, he also felt that in the same experiment, it was confirmed that journalized Tactics and game management contributed to golf score reduction. "My golfers kept journals which showed the mind's eye actually was functioning. I felt that the experiment found a large 7 stroke drop in 18 holes", he stated.

Additional Research

The next Research focus took about 8 years of part time effort to bring to final completion. Using Silver Springs (Calgary, Canada) private Golf Club members, their putting green, videotape compared to straight image exercises from 'memory' cards, we compared separately, junior golfers, women players and men players on putting improvement. My Research assistant, Lloyd Boody soon enough found out that imagery improves putting and that videotapes of their own repeated successful putts committed to their mind's eye brain was functional in improving putting to a 15' target. Women improved significantly, juniors improved somewhat and men had lean improvement.

PURE VISUALIZATION EXERCISES

Let us set out the key area to concentrate upon in our sport visualization exercises. Use a Simple Guideline. Better concentration, better relaxation and sport vision produces better images in golf. You must be motivated but relaxed and in a state of what is called "easy" concentration. Forcing visualization tends to extinguish it just as the visual starts to appear, which is why you should practice the following exercises for short, relaxed periods of time. Visualization is very individual and your colors may vary with the "original" scene you are imitating in your mind's eye. When people first begin to visualize, the images they see are often different from the images you "get" from the retina of your eye. These "different" images can still be sport-effective however.

It is quite often found that the imager almost feels that they are "making up" mind pictures. Mental images often have more resemblance to thoughts and ideas than to sights. After practicing for several days, you will begin to be pleased with the development of the actual "sight" images that you generate. These images will become more like the golf accurate scenes you require. Almost all my images on putting greens are done with my eyes open (with my two hands shading my eyes) but you should practice these exercises with your eyes closed. I believe that eyes closed imagery is the more effective form of using images in golf. Personally, however, I sometimes have my eyes open and try to imagine the ball rotating to the hole. Also, my eyes are open for ball tracking and ball bounce and roll imaging. Practice these exercises with eyes closed and you will later find that brief eyes closed golf scenes come to you more readily on the golf course.

Exercise 1: Concentrated Breathing

One effective way to get ready for visualization practice is to count breaths for sixty seconds or longer. Visualize yourself sitting back in a soft chair, relaxing your body until it produces tension-free tingling while you start noticing your inhale, exhale cycle. Count these cycles. Concentrate only on your breathing and when extraneous thoughts enter into your mind, let them pass through. Expect distractions but simply shuttle them on through without any effect at all. Return to counting breaths. Slowly improve your concentrated breathing ability. If you lose track of your count, try again. Use the *Zen* metaphor for intruding thoughts - thoughts are like birds flying across the sky of your mind. They will pass through - let them. This is a handy skill on the golf course. Notice that you are better off if you concentrate on one image. Notice too, that you are capable what of the Yogas and sufis call heightened awareness. Return to this exercise each day you practice. You can easily combine an image of a lung inflating and deflating as you count. The key, however, is to learn to concentrate and be in control. Later this skill will be used to narrow down to the one key golf image you require.

Exercise 2: Visualizing a Triangle

Place this triangle illustration in line with your eyes. Sit in your soft chair and feel your body progressively relax. Take the time to feel the difference between tense and relaxed muscles. Breath smoothly and deeply. Look at all aspects of the triangle and see the gradations of grey in the background. Close your eyes and bring the triangle to your mind's eye. See as much detail of color and shape as you can. The geometric shape produces a visualization of grey and black background and white contrast. Some people see shades of reds (I tend to see reds and shades of red) for the triangle or some other color contrast in the mind's eye. The triangle visualization produces vivid or sharper imagery and also illustrates that we must accept various levels of visual ability.

Exercise 3: Visualizing a Small Object

Use a light bulb, a shiny apple, or a glossy golf tee for this exercise. Take in the whole object, let's say the golf tee, as you view it. Look directly at it. Eyes open. Think only of the object. Notice its size, its shine, its shape, its smoothness, its color, its grain and its varying roundness. If intruding thoughts come to you, let them pass and go back to concentrating. How well can you concentrate? Is a minute a standard you can attain? Your mind may want to wander but don't let it. This ability to concentrate and then use an image of the object will be the same as your improved golf course ability to concentrate on and image an exact landing sport on a golf shot.

After viewing the object, close your eyes and see if you can bring the object before your mind's eye. Relax and don't try too hard. Be "soft" with your attempts to visualize and you will soon improve your visualization skill.

Exercise 4: Visualizing a Favorite Room

Use visualization to visit a favorite room from your childhood or a favorite clubhouse. See the details that you remember the best. See favorite chairs, the woodwork and the "comfort" of the room. See yourself relaxing in this room and visualizing the views that come easily to your mind. Psychologists feel that this is one of the easiest visualizations to recollect. Visualize some of the activities that you used to do in this favorite room.

If it is a golf clubhouse with good views of a golf course, visualize the best of the views.

Exercise 5: A Visualization of Moving Around an object

Use your visualization to move around the outside of a favorite house or golf clubhouse. Walk around all sides and examine it closely. "Zoom" in for a close up of some details. See a full view of some of the features that interest you. See your favorite view lines of the house or clubhouse as if you were looking at them from your most recollectible sight lines. Can you visualize some of the classic clubhouses in golf such as Pinehurst, Royal Troon or St. Andrews?

Exercise 6: See Around a Detailed Object and an Object that has Subtle Differences in It

Stand a favorite golf bag up in a tripod golf stand and view it from all angles. Walk around it and move your visualization angles constantly. View it from above. See the sides and the front view. See a visualization of the bag lying on the green grass. You consciousness that supplies images can move at your will. See that your mind is a slide projector with an infinite number of slides in its storage files. Without moving greatly, you have seen a great variety of viewing angles.

Visualize the subtle differences of the 3 iron through the 9 iron in the graphic at right. Close your eyes and see the difference between the 3, 6 and 9 iron. You can almost see the all leaving these clubfaces at three different angles. Observe your own irons for every detail of their character as well.

Exercise 7: Visualizing Golf Balls

Imagine that you are seeing the three balls from above, below and from the side. Visualize the three labels

noticing the style of print and the various angles of the lettering. As a self test, can you recollect in your imagery the lettering styles of the Titleist, the Pro Staff and the Top Flite balls? Visualize three other balls such as the Ping, the Golden Ram and the Tracer.

Visualize the balls rolling towards you as you crouch behind the hole sighting in a putt. Do this with eyes closed and then with eyes open. Visualize the ball roll and the letters rotate as if they are moving without any wobble. See the letters fall into the exact middle of the golf hole. Visualize for each color in your mind's eye. Use a Ping two tone ball and you will be able to path a rolling putt with exacting effectiveness. Visualize that you are practicing a variety of chip shot angles with colored or optic golf balls. You will soon chip more effectively since you will have stored images for ball path and various angles of ball movement off golf clubs of various lofts.

Notice that you are now combining Imagination with Imagery.

Try holding a labelled, colored golf ball and rotate it as if it were rolling towards the cup or hole on a green. Sight just over the top of the ball towards a real golf hole. Then set the ball down, lettering facing the exact middle of the hole and putt the ball into the cup. Practice all of your visualizations of ball rotations three

times each so that you will remember to do the same on the golf course.

**Visualize the ball
rolling into the cup**

Exercise 8: Controlling Your Image

Visualize yourself returning to a familiar golf locker room. As you enter, turn on the light and notice the familiar parts of the room. Turn the switch off and on, and recheck the details in your visualization. Go over to a window that overlooks a putting green. Use this opportunity to "float" out the window and view the contour of the green. Notice the putts that will be subjected to considerable contour roll. Gently "float" down to the green, putt on the holes that you had noticed. Notice that you are now exhibiting considerable control over your images. You control the light and the dark and the angles of view just as required in *Tactics Imagexercising©*.

Exercise 9: Visualize a Person

Visualize another golfer with whom you can play a game. Notice his golf glove. Notice the shoes he chooses to wear. Notice his facial expression. Do you see a calm, impatient or harried look on his face?

Now visualize his movement as he does a basic skill such as teeing up a ball or taking a practice swing with his driver. This exercise teaches you to visualize another person who is moving or doing movements. Realize that your daydreams re infinitely rich visualizations. Use these daydreams for improving image control.

Exercise 10: Visualize Yourself and Your Movements

Imagine yourself from the time you are in a locker room to the time you walk onto the practice or 1st tee. Join some friends and see yourself hit a few balls as you chat with them. Step outside of "yourself" as you do an external image of one of your golf swing movements. Imagine the feel you get on those first few hits! See yourself as taking it really easy as you build up to a nice tempo in your swing. Zoom in for a close-up of your hand-action and see and feel little hand tension. Hear a click of center-to-center contact between ball and club. Hear yourself explaining your good golf swing.

**Zoom in on a part of
the golf swing**

Do not be impressed by the good players practicing, rather see an image of your own practice system and your own thorough preparation. Do not tire yourself out, instead get your golf mind prepared.

Exercise 11: Visualization of Your Favorite Scene

Close your eyes and relax your muscles as you ease your mind's eye into one of your favorite visual reveries.

Notice the fine details of your scene, the light dancing on the water, the sunrise or sunset that allows you to visualize with ease. Pick out a favorite action you might enjoy and imagine your own details.

Notice how you tend to feel happy and sure of yourself. Enjoy a fine moment for you and your consciousness.

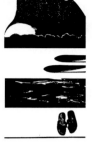

What would you be doing in your favorite scene? What does your visualization have your sense of hearing, feel, touch and smell doing?

Exercise 12: Body Response to Your Visualization Practice

Imagine that one arm is holding a couple of books or boxes of golf balls. The other is being "supported" by a balloon that floats above your arm.

As you close your eyes and visualize this exercise, you will feel your arms slightly in response to the imagined resistances. Your body does respond to Visual Images. "Feel" your golf clubs via the same exercise in your imagination.

Exercise 13: Visualization of a Special Image Viewing Room or Studio

Visualization practice is often done in a private area or favorite room. Use this exercise to further develop this facility. Include a viewing screen so that you can preview your golf technique, the golf course you intend to play and the *Tenacity Imagexercise©* you will require for mentally productive golf.

As you visualize your viewing "retreat", make it as comfortable and as "sports" enhance as you would if you could actually design and build such a facility. Note all the details of warmth and color. Add a clock so that you can complete imagery exercises for many programs of golf preparation.

Also notice in your mind's eye that you can devise new images for lowering your golf score while practicing in your image viewing room.

This viewing room is a facility or space that you can return to anytime you wish, not matter what you may be involved in at the moment. Return anytime that you wish, to work, to think, ti imagine, or just to feel good. Artists and writers need such a space and so does a creative golfer. Plan your golf practice sessions by visualization in your viewing room.

Exercise 14: Using Confidence Rather than Doubt Exercise

In this exercise, you use a "saying" or strategy statement as a suggestion to your visualization brain. As in a prayer, you visualize and associate with confidence, not with doubt. Follow up this exercise with golf visualizations,

Visualize the ball tracking and dropping into the hole

It is not true that visualization "turns-on" one day and "turns off" the next, although this will happen if you let it, if you don't use exercises such as Exercise 14.

Exercises 13 and 14 are designed to make visualization a daily occurrence.

To further develop confidence in your visual imagery ability, see the books by Singer, Horowitz, McKim and Castenada listed in the Bibliography.

Exercise 15: Strategy Statement for   Confident *Imagexercise©*

Relax as you close your eyes and visually travel to the most comforting golf course or retreat you have ever visited. Tell yourself how "deeply" relaxed you are. Sit down and view the deep serenity of this peaceful area of green space and growth. Your mind is clear and satisfied, and your body is strong and supportive. See how receptive your mind is to your clear golf images and strengthen these images.

Exercise 16: Getting in Touch with Your Present Visualization

To change or upgrade your present visualizations about golf (or other visualizations), it will be necessary to get in touch with your present ones. Return to your image viewing room or studio and start to assess some of your current images in golf. Look at those that appear to be uncertain.

Then replan a series of changed images based on new, accurate and specific golf information for technique, tactics and tenacity. Review a few of these on your golf viewing screen until you are able to visualize them with confidence.

Exercise 17: Repetitive Imagery Rehearsal

It is extremely effective to exercise the same image sequence repeatedly in golf. For example, a full *Tactics* rehearsal of a golf course can be completed in a few minutes. Repeat this exercise six or eight times and your right brain and subconscious brain will be fully available to make certain you play the course in the best way you have visualized it.

The Key to Exercise 17 is repeatability in Imagexercise©.

Detailed and repeated visualization of skills and assets you may wish to acquire can be done. It is best to keep these wishes private and confidential but rest assured that you can, in fact, acquire them via visualization. Read about creative visualization in the book by Wiehl and Opthiel for further ideas.

Some Tips in Carrying Out Exercise for Improved Imagery

• Easy concentration or easy imagining practice days are the days that you can image with added vividness. Ability to hold an image is directly affected by ease of concentration in imagining.

• Improvement in ability to hold clear golf images will be gradual.

• The colors of your imagery will gradually improve.

• Do not stress verbal reactions or start to label images in exercising for images; instead stress feelings and the experience that the object itself suggests.

• Learn to control intruding thoughts while practicing imagery by letting those thoughts pass by.

• Set some easily attainable goals (thirty second; sixty second; two minutes; five minutes; or occasionally longer sessions per exercise).

• Practice zooming in on an image as if you were a movie or video camera.

• See an object from various points of view. For example, in Exercise 3, see a low tee, see a high tee, see a row of tees or see a tee forming a V with another tee. See various golfers holding those tees. Break away from habitual ways of viewing things! Break away from habitual labels and see the added potential of the way in which you view things. This creates a self-view as if you were continuing to become a proficient user of visualization/imagery skills.

• Set a number of small objects on a green table cloth and see how many objects you can hold in your mind's eye imagery. Check the details by opening your eyes and then check the details of your images accuracy.

Some Key Tips On Relaxing Your Body

1. Learn the difference in the feeling of a muscle tightening and a muscle loosening or relaxing.

2. Practice by progressively putting a muscle under tension and slowly making that same muscle relax.

3. Go through all the major muscle groups and practice muscle relaxing one group or one body part at a time.

4. Start with large muscles and progress towards smaller muscles.

5. Use images that suggest to your subconscious a relaxed state or stretch.

6. Practice relaxing in a comfortable lying position (often lying on your side).

7. Practice relaxing while sitting with your legs stretched out in front of you.

Other Titles
By Golf Technology
Calgary (1984)
Imprints of A2Z Publishing

All Titles Available From:
A2ZPublishing@shaw.ca
or
EBay internet-golf book

Six 1 Putts ... Minimum ... to CURE a Sick Golf Score
Authors: Geoffrey Lucas, with Frank F. Sanchez, Jr. and
Jerry Borro
ISBN: 09-692902-3-3
Price: $39.95 US $45.50 CAN
260 Color pictures with 55 exercises including 17 original
visualization exercises devised by the main author. All exercises
are aimed at perfecting one putting and lowering putt average
for TOUR/College and competitive fun golfers trying to win a
flight event at their local golf course. For putting green and for
smooth at home surfaces.
Someday soon the average golfer will be able to talk about the number of putts
they used in 18 holes and indeed, for four rounds. This is an exciting new part of
golf because it is a part of the game where equality in play can exists.

**The NEW Images of Golf: The Fundamentals of
Visualization and Scoring
2nd Edition**
Author: Geoffrey Lucas
ISBN: 09-692902-4-1
Price: $16.95 US $19.35 CAN
This classy little book sold over 10,000 copies in Canada alone
among golfers despite not being published in the USA or
Internationally. It has been re-written in 2005 by Geoffrey Lucas,
a learning design specialist from the University of Oregon
curriculum program and advanced golf and skating and hockey teacher at the
University level. The book includes the original 17 Visualization exercises devised
by the author.
It is said that visualization is used by every TOUR golfer and most prominent
amateur golfers. However, all techniques get better over time and this is just what
visualization and scoring in golf has done, got better. Prominent TOUR platers
have called internal images their secret weapon in scoring. Learn the Imagexercise
System of applying consistency to your golf with the power of visualization and
self confidence.

Golf Aiming Skills via Mind's Eye Imagery with Biographies

Author: Geoffrey Lucas

ISBN: 09-692902-5-X

Price: $22.35 US $25.45 CAN

An immediate golf battle ensues in Chapter 1 featuring Lonnie Nielsen, Nolan Henke, rookie Marc Blais and Dana Quigley at the Beck's Challenge Florida TOUR event. The players use mental skills such as eyes closed calm rehearsals of what the golfer intends, mind's eye swing preparations, and an analysis of success/failure when a young TOUR rookie shoots 65 on day 1 and follows with a disasterous 77 on day 2 when nothing at all can calm his play even despite calming comments to him by TOUR nice guy Dana Quigley. The author was there in the foursome as a Caddy and uses his golf teaching skills and experience to explain the happenings at this TOUR event.

Many more TOUR battles take place in the book and Karrie Webb, Billy Mayfair, Michael Bradley and John Huston help illustrate what this gameis all about.

Biographies include Marisa Baena, Natalie Gulbis, Lonnie Nielsen and others. Read about Natalie Gulbis who as a very young mind's eye battler as we caddied out in California at the Long's Drugstore chain LPGA event will soon enough become a TOUR winner as well as the TOUR's calendar girl!

About the Authors

Geoffrey Lucas is a learning design specialist from the University of Oregon and the Golf Tours (performance coach, caddy) and advanced golf and skating Professor. He is well known for a Visualization research study series in which women and junior golfers improve to a stat. significant amount in putting and golf learners improved significantly in iron accuracy.

Geoffrey Lucas played Midget AAA hockey with the Canadians in Edmonton, was mvp Lineman in University football as long snap, center and guard with Alberta Golden Bears and also made starter in basketball at University after being Provincial Champions at Scona Composite High School. He is past Champion in the Vulcan Open golf tourney shooting 72 in the final day to win that event. He kayaks and bikes as well as golfs.

Frank Sanchez Jr. is a PGA certified Instructor in Golf and is especially talented in the short game and the variations used in putting. He is a competitive Professional golfer and is a past Champion in the Maui Open.He can be contacted at the Alai Wai Golf course practice area in Honolulu, Hawaii.

Jerry Borro teaches golf in Hawaii and also is well known at the New Mexico Golf School. He is well respected for Golf Tips and vital information and skills in putting and the short game.